Biology 2

Mary Jones

Jennifer Gregory

Series editor: Mary Jones

CAMBRIDGE
UNIVERSITY PRESS

PUBLISHED BY THE PRESS SYNDICATE OF THE UNIVERSITY OF CAMBRIDGE
The Pitt Building, Trumpington Street, Cambridge, United Kingdom

CAMBRIDGE UNIVERSITY PRESS
The Edinburgh Building, Cambridge CB2 2RU, UK
40 West 20th Street, New York, NY 10011-4211, USA
477 Williamstown Road, Port Melbourne, VIC 3207, Australia
Ruiz de Alarcón 13, 28014 Madrid, Spain
Dock House, The Waterfront, Cape Town 8001, South Africa

http://www.cambridge.org

© Cambridge University Press 2001

First published 2001
Fifth printing 2004

Printed in Dubai by Oriental Press

Typeface Swift   *System* QuarkXPress®

A catalogue record for this book is available from the British Library

ISBN 0 521 79714 4 paperback

Produced by Gecko Ltd, Bicester, Oxon

Front cover photograph: False-colour SEM of tracheal epithelium/SPL

Contents

Introduction

Cambridge Advanced Sciences

The *Cambridge Advanced Sciences* series has been developed to meet the demands of all the new AS and A level science examinations. In particular, it has been endorsed by OCR as providing complete coverage of their specifications. The AS material is presented as a single text for each of biology, chemistry and physics. Material for the A2 year comprises six books in each subject: one of core material and one for each option. Some material has been drawn from the existing *Cambridge Modular Sciences* books; however, many parts are entirely new.

During the development of this series, the opportunity has been taken to improve the design, and a complete and thorough new writing and editing process has been applied. Much more material is now presented in colour. Although the existing *Cambridge Modular Sciences* texts do cover most of the new specifications, the *Cambridge Advanced Sciences* books cover every OCR learning objective in detail. They are the key to success in the new AS and A level examinations.

OCR is one of the three unitary awarding bodies offering the full range of academic and vocational qualifications in the UK. For full details of the new specifications, please contact OCR:

OCR, 1 Hills Rd, Cambridge CB1 2EU
Tel: 01223 553311

The presentation of units

You will find that the books in this series use a bracketed convention in the presentation of units within tables and on graph axes. For example, ionisation energies of $1000\,kJ\,mol^{-1}$ and $2000\,kJ\,mol^{-1}$ will be represented in this way:

Measurement	Ionisation energy ($kJ\,mol^{-1}$)
1	1000
2	2000

OCR examination papers use the solidus as a convention, thus:

Measurement	Ionisation energy / $kJ\,mol^{-1}$
1	1000
2	2000

Biology 2 – the A2 biology text

Biology 2 covers all of the core material required for the second year of A level study. It is designed to be accessible to students with a double-award science GCSE background and an AS in biology. This book combines entirely new text and illustrations with revised and updated material from *Foundation Biology, Ecology and Conservation, Central Concepts in Biology,* and *Transport, Regulation and Control,* formerly available in the *Cambridge Modular Sciences* series.

Chapters 1 and 2 are based on *Central Concepts* chapters 1 and 2, with the content rearranged and expanded upon. Chapter 3 draws upon *Central Concepts* chapter 3 and *Ecology and Conservation* chapters 2 and 3 (converted into full colour), with additional information on sustainable production, including that of timber. Chapter 4 combines part of *Foundation Biology* chapter 2 with an expanded version of *Central Concepts* chapter 5 and new coverage of the chi-squared test. Chapter 5 is based on *Central Concepts* chapter 6, with more extensive explanations of key concepts. Chapter 6 is a combination of *Transport, Regulation and Control* chapters 4 and 5 and new material on plant growth regulators.

The writing style and visual design have been improved throughout for greater clarity, and the book benefits from an extensive glossary. In addition, each chapter ends with 'synoptic' questions designed to bring together knowledge gained from across the course as a whole.

Acknowledgements

Photographs

1.14, Dr Keith Porter/Science Photo Library; 1.15, Dr J E Walker, MRC Cambridge; 2.7, 2.8, ©Andrew Syred; 2.10, 6.22, Electron Microscopy Unit, Royal Holloway, University of London; 2.11, 4.3, 6.6a, 6.6b, 6.18, 6.29, 6.42, 6.45, Biophoto Associates; 3.2 , ©Roger Wilmshurst/FLPA; 3.4b, Ferrero/Labat/Ardea London Ltd; 3.4c, Kenneth W Fink/Ardea London Ltd; 3.6b, 3.18, Ecoscene; 3.7, Oman/Combs/Geoscience Features; 3.9, Geoff Jones; 3.10, John Walmsley; 3.12, Eleanor Jones; 3.16, Ardea London Ltd; 4.6a, Wayne Hutchison/Holt Studios; 4.6b, G I Bernard/Oxford Scientific Films; 4.6c, John Daniels/Ardea London Ltd; 4.6d, Hans Reinhard/Bruce Coleman; 4.9, Eye of Science/Science Photo Library; 5.2, Popperfoto; 5.3, Jane Burton/Bruce Coleman; 5.6, Dick Roberts/Holt Studios; 5.7, Eric Dragesco/Ardea London Ltd; 5.8, John Durham/Science Photo Library; 5.9a, 5.9b, J L Mason/Ardea London Ltd; 5.11, Wellcome Trust Medical Photographic Library; 5.13 (from top), P Morris/Ardea London Ltd, J B & S Bottomley/Ardea London Ltd; 5.14, unknown; 5.15a, NIBSC/Science Photo Library; 5.15b, Biophoto Associates/Science Photo Library; 5.16c, Simon Fraser/Science Photo Library; 5.17c (from top), Manfred Kage/Science Photo Library, Wildlife Matters Photographic Library, Dr Jeremy Burgess/Science Photo Library, David Scharff/Science Photo Library; 5.18b, Ken Gibson/Garden Matters Photographic Library; 5.18c, Garden Matters Photographic Library; 5.18d, Colin Milkins/Garden Matters Photographic Library; 5.19b, Gilbert S Grant/Science Photo Library; 5.19c, Dr Tony Brain/Science Photo Library; 5.19d, Renee Lynn/Science Photo Library; 6.24, St Bartholomew's Hospital/SPL; 6.38, H. Lindscog/Geoscience Features; 6.47, Nigel Cattlin/Holt Studios.

Picture research: Maureen Cowdroy

Diagrams

3.14, from *The Nitrogen Cycle of the United Kingdom*, 1983, The Royal Society, London; 3.15, from *Research on the Nitrogen cycle − A Sixth Form Study Resource*, Agricultural and Food Research Centre and the National Centre for Biotechnology Education; 6.49, Geoff Jones.

CHAPTER 1

Energy and respiration

By the end of this chapter you should be able to:

1 outline the need for energy in living organisms;

2 describe the structure of ATP as a phosphorylated nucleotide;

3 describe the universal role of ATP as the energy 'currency' in living organisms;

4 explain that the synthesis of ATP is associated with the electron transport chain on the membranes of the mitochondrion;

5 outline glycolysis as the phosphorylation of glucose and the subsequent splitting of hexose phosphate (6C) into two triose phosphate molecules which are then further oxidised with a small yield of ATP and reduced NAD;

6 explain that, when oxygen is available, pyruvate is converted to acetyl (2C) coenzyme A, which then combines with oxaloacetate (4C) to form citrate (6C);

7 outline the Krebs cycle, explaining that citrate is reconverted to oxaloacetate in a series of small steps in the matrix of the mitochondrion;

8 explain that these processes involve decarboxylation and dehydrogenation, and describe the role of NAD;

9 outline the process of oxidative phosphorylation, including the role of oxygen;

10 explain the production of a small yield of ATP from anaerobic respiration and the formation of ethanol in yeast and lactate in mammals;

11 explain the relative energy values of carbohydrate, lipid and protein as respiratory substrates;

12 define the term *respiratory quotient* (RQ);

13 know how to use a simple respirometer to measure RQ and the effect of temperature on respiration rate.

The need for energy in living organisms

All living organisms require a continuous supply of energy to stay alive, either from the absorption of light energy or from chemical potential energy. The process of photosynthesis transfers light energy to chemical potential energy and so almost all life on Earth depends on photosynthesis, either directly or indirectly. Photosynthesis supplies living organisms with two essential requirements: an energy supply and usable carbon compounds.

All biological macromolecules, such as carbohydrates, lipids, proteins and nucleic acids, contain carbon. All living organisms therefore need a source of carbon. Organisms which can use an inorganic carbon source in the form of carbon dioxide are called **autotrophs**. Those needing a ready-made organic supply of carbon are **heterotrophs**. (An *organic* molecule is a compound including carbon and hydrogen. The term originally meant a molecule derived from an organism, but now includes all compounds of carbon and hydrogen even if they do not occur naturally.)

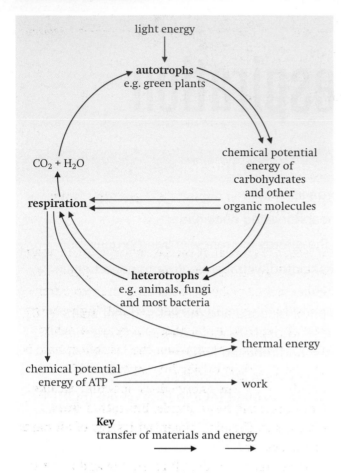

Key
transfer of materials and energy

● **Figure 1.1** Transfer of materials and energy in an ecosystem.

Organic molecules can be used by living organisms in two ways. They can serve as 'building bricks' for making other organic molecules that are essential to the organism, and they can represent chemical potential energy which can be released by breaking down the molecules in respiration (page 5). This energy can then be used for all forms of work. Heterotrophs depend on autotrophs for both materials and energy (*figure 1.1*).

Work

Work in a living organism includes:
■ the synthesis of complex substances from simpler ones (anabolic reactions) such as the synthesis of polypeptides from amino acids;
■ the active transport of substances against a diffusion gradient such as the activity of the sodium-potassium pump;
■ mechanical work such as muscle contraction and other cellular movements, for example the movement of cilia and flagella, amoeboid

movement and the movement of vesicles through cytoplasm;
■ in a few organisms, bioluminescence and electrical discharge.

Mammals and birds use thermal energy from metabolic reactions to maintain a constant body temperature.

Two of these forms of work, active transport and muscle contraction, will be looked at in more detail later (*boxes 1A* and *1B*).

For a living organism to do work, energy-requiring reactions must be linked to those that yield energy. In the complete oxidation of glucose ($C_6H_{12}O_6$) in aerobic conditions a large quantity of energy is made available:

$$C_6H_{12}O_6 + 6O_2 \rightarrow 6CO_2 + 6H_2O + 2870 \, kJ$$

Reactions such as this take place in a series of small steps, each releasing a small quantity of the total available energy. You may remember that multi-step reactions allow precise control via feed-back mechanisms (*Biology 1,* chapter 3) but this and other such advantages are in addition to the basic fact that the cell could not usefully harness the total available energy if all of it were made available at one instant.

Although the complete oxidation of glucose to carbon dioxide and water has a very high energy yield, the reaction does not happen easily. Glucose is actually quite stable, because of the **activation energy** that has to be overcome before any reaction takes place (*figure 1.2*). In living organisms

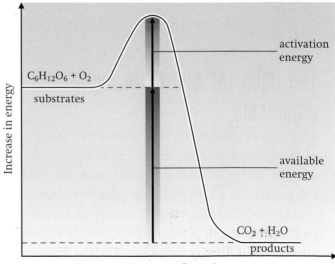

● **Figure 1.2** Oxidation of glucose.

this is overcome by lowering the activation energy using enzymes (see *Biology 1*, page 43) and also by raising the energy level of the glucose by phosphorylation (page 7).

Theoretically, the energy released from each step of respiration could be harnessed directly to some form of work in the cell. However, a much more flexible system actually occurs in which energy-yielding reactions in *all* organisms are linked to the production of an intermediary molecule, **ATP** (adenosine triphosphate).

ATP

ATP as energy 'currency'

The structure of adenosine triphosphate (ATP) is shown in *figure 1.3*. It consists of adenine (an organic base) and ribose (a pentose sugar), which together make adenosine (a nucleoside). This is combined with three phosphate groups to make ATP. ATP is therefore a nucleotide (*Biology 1*, page 66). ATP is a small, water-soluble molecule. This allows it to be easily transported around the cell.

When a phosphate group is removed from ATP, adenosine diphosphate (ADP) is formed and $30.5 \, \text{kJ} \, \text{mol}^{-1}$ of energy is released. Removal of a second phosphate produces adenosine monophosphate (AMP) and $30.5 \, \text{kJ} \, \text{mol}^{-1}$ of energy is again

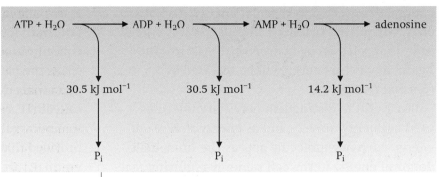

● **Figure 1.4** Hydrolysis of ATP. (P_i is inorganic phosphate, H_3PO_4.)

released. Removal of the last phosphate, leaving adenosine, releases only $14.2 \, \text{kJ} \, \text{mol}^{-1}$ (*figure 1.4*). In the past, the bonds attaching the two outer phosphate groups have been called 'high-energy bonds', because more energy is released when they are broken than when the last phosphate is removed. This is misleading and should be avoided since the energy does not come simply from breaking those bonds, but rather from changes in chemical potential energy of all parts of the system.

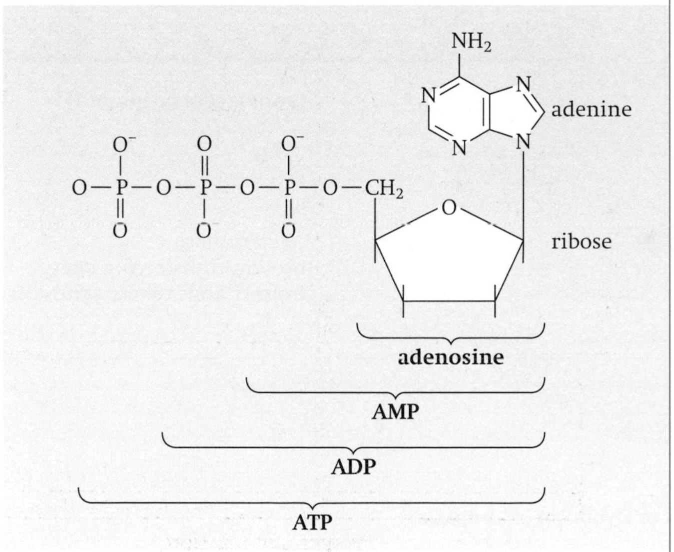

These reactions are all reversible and it is the interconversion of ATP and ADP that is all-important in providing energy for the cell:

$$ATP + H_2O \rightleftharpoons ADP + H_3PO_4 \pm 30.5 \, \text{kJ}$$

The rate of interconversion, or turnover, is enormous. It is estimated that a resting human uses about 40 kg of ATP in 24 hours, but at any one time contains only about 5 g of ATP. During strenuous exercise, ATP breakdown may be as much as 0.5 kg per minute.

The cell's energy-yielding reactions are linked to ATP synthesis. The ATP is then used by the cell in all forms of work. ATP is the universal intermediary molecule between energy-yielding and energy-requiring reactions used in a cell, whatever its type. In other words, ATP is the 'energy currency' of the cell. The cell 'trades' in ATP rather than making use of a number of different intermediates.

Energy transfers are inefficient. Some energy is converted to thermal energy whenever energy is transferred. At the different stages in a multi-step reaction, such as respiration, the energy made available may not perfectly correspond with the energy needed to synthesise ATP. Any 'excess'

● **Figure 1.3** Structure of ATP.

energy is converted to thermal energy. Also, many energy-requiring reactions in cells use less energy than that released by hydrolysis of ATP to ADP. Again, any extra energy will be released as thermal energy.

Be careful to distinguish between molecules used as energy *currency* and as energy *storage*. An energy currency molecule acts as the immediate donor of energy to the cell's energy-requiring reactions. An energy storage molecule is a short-term (glucose or sucrose) or long-term (glycogen, starch or triglyceride) store of chemical potential energy.

Synthesis of ATP

Energy for ATP synthesis can become available in two ways. In respiration, energy released by reorganising chemical bonds (chemical potential energy) during glycolysis and the Krebs cycle (pages 6–9) is used to make some ATP. However, most ATP in cells is generated using electrical potential energy. This energy is from the transfer of electrons by electron carriers in mitochondria and chloroplasts (page 9). It is stored as a difference in hydrogen ion concentration across some phospholipid membranes in mitochondria and chloroplasts which are essentially impermeable to hydrogen ions. Hydrogen ions are then allowed to flow down their concentration gradient through a protein which spans the phospholipid bilayer. Part of this protein acts as an enzyme which synthesises ATP, and is called **ATP synthase**. The transfer of three hydrogen ions allows the production of one ATP molecule provided that ADP and an inorganic phosphate group (P_i) are available inside the organelle. This process occurs in both mitochondria (page 11) and chloroplasts (page 24) and is summarised in *figure 1.5*. The process was first proposed by Peter Mitchell in 1961 and is called **chemiosmosis**.

ATP synthase has three binding sites (*figure 1.6*) and a part of the molecule (γ) that rotates as hydrogen ions pass. This produces structural changes in the binding sites and allows them to pass sequentially through three phases:

- binding ADP and P_i;
- forming tightly bound ATP;
- releasing ATP.

SAQ 1.1

Write the equation for the reaction catalysed by ATP synthase.

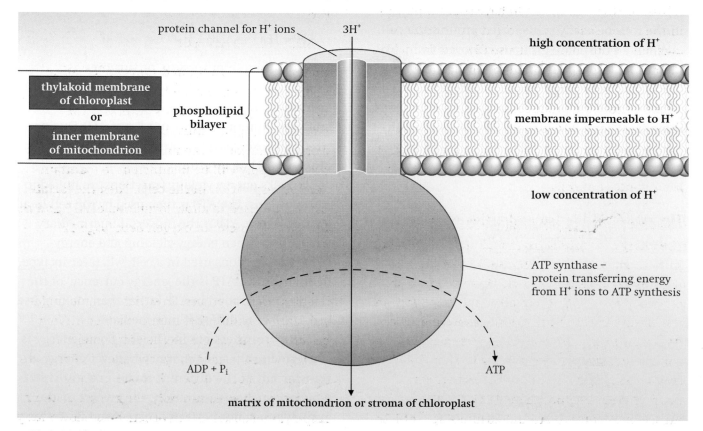

protein channel for H⁺ ions — 3H⁺

high concentration of H⁺

thylakoid membrane of chloroplast

or

inner membrane of mitochondrion

phospholipid bilayer

membrane impermeable to H⁺

low concentration of H⁺

ATP synthase – protein transferring energy from H⁺ ions to ATP synthesis

ADP + P_i

ATP

matrix of mitochondrion or stroma of chloroplast

● **Figure 1.5** ATP synthesis.

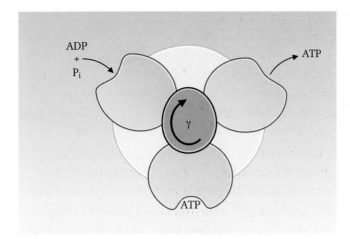

● **Figure 1.6** Transverse section (TS) of ATP synthase showing its activity.

The role of ATP in active transport

Active transport is the movement of molecules or ions across a differentially permeable membrane against a concentration gradient. Energy is needed, in the form of ATP, to counteract the tendency of these particles to move by diffusion down the gradient.

All cells show differences in concentration of ions, in particular sodium and potassium ions, inside the cell with respect to the surrounding solution. Most cells seem to have sodium pumps in the plasma membrane which pump sodium ions out of the cell. This is usually coupled with the ability to pump potassium ions from the surrounding solution into the cell (*box 1A*).

The importance of active transport in ion movement into and out of cells should not be underestimated. About 50% of the ATP used by a resting mammal is devoted to maintaining the ionic content of cells.

The role of ATP in the contraction of muscle

The energy for muscle contraction (*box 1B*) comes from the hydrolysis of ATP to ADP and inorganic phosphate. In resting muscle there is only a small concentration of ATP, and although this supplies the energy which is turned into muscular work, its concentration is about the same in resting and contracting muscle. During contraction the ATP is continually regenerated by a system which involves creatine phosphate (PCr). A resting muscle may contain around $20 \, \text{mmol kg}^{-1}$ of PCr compared with $6 \, \text{mmol kg}^{-1}$ of ATP.

Box 1A The sodium–potassium pump

The sodium–potassium pump is a protein which spans the plasma membrane. It has binding sites for sodium ions (Na^+) and for ATP on the inner side, and for potassium ions (K^+) on the outer side. The protein acts as an ATPase, and catalyses the hydrolysis of ATP to ADP and inorganic phosphate, releasing energy to drive the pump. Changes in the shape of the protein move sodium and potassium ions across the membrane in opposite directions. For each ATP used, two potassium ions move into the cell and three sodium ions move out of the cell. Since only two potassium ions are added to the cell contents for every three sodium ions removed, a potential difference is created across the membrane which is negative inside with respect to the outside. Both sodium and potassium ions leak back across the membrane, down their diffusion gradients. However plasma membranes are much less permeable to sodium ions than potassium ions, so this diffusion actually increases the potential difference across the membrane.

This potential difference is most clearly seen as the resting potential of a nerve cell (see page 108). One of the specialisations of a nerve cell is an exaggeration of the potential difference across the plasma membrane as a result of the activity of the sodium–potassium pump.

The ADP produced during muscle contraction is reconverted to ATP by transferring a phosphate group from creatine phosphate, leaving creatine (Cr).

$$ADP + PCr \rightarrow ATP + Cr$$

However, there is a limited supply of creatine phosphate. It is adequate for a sudden, short sprint lasting a few seconds. After this the creatine phosphate must be replenished via ATP from respiration. If the muscle is very active, the oxygen supply will be insufficient to maintain aerobic respiration in the cells. Then the lactate pathway is used to allow formation of ATP and the muscle cells incur an oxygen debt (page 12).

Respiration

Respiration is a process in which organic molecules act as a fuel. These are broken down in a series of stages to release chemical potential energy which is used to synthesise ATP. The main fuel for most cells is carbohydrate, usually glucose. Many cells can only use glucose as their respiratory substrate, but others break down fatty acids, glycerol and amino acids in respiration.

Box 1B Muscle contraction

A sarcomere contracts by sliding the thin **actin** filaments over the thick **myosin** filaments. Myosin filaments are made up of many myosin molecules, each with a flexible 'head'. This head is an ATPase molecule, which can hydrolyse ATP to ADP and P_i. In resting muscle, the ADP and P_i are bound to the head.

When the muscle is activated by a nerve impulse, calcium ions are released from the **sarcoplasmic reticulum** (specialised endoplasmic reticulum). They allow the myosin head to bind to the portion of actin filament next to it. The myosin head then tilts about 45°, moving the attached actin filament about 10 nm in relation to the myosin, towards the centre of the sarcomere. This is the 'power stroke'. The combined effect of millions of such power strokes makes the muscle contract. At the same time, the ADP and P_i are released from the head.

Then another ATP binds to the head and is hydrolysed to ADP and P_i, releasing energy that allows the actin and myosin to separate. The head tilts back to its original position, ready for the cycle to repeat – which can happen about five times per second. Note that the hydrolysis of ATP and the power stroke do not occur at the same time.

When excitation ceases, ATP is again needed to pump calcium ions back into the sarcoplasmic reticulum.

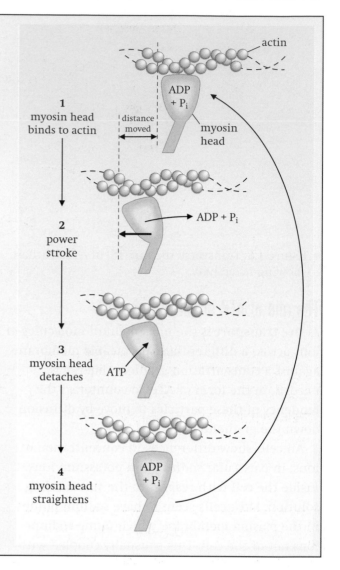

● **Figure 1.7** The action of ATP in muscle contraction.

Glucose breakdown can be divided into four stages: **glycolysis**, the **link reaction**, the **Krebs cycle** and **oxidative phosphorylation** (*figure 1.8*).

The glycolytic pathway

Glycolysis is the splitting, or **lysis** of glucose. It is a multi-step process in which a glucose molecule with six carbon atoms is eventually split into two molecules of pyruvate, each with three carbon atoms. Energy from ATP is needed in the first steps, but energy is *released* in later steps, when it can be used to make ATP. There is a net gain of two ATP

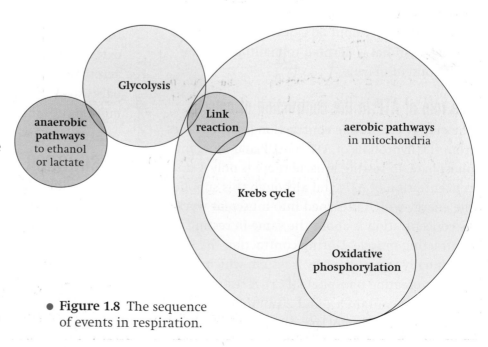

● **Figure 1.8** The sequence of events in respiration.

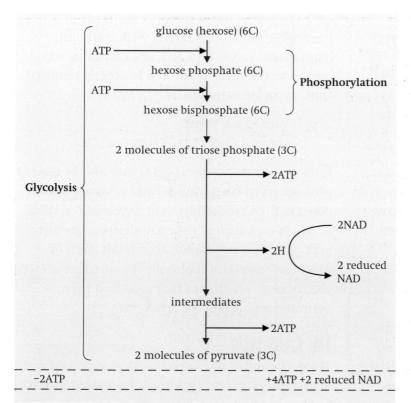

Figure 1.9 The glycolytic pathway.

molecules per molecule of glucose broken down. Glycolysis takes place in the cytoplasm of a cell. A simplified flow diagram of the pathway is shown in *figure 1.9*.

In the first stage, **phosphorylation**, glucose is phosphorylated using ATP. As we saw on page 2, glucose is energy-rich, but does not react easily. To tap the bond energy of glucose, energy must first be used to make the reaction easier (*figure 1.2*). Two ATP molecules are used for each molecule of glucose to make hexose bisphosphate, which breaks down to produce two molecules of triose phosphate.

Hydrogen is then removed from triose phosphate and transferred to the carrier molecule NAD (nicotinamide adenine dinucleotide). The structure of NAD is shown in *box 1C, figure 1.10*. Two molecules of reduced NAD are produced for each molecule of glucose entering glycolysis. The hydrogens carried by reduced NAD can easily be transferred to other molecules and are used in oxidative phosphorylation to generate ATP (page 9).

Box 1C Hydrogen carrier molecules: NAD, NADP and FAD

NAD (nicotinamide adenine dinucleotide) is made of two linked nucleotides. Both nucleotides contain ribose. One nucleotide contains the nitrogenous base adenine. The other has a nicotinamide ring, which can accept a hydrogen ion and two electrons, thereby becoming reduced.

NAD + 2H $\rightleftharpoons$ reduced NAD
$NAD^+ + 2H \rightleftharpoons NADH^+ + H^+$

A slightly different form of NAD has a phosphate group instead of the hydrogen on carbon 1 in one of the ribose rings. This molecule is called NADP (nicotinamide adenine dinucleotide phosphate) and is used as a hydrogen carrier molecule in photosynthesis.

FAD (flavin adenine dinucleotide) is similar in function to NAD and is used in respiration in the Krebs cycle (page 8). It is made of one nucleotide containing ribose and adenine and one with an unusual structure involving a linear molecule, ribitol, instead of ribose.

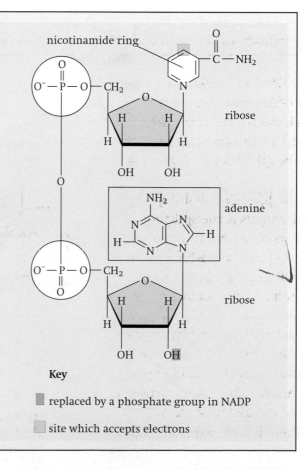

Key

replaced by a phosphate group in NADP

site which accepts electrons

Figure 1.10 NAD.

The end-product of glycolysis, pyruvate, still contains a great deal of chemical potential energy. When free oxygen is available, some of this energy can be released via the Krebs cycle and oxidative phosphorylation. However, the pyruvate first enters the link reaction, which takes place in the mitochondria (page 11).

SAQ 1.2

How does the linkage between the nucleotides in NAD differ from that in a polynucleotide? (You may need to refer back to *Biology 1*, page 68 to answer this question.)

The link reaction

Pyruvate passes by active transport from the cytoplasm, through the outer and inner membranes of a mitochondrion and into the mitochondrial matrix. Here it is decarboxylated (that is carbon dioxide is removed), dehydrogenated and combined with coenzyme A (CoA) to give acetyl coenzyme A. This is known as the **link reaction** (*figure 1.11*). Coenzyme A is a complex molecule of a nucleoside (adenine + ribose) with a vitamin (pantothenic acid), and acts as a carrier of acetyl groups to the Krebs cycle. The hydrogen removed from pyruvate is transferred to NAD.

$$\text{pyruvate} + \text{CoA} + \text{NAD}$$
$$\rightleftharpoons \text{acetyl CoA} + CO_2 + \text{reduced NAD}$$

Fatty acids from fat metabolism may also be used to produce acetyl coenzyme A. Fatty acids are broken down in the mitochondrion in a cycle of reactions in which each turn of the cycle shortens the fatty acid chain by a two-carbon acetyl unit. Each of these can react with coenzyme A to produce acetyl coenzyme A, which, like that produced from pyruvate, now enters the Krebs cycle.

The Krebs cycle

The Krebs cycle (also known as the citric acid cycle or tricarboxylic acid cycle) was discovered in 1937 by Hans Krebs. It is shown in *figure 1.11*.

The Krebs cycle is a closed pathway of enzyme-controlled reactions:

- acetyl coenzyme A combines with a four-carbon compound (oxaloacetate) to form a six-carbon compound (citrate);
- the citrate is decarboxylated and dehydrogenated in a series of steps, to yield carbon dioxide, which is given off as a waste gas, and hydrogens which are accepted by the carriers NAD and FAD (flavin adenine dinucleotide) (*box 1C*);
- oxaloacetate is regenerated to combine with another acetyl coenzyme A.

For each turn of the cycle, two carbon dioxide molecules are produced, one FAD and three NAD molecules are reduced, and one ATP molecule is generated via an intermediate compound.

Although part of aerobic respiration, the reactions of the Krebs cycle make no use of molecular oxygen. However, oxygen is necessary for the final stage which is called oxidative phosphorylation.

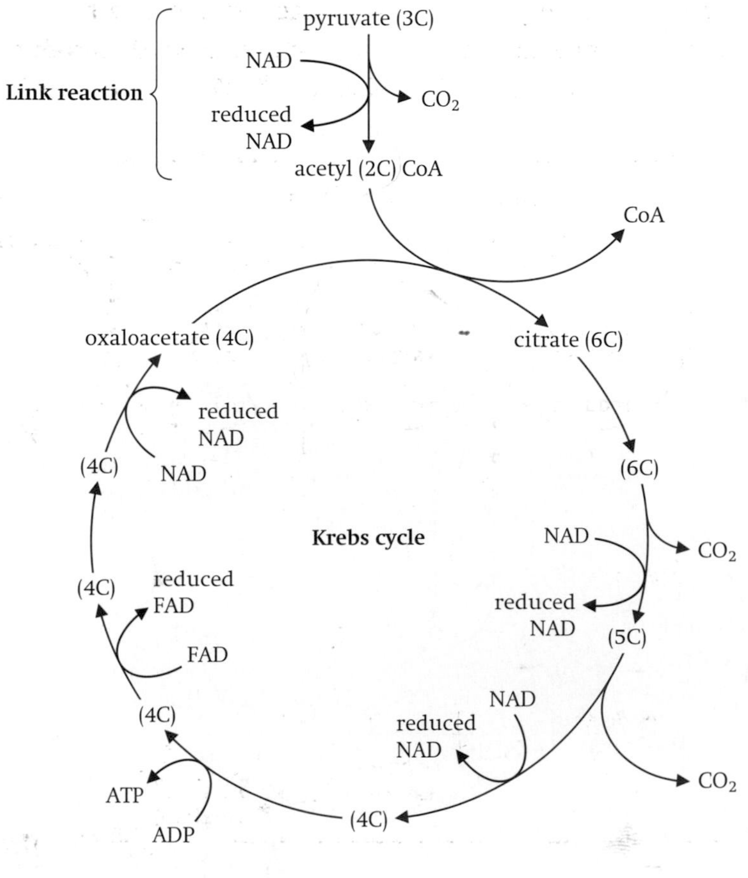

• **Figure 1.11** The link reaction and the Krebs cycle.

The most important contribution of the Krebs cycle to the cell's energetics is the release of hydrogens, which can be used in oxidative phosphorylation to provide energy to make ATP.

SAQ 1.3 _____

Explain how the events of the Krebs cycle can be cyclical.

Oxidative phosphorylation and the electron transport chain

In the final stage of aerobic respiration, the energy for the phosphorylation of ADP to ATP comes from the activity of the electron transport chain. This takes place in the mitochondrial membranes.

Reduced NAD and reduced FAD are passed to the electron transport chain. Here, hydrogens are removed from the two hydrogen carriers and each is split into its constituent hydrogen ion (H^+) and electron. The electron is transferred to the first of a series of electron carriers (*box 1D*), whilst the hydrogen ion remains in solution in the mitochondrial matrix. Once the electron is transferred to oxygen (also in solution in the matrix), a hydrogen ion will be drawn from solution to reduce the oxygen to water (*figure 1.12*).

The transfer of electrons along the series of electron carriers makes energy available which is used to convert ADP + P_i to ATP. As an electron passes from a carrier at a higher energy level to one that is lower, energy is released. This is usually lost as heat, but at particular points in the chain the energy released is sufficient to produce ATP.

Potentially, three molecules of ATP can be produced from each reduced NAD molecule and two ATP from each reduced FAD molecule (*figure 1.12*). However, this yield cannot be realised unless ADP and P_i are available inside the mitochondrion. About 25% of the total energy yield of electron transfer is used to transport ADP into the mitochondrion, and ATP into the cytoplasm. Hence, each reduced NAD molecule entering the chain produces on average two and a half molecules of ATP and each reduced FAD produces one and a half molecules of ATP.

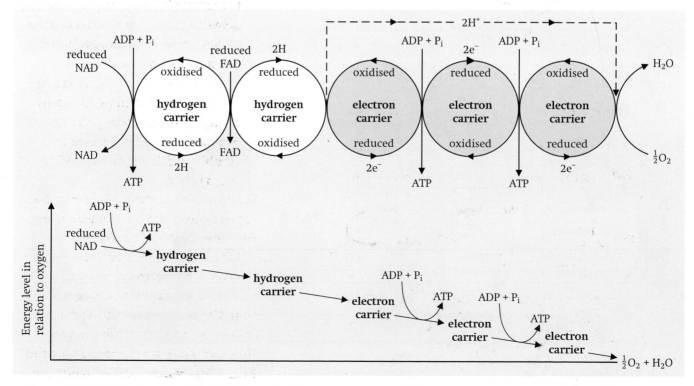

● **Figure 1.12** Oxidative phosphorylation: the electron transport chain.

The most widely accepted explanation for the synthesis of ATP in oxidative phosphorylation is that of chemiosmosis (page 4). The energy released by the electron transport chain is used to pump hydrogen ions from the mitochondrial matrix into the space between the two membranes of the mitochondrial envelope. The concentration of hydrogen ions in the intermembrane space therefore becomes higher than that in the matrix, so a concentration gradient is set up. Hydrogen ions pass back into the mitochondrial matrix through protein channels in the inner membrane. Associated with each channel is the enzyme ATP synthase. As the ions pass through the channel, their electrical potential energy is used to synthesise ATP (*figure 1.5*).

The sequence of events in respiration and their sites are shown in *figure 1.13*. The balance sheet of ATP use and synthesis for each molecule of glucose entering the respiration pathway is shown in *table 1.1*.

	ATP used	ATP made	Net gain in ATP
Glycolysis	−2	4	+2
Link reaction	0	0	0
Krebs cycle	0	2	+2
Oxidative phosphorylation	0	28	+28
Total	−2	34	+32

● **Table 1.1** Balance sheet of ATP use and synthesis for each molecule of glucose entering respiration.

SAQ 1.4

Calculate the number of reduced NAD and reduced FAD molecules produced for each molecule of glucose entering the respiration pathway when oxygen is available.

SAQ 1.5

Using your answer to SAQ 1.4, calculate the number of ATP molecules produced for each molecule of glucose in oxidative phosphorylation.

SAQ 1.6

Explain why the important contribution of the Krebs cycle to cellular energetics is the release of hydrogens and not the direct production of ATP.

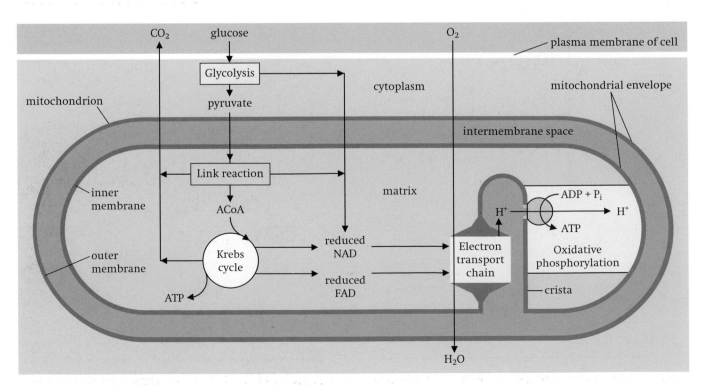

● **Figure 1.13** The sites of the events of respiration in a cell.

Mitochondrial structure and function

In eukaryotic organisms, the mitochondrion is the site of the Krebs cycle and the electron transport chain. Mitochondria are rod-shaped or filamentous organelles about 0.5–1.0 µm in diameter. Time-lapse photography shows that they are not rigid, but can change their shape. The number of mitochondria in a cell depends on its activity. Mammalian liver cells contain between 1000 and 2000 mitochondria, occupying 20% of the cell volume.

The structure of a mitochondrion is shown in *figure 1.14*. Like a chloroplast, each mitochondrion is surrounded by an **envelope** of two phospholipid membranes (*Biology 1*, page 52). The outer membrane is smooth, but the inner is much folded inwards to form **cristae** (singular **crista**). These give the inner membrane a large total surface area. Cristae in mitochondria from different types of cells show considerable variation, but, in general, mitochondria from active cells have longer, more densely packed cristae than those from less active cells. The two membranes have different compositions and properties. The outer membrane is relatively permeable to small molecules, whilst the inner membrane is less permeable. The inner membrane is studded with

tiny spheres, about 9 nm in diameter, which are attached to the inner membrane by stalks (*figure 1.15*). The spheres are the enzyme **ATP synthase**.

The inner membrane is the site of the electron transport chain and contains the proteins necessary for this. The space between the two membranes of the envelope usually has a lower pH than the matrix of the mitochondrion as a result of the hydrogen ions that are released into the intermembrane space by the activity of the electron transport chain.

The **matrix** of the mitochondrion is the site of the link reaction and the Krebs cycle, and contains the enzymes needed for these reactions. It also contains small (70 S) **ribosomes** and several identical copies of looped mitochondrial **DNA**.

ATP is formed in the matrix by the activity of ATP synthase on the cristae. The energy for the production of ATP comes from the hydrogen ion gradient between the intermembrane space and the matrix. The ATP can be used for all the energy-requiring reactions of the cell, both inside and outside the mitochondrion.

SAQ 1.7

Explain how the structure of a mitochondrion is adapted for its functions in aerobic respiration.

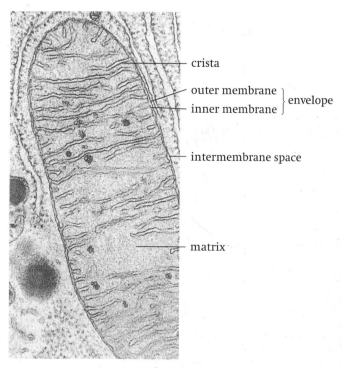

● **Figure 1.14** Transmission electron micrograph of a mitochondrion from a pancreas (× 15 000).

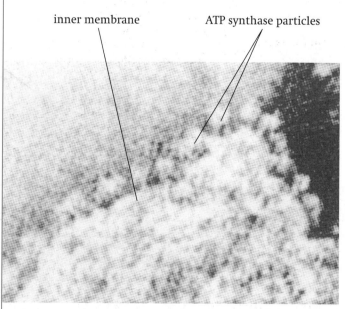

● **Figure 1.15** TEM of ATP synthase particles on the inner membrane of a mitochondrion.

Anaerobic respiration

When free oxygen is not present, hydrogen cannot be disposed of by combination with oxygen. The electron transfer chain therefore stops working and no further ATP is formed by oxidative phosphorylation. If a cell is to gain even the two ATP molecules for each glucose yielded by glycolysis, it is essential to pass on the hydrogens from the reduced NAD that are also made in glycolysis. There are two different anaerobic pathways which solve the problem of 'dumping' hydrogen. Both pathways take place in the cytoplasm of the cell.

In various microorganisms such as yeast, and in some plant tissues, the hydrogen from reduced NAD is passed to ethanal (CH_3CHO). This releases the NAD and allows glycolysis to continue. The pathway is shown in *figure 1.16*. First, pyruvate is decarboxylated to ethanal; then the ethanal is reduced to ethanol (C_2H_5OH) by the enzyme alcohol dehydrogenase. The conversion of glucose to ethanol is referred to as **alcoholic fermentation**.

In other microorganisms, and in mammalian muscles when deprived of oxygen, pyruvate acts as the hydrogen acceptor and is converted to lactate by the enzyme lactate dehydrogenase (named after the reverse reaction, which it also catalyses). Again, the NAD is released and allows glycolysis to continue in anaerobic conditions. This pathway is shown in *figure 1.17*.

These reactions 'buy time'. They allow the continued production of at least some ATP even

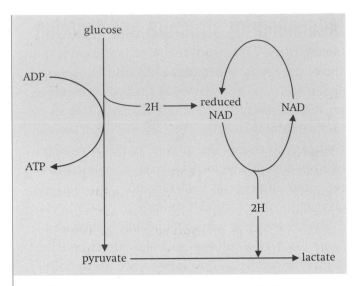

● **Figure 1.17** Anaerobic respiration: the lactate pathway.

though oxygen is not available as the hydrogen acceptor. However, since the products of anaerobic reaction, ethanol or lactate, are toxic, the reactions cannot continue indefinitely. The pathway leading to ethanol cannot be reversed and the remaining chemical potential energy of ethanol is wasted. The lactate pathway can be reversed in mammals. Lactate is carried by the blood plasma to the liver and converted back to pyruvate. The liver oxidises some (20%) of the incoming lactate to carbon dioxide and water via aerobic respiration when oxygen is available again. The remainder of the lactate is converted by the liver to glycogen. The oxygen needed to allow this removal of lactate is called the **oxygen debt**.

Respiratory substrates

Although glucose is the essential respiratory substrate for some cells, such as neurones in the brain, red blood cells and lymphocytes, other cells can oxidise lipids and amino acids. When lipids are respired, carbon atoms are removed in pairs, as acetyl CoA, from the fatty acid chains and fed into the Krebs cycle. The carbon–hydrogen skeletons of amino acids are converted into pyruvate or into acetyl CoA.

Energy values of respiratory substrates

Most of the energy liberated in aerobic respiration comes from the oxidation of hydrogen to water

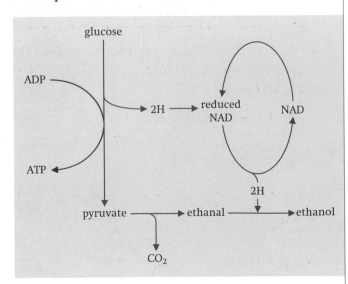

● **Figure 1.16** Anaerobic respiration: the ethanol pathway.

Respiratory substrate	Energy density ($kJ\,g^{-1}$)
carbohydrate	15.8
lipid	39.4
protein	17.0

● **Table 1.2** Typical energy values.

when reduced NAD and reduced FAD are passed to the electron transport chain. Hence, the greater the number of hydrogens in the structure of the substrate molecule, the greater the energy value. Fatty acids have more hydrogens per molecule than carbohydrates and so lipids have a greater energy value per unit mass, or **energy density**, than carbohydrates or proteins.

The energy value of a substrate is determined by burning a known mass of the substance in oxygen in a **calorimeter** (*figure 1.18*).

The energy liberated by oxidising the substrate can be determined from the rise in temperature of a known mass of water in the calorimeter. Typical energy values are shown in *table 1.2*.

Respiratory quotient (RQ)

The overall equation for the aerobic respiration of glucose shows that the number of molecules, and hence the volumes, of oxygen used and carbon dioxide produced are the same:

$$C_6H_{12}O_6 + 6O_2 \rightarrow 6CO_2 + 6H_2O + energy$$

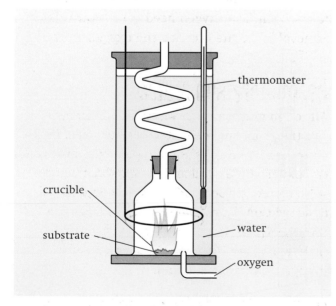

● **Figure 1.18** A simple calorimeter in which the energy value of a respiratory substrate can be measured.

So the **ratio** of O_2 taken in and CO_2 released is 1:1. However, when other substrates are respired, the ratio of the volumes of oxygen used and carbon dioxide given off differ. It follows that measuring this ratio, called the **respiratory quotient** (**RQ**), shows what substrate is being used in respiration. It can also show whether or not anaerobic respiration is occurring.

$$RQ = \frac{\text{volume of carbon dioxide given out in unit time}}{\text{volume of oxygen taken in in unit time}}$$

Or, from an equation,

$$RQ = \frac{\text{moles or molecules of carbon dioxide given out}}{\text{moles or molecules of oxygen taken in}}$$

For the aerobic respiration of glucose,

$$RQ = \frac{CO_2}{O_2} = \frac{6}{6} = 1.0$$

When the fatty acid oleic acid (from olive oil) is respired aerobically the equation is:

$$C_{18}H_{34}O_2 + 25.5\,O_2 \rightarrow 18CO_2 + 17H_2O + energy$$

For the aerobic respiration of oleic acid,

$$RQ = \frac{CO_2}{O_2} = \frac{18}{25.5} = 0.7$$

Typical RQs for the aerobic respiration of different substrates are shown in *table 1.3*.

SAQ 1.8

Calculate the RQ for the aerobic respiration of the fatty acid, stearic acid ($C_{18}H_{36}O_2$).

What happens when respiration is anaerobic? The equation for the alcoholic fermentation of glucose in a yeast cell is:

$$C_6H_{12}O_6 \rightarrow 2C_2H_5OH + 2CO_2 + energy$$

$$RQ = \frac{CO_2}{O_2} = \frac{2}{0} = \infty$$

Respiratory substrate	Respiratory quotient (RQ)
carbohydrate	1.0
lipid	0.7
protein	0.9

● **Table 1.3** Respiratory quotients of different substrates.

In reality, some respiration in the yeast cell will be aerobic and so a small volume of oxygen will be taken up and the RQ will be <2. High values of RQ indicate that anaerobic respiration is occurring: note that no RQ can be calculated for muscle cells using the lactate pathway since no carbon dioxide is produced:

glucose ($C_6H_{12}O_6$)

→ 2 lactic acid ($C_3H_6O_3$) + energy

Oxygen uptake during respiration can be measured using a **respirometer**. A respirometer suitable for measuring the rate of oxygen consumption of small terrestrial invertebrates at different temperatures is shown in *figure 1.19*.

Carbon dioxide produced in respiration is absorbed by a suitable chemical, such as soda-lime or a concentrated solution of potassium hydroxide or sodium hydroxide. Any decrease in the volume of air surrounding the organisms results from their oxygen consumption. Oxygen consumption in unit time can be measured by reading the level of the manometer fluid against the scale. Changes in temperature and pressure alter the volume of air in the apparatus and so the temperature of the surroundings must be kept constant whilst readings are taken, for example by using a thermostatically controlled water bath. The presence of a control tube containing an equal volume of inert material to the volume of the organisms used helps to compensate for changes in atmospheric pressure. Once measurements have been taken at a series of temperatures, a graph can be plotted of oxygen consumption against temperature.

The same apparatus can be used to measure the RQ of an organism. First, oxygen consumption at a particular temperature is found (x cm^3 min^{-1}). Then the respirometer is set up with the same organism at the same temperature, but with no chemical to absorb carbon dioxide. The manometer scale will show whether the volumes of oxygen absorbed and carbon dioxide produced are the same. When the volumes *are* the same, the level of the manometer fluid will not change and the RQ = 1. When more carbon dioxide is produced than oxygen absorbed, the scale will show an increase in the volume of air in the respirometer (by y cm^3 min^{-1}). The RQ can then be calculated:

$$RQ = \frac{CO_2}{O_2} = \frac{x + y}{x}$$

Conversely, when less carbon dioxide is produced than oxygen absorbed, the volume of air in the respirometer will decrease (by z cm^3 min^{-1}) and the calculation will be:

$$RQ = \frac{CO_2}{O_2} = \frac{x - z}{x}$$

SAQ 1.9

Outline the steps you would take to investigate the effect of temperature on respiration rate.

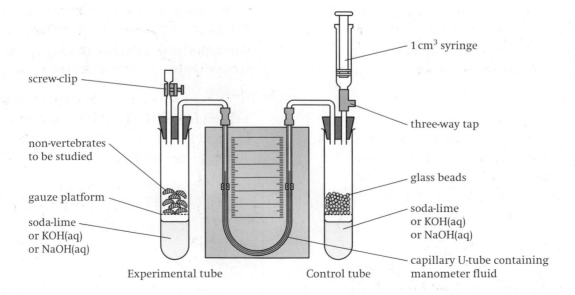

Figure 1.19 A respirometer.

SUMMARY

◆ Organisms must do work to stay alive. The energy input necessary for this work is either light, for photosynthesis, or the chemical potential energy of organic molecules. Photosynthesis traps light energy as chemical bond energy which can later be released and used by cells.

◆ Work includes anabolic reactions, active transport and mechanical work.

◆ Reactions which release energy must be harnessed to energy-requiring reactions. This 'harnessing' involves an intermediary molecule, ATP. This can be synthesised from ADP and phosphate using energy, and hydrolysed to ADP and phosphate to release energy. ATP therefore acts as an energy currency.

◆ Respiration is the sequence of enzyme-controlled steps by which an organic molecule, usually glucose, is broken down so that its chemical potential energy can be used to make the energy currency, ATP.

◆ In aerobic respiration, the sequence involves four main stages: glycolysis, the link reaction, the Krebs cycle and oxidative phosphorylation.

◆ In glycolysis, glucose is first phosphorylated and then split into two triose phosphate molecules. These are further oxidised to pyruvate, giving a small yield of ATP and reduced NAD. Glycolysis occurs in the cell cytoplasm.

◆ When oxygen is available (aerobic respiration), the pyruvate passes to the matrix of a mitochondrion. There, in the link reaction, it is decarboxylated and dehydrogenated and the remaining 2C acetyl unit combined with coenzyme A to give acetyl coenzyme A.

◆ The acetyl coenzyme A enters the Krebs cycle and donates the acetyl unit to oxaloacetate (4C) to make citrate (6C).

◆ The Krebs cycle decarboxylates and dehydrogenates citrate to oxaloacetate in a series of small steps. The oxaloacetate can then react with another acetyl coenzyme A from the link reaction.

◆ Dehydrogenation provides hydrogen atoms which are accepted by the carriers NAD and FAD. These pass to the inner membrane of the mitochondrial envelope where the hydrogens are split into hydrogen ions and electrons.

◆ The electrons are passed along a series of carriers. Some of the energy released in this process is used to phosphorylate ADP to ATP. The phosphorylation depends on a gradient of hydrogen ions set up across the inner membrane of the mitochondrial envelope.

◆ At the end of the carrier chain, electrons and protons are recombined and reduce oxygen to water.

◆ In the absence of oxygen as a hydrogen acceptor (anaerobic respiration), a small yield of ATP is made by dumping hydrogen into other pathways in the cytoplasm which produce ethanol or lactate.

◆ The energy values of respiratory substrates depend on the number of hydrogen atoms per molecule. Lipids have a higher energy density than carbohydrates or proteins.

◆ The respiratory quotient (RQ) is the ratio of the volumes of oxygen absorbed and carbon dioxide given off in respiration. The RQ reveals the nature of the substrate being respired.

◆ Oxygen uptake, and hence RQ, can be measured by using a respirometer.

Questions

1 Describe the structure of ATP and explain its role as an energy currency.

2 Describe how energy-yielding and energy-requiring reactions are linked in living cells.

3 Discuss the parts played in aerobic respiration by:
   a the phosphorylation of glucose;
   b acetyl coenzyme A;
   c the oxidative decarboxylation of pyruvate;
   d the electron transfer chain.

4 Explain why anaerobic respiration produces much less available energy than aerobic respiration.

5 a Outline the biochemical pathways by which energy is released from glucose in anaerobic conditions.
   b State what happens to the products of anaerobic respiration when oxygen becomes available.

6 Describe oxidative phosphorylation and distinguish it from oxidative decarboxylation.

7 Describe the functions of the various enzymes involved in respiration.

8 Outline the synthesis of ATP in respiration.

To answer the following questions you will need to bring together information from other areas of your course, as well as from this chapter.

9 a Describe the structure of a fluid mosaic membrane.
   b Describe the role of the proteins in the envelope of a mitochondrion in the process of aerobic respiration.

10 a Relate the roles of the different carbohydrates used in the storage and release of energy to their different structures.
   b Explain why carbohydrates and lipids used as respiratory substrates have different energy values and different respiratory quotients (RQs).

11 a Describe the roles of passive diffusion and facilitated diffusion in the process of aerobic respiration in a cell.
   b Explain how exercise leads to an oxygen debt.

CHAPTER 2

Photosynthesis

By the end of this chapter you should be able to:

1 explain that photosynthesis traps light energy as chemical energy in organic molecules, and that respiration releases this energy in a form which can be used by living organisms;

2 describe the photoactivation of chlorophyll that results in the conversion of light energy into chemical energy of ATP and reduction of NADP;

3 describe in outline the Calvin cycle involving the light-independent fixation of carbon dioxide by combination with a five-carbon compound (RuBP) to yield a three-carbon compound, GP (PGA), and the subsequent conversion of this compound into carbohydrates, amino acids and lipids;

4 describe the structure of a dicotyledonous leaf, a palisade cell and a chloroplast and relate these structures to their roles in photosynthesis;

5 discuss limiting factors in photosynthesis.

An energy transfer process

As you have seen at the beginning of chapter 1, the process of photosynthesis transfers light energy into chemical potential energy of organic molecules. This energy can then be released for work in respiration (*figure 1.1*). Almost all the energy transferred to all the ATP molecules in all living organisms is derived from light energy used in photosynthesis by autotrophs. Such **photoautotrophs** are green plants, the photo-synthetic prokaryotes and both single-celled and many-celled protoctists (including the green, red and brown algae). A few autotrophs do *not* depend on light energy, but use chemical energy sources. These **chemoautotrophs** include the nitrifying bacteria which are so important in the nitrogen cycle. These bacteria obtain their energy from oxidising ammonia to nitrite, or nitrite to nitrate.

An outline of the process

Photosynthesis is the trapping (fixation) of carbon dioxide and its subsequent reduction to carbohy-drate, using hydrogen from water.

An overall equation for photosynthesis in green plants is:

$$nCO_2 + nH_2O \xrightarrow[\text{in the presence of chlorophyll}]{\text{light energy}} (CH_2O)n + nO_2$$

carbon dioxide + water → carbohydrate + oxygen

Hexose sugars and starch are commonly formed, so the following equation is often used:

$$6CO_2 + 6H_2O \xrightarrow[\text{in the presence of chlorophyll}]{\text{light energy}} C_6H_{12}O_6 + 6O_2$$

carbon dioxide + water → carbohydrate + oxygen

Two sets of reactions are involved. These are the **light-dependent reactions**, for which light energy is necessary, and the **light-independent reactions**, for which light energy is not needed. The light-dependent reactions only take place in the presence of suitable pigments which absorb certain wavelengths of light. Light energy is necessary for the splitting of water into hydrogen and oxygen; oxygen is a waste product. Light energy is also needed to provide chemical energy (ATP) for the reduction of carbon dioxide to carbohydrate in the light-independent reactions.

Trapping light energy

Light energy is trapped by photosynthetic pigments. Different pigments absorb different wavelengths of light. The photosynthetic pigments of higher plants form two groups: the **chlorophylls** and the **carotenoids** (table 2.1).

Chlorophylls absorb mainly in the red and blue-violet regions of the light spectrum. They reflect

Pigment		Colour
Chlorophylls:	chlorophyll *a*	yellow-green
	chlorophyll *b*	blue-green
Carotenoids:	β carotene	orange
	xanthophyll	yellow

● **Table 2.1** The colours of the commonly occurring photosynthetic pigments.

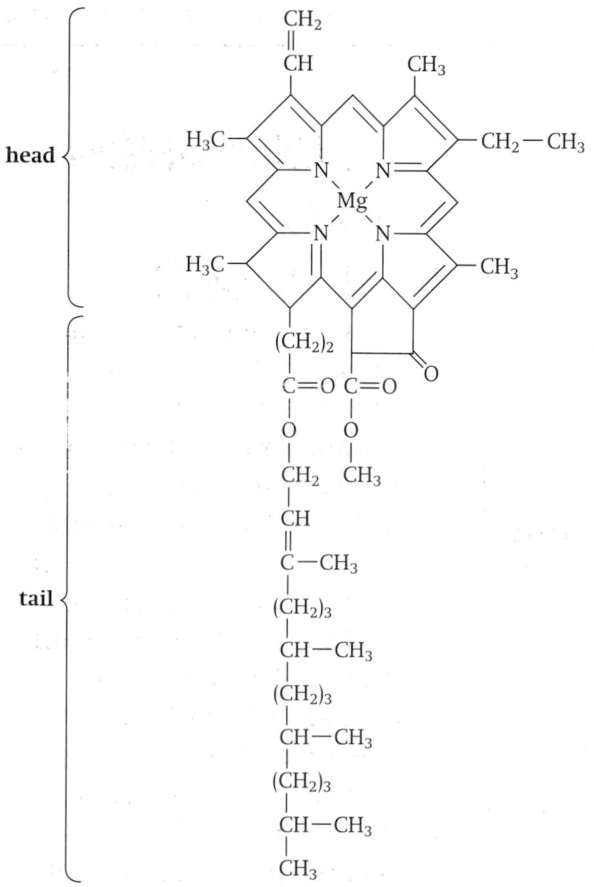

● **Figure 2.1** Structure of chlorophyll *a*.

green light, which is why plants look green. The structure of chlorophyll *a* is shown in *figure 2.1*. The carotenoids absorb mainly in the blue-violet region of the spectrum.

An **absorption spectrum** is a graph of the absorbance of different wavelengths of light by a pigment. The absorption spectra of chlorophyll *a* and *b*, and of the carotenoids can be seen in *figure 2.2a*.

An **action spectrum** is a graph of the rate of photosynthesis at different wavelengths of light (*figure 2.2b*). This shows the effectiveness of the different wavelengths, which is, of course, related to their absorption and to their energy content. The shorter the wavelength, the greater the energy it contains.

In the process of photosynthesis, the light energy absorbed by the photosynthetic pigments is converted to chemical energy. The absorbed light energy excites electrons in the pigment molecules. If you illuminate a solution of chlorophyll *a* or *b* with ultraviolet light, you will see a red fluorescence. (In the absence of a safe ultraviolet light, you can illuminate the pigment with a standard fluorescent tube.) The ultraviolet light is absorbed and electrons are excited but, in a solution which only contains extracted pigment, the absorbed energy cannot usefully be passed on to do work. The electrons return to their unexcited state and the absorbed energy is transferred to the surroundings as thermal energy and as light at a longer (less energetic) wavelength than that which was absorbed, and is seen as the red fluorescence. In the functioning photosynthetic system it is this energy that drives the process of photosynthesis.

The photosynthetic pigments fall into two categories: **primary pigments** and **accessory pigments**. The primary pigments are two forms of chlorophyll *a* with slightly different absorption peaks. The accessory pigments include other forms of chlorophyll *a*, chlorophyll *b* and the carotenoids. The pigments are arranged in light-harvesting clusters called **photosystems**. In a photosystem, several hundred accessory pigment molecules surround a primary pigment molecule and the energy of the light absorbed by the different pigments is passed to the primary pigment (*figure 2.3*). The primary pigments are said

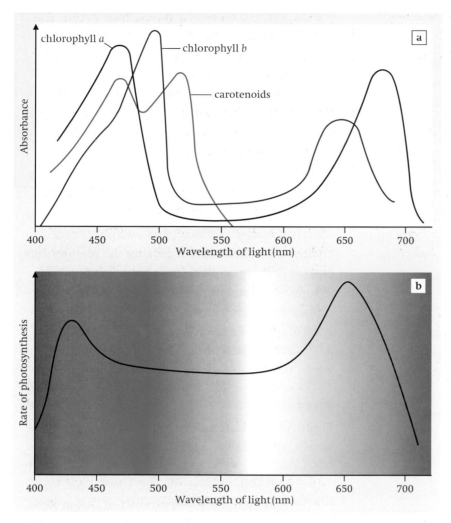

● **Figure 2.2**
a Absorption spectra of chlorophyll *a*, *b* and carotenoid pigments.
b Photosynthetic action spectrum.

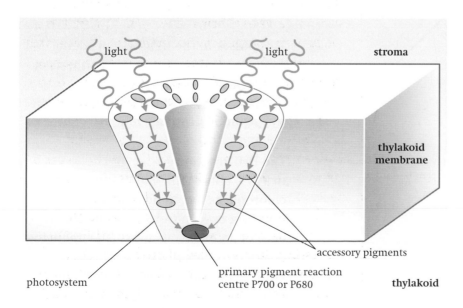

● **Figure 2.3** A photosystem: a light-harvesting cluster of photosynthetic pigments in a chloroplast thylakoid membrane. Only a few of the pigment molecules are shown.

to act as **reaction centres**. **Photosystem I** is arranged around a molecule of chlorophyll *a* with a peak absorption at 700 nm. The reaction centre of photosystem I is therefore known as **P700**. **Photosystem II** is based on a molecule of chlorophyll *a* with a peak absorption of 680 nm. The reaction centre of photosystem II is therefore known as **P680**.

SAQ 2.1 _____

Compare the absorption spectra shown in *figure 2.2a* with the action spectrum shown in *figure 2.2b*.
a Identify and explain any similarities in the absorption and action spectra.
b Identify and explain any differences between the absorption and action spectra.

The light-dependent reactions of photosynthesis

These reactions include the synthesis of ATP in photophosphorylation and the splitting of water by photolysis to give hydrogen ions. The hydrogen ions combine with a carrier molecule NADP (*box 1C* on page 7) to make reduced NADP. ATP and reduced NADP are passed from the light-dependent to the light-independent reactions.

Photophosphorylation of ADP to ATP can be cyclic or non-cyclic depending on the pattern of electron flow in one or both photosystems.

Cyclic photophosphorylation

Cyclic photophosphorylation involves only photosystem I. Light is absorbed by photosystem I and is passed to chlorophyll *a* (P700). An electron in the chlorophyll *a* molecule is excited to a higher energy level and is emitted from the chlorophyll molecule. Instead of falling back into the photosystem and losing its energy as fluorescence, it is captured by an electron acceptor and passed back to a chlorophyll *a* (P700) molecule via a chain of electron carriers. During this process enough energy is released to synthesise ATP from ADP and an inorganic phosphate group (P_i). The ATP then passes to the light-independent reactions.

Non-cyclic photophosphorylation

Non-cyclic photophosphorylation involves both photosystems in the so-called 'Z scheme' of electron flow (*figure 2.4*). Light is absorbed by both photosystems and excited electrons are emitted from the primary pigments of both reaction centres (P680 and P700). These electrons are

> ### Box 2A Redox reactions
> These are oxidation–reduction reactions and involve the transfer of electrons from an electron donor (reducing agent) to an electron acceptor (oxidising agent). Sometimes hydrogen atoms are transferred, so that dehydrogenation is equivalent to oxidation. Chains of electron carriers involve electrons passing via redox reactions from one carrier to the next. Such chains occur in both chloroplasts and mitochondria. During their passage, electrons fall from higher to lower energy states.

absorbed by electron acceptors and pass along chains of electron carriers leaving the photosystems positively charged. The P700 of photosystem I absorbs electrons from photosystem II. P680 receives replacement electrons from the splitting (photolysis) of water. As in cyclic photophosphorylation, ATP is synthesised as the electrons lose energy whilst passing along the carrier chain.

Photolysis of water

Photosystem II includes a water-splitting enzyme which catalyses the breakdown of water:

$$H_2O \rightarrow 2H^+ + 2e^- + \tfrac{1}{2}O_2$$

Oxygen is a waste product of this process. The hydrogen ions combine with electrons from photosystem I and the carrier molecule NADP to give reduced NADP.

$$2H^+ + 2e^- + NADP \rightarrow \text{reduced NADP}$$

This passes to the light-independent reactions and is used in the synthesis of carbohydrate.

The photolysis of water can be demonstrated by the Hill reaction.

The Hill reaction

In 1939, Robert Hill showed that isolated chloroplasts had 'reducing power', and liberated oxygen from water in the presence of an oxidising agent. The 'reducing power' was demonstrated by using a redox agent (*box 2A*) which changed colour on reduction. Hill used Fe^{3+} ions as his acceptor, but various redox agents, such as the blue dye DCPIP (dichlorophenolindophenol), can substitute for the

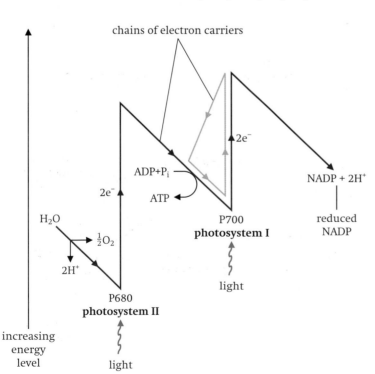

Key — flow of electrons in non-cyclic photophosphorylation
— flow of electrons in cyclic photophosphorylation

chains of electron carriers

$2e^-$

ADP+P_i

ATP

NADP + 2H$^+$

$2e^-$

H_2O

$\tfrac{1}{2}O_2$

$2H^+$

P700
photosystem I

reduced NADP

light

P680
photosystem II

light

increasing energy level

- **Figure 2.4** The 'Z scheme' of electron flow in photophosphorylation.

plant's NADP in this system. DCPIP becomes colourless when reduced:

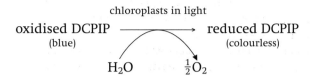

chloroplasts in light

oxidised DCPIP $\longrightarrow$ reduced DCPIP
(blue)   (colourless)

H_2O $\frac{1}{2}O_2$

Figure 2.5 shows classroom results of this reaction.

SAQ 2.2 _____

Examine the two curves shown in *figure 2.5* and explain:

a the downward trend of the two curves;
b the differences between the two curves.

SAQ 2.3 _____

Explain what contribution the discovery of the Hill reaction made to an understanding of the process of photosynthesis.

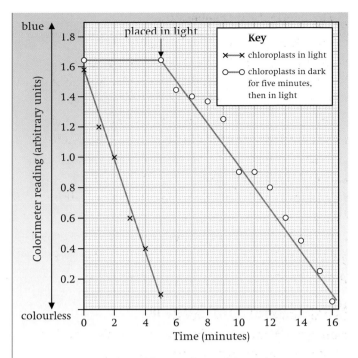

● **Figure 2.5** The Hill reaction. Chloroplasts were extracted from lettuce and placed in buffer solution with DCPIP. The colorimeter reading is proportional to the amount of DCPIP remaining unreduced.

The light-independent reactions of photosynthesis

The fixation of carbon dioxide is a light-independent process in which carbon dioxide combines with a five-carbon sugar, ribulose bisphosphate (RuBP), to give two molecules of a three-carbon compound, glycerate 3-phosphate (GP). (This compound is also sometimes known as PGA.)

GP, in the presence of ATP and reduced NADP from the light-dependent stages, is reduced to triose phosphate (three-carbon sugar).

This is the point at which carbohydrate is produced in photosynthesis. Some of these triose phosphates condense to form hexose phosphates, sucrose, starch and cellulose or are converted to acetylcoenzyme A (page 8) to make amino acids and lipids. Others regenerate RuBP. This cycle of events was worked out by Calvin, Benson and Bassham between 1946 and 1953, and is usually called the Calvin cycle

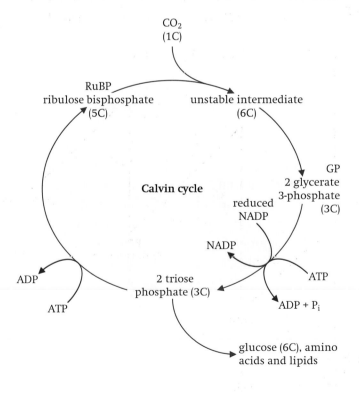

● **Figure 2.6** The Calvin cycle.

(*figure 2.6*). The enzyme ribulose bisphosphate carboxylase (rubisco), which catalyses the combination of carbon dioxide and RuBP, is the most common enzyme in the world.

Leaf structure and function

The leaf is the main photosynthetic organ in dicotyledons. It has a broad, thin lamina, a midrib and a network of veins. It may also have a leaf stalk (petiole). *Figure 2.7* is a photomicrograph of a section of a typical leaf from a mesophyte, that is a plant adapted for 'middling' terrestrial conditions (it is adapted neither for living in water nor for withstanding excessive drought).

To perform its function the leaf must:

- contain chlorophyll and other photosynthetic pigments arranged in such a way that they can absorb light;
- absorb carbon dioxide and dispose of the waste product oxygen;
- have a water supply and be able to export manufactured carbohydrate to the rest of the plant.

The large surface area of the lamina makes it easier to absorb light, and its thinness minimises the diffusion pathway for gaseous exchange. The arrangement of leaves on the plant (the leaf mosaic) helps the plant to absorb as much light as possible.

The upper **epidermis** is made of thin, flat, transparent cells which allow light through to the

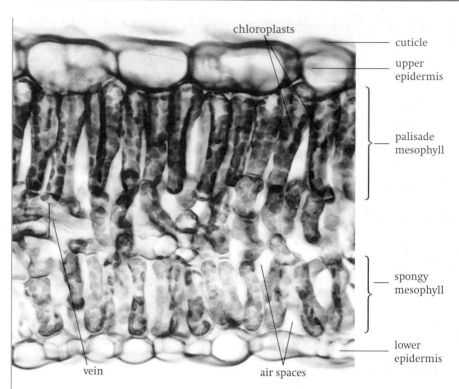

● **Figure 2.7** Photomicrograph of a TS of *Hypericum* leaf (× 1600).

cells of the mesophyll below, where photosynthesis takes place. A waxy transparent **cuticle**, which is secreted by the epidermal cells, provides a watertight layer. The cuticle and epidermis together form a protective layer.

The structure of the lower epidermis is similar to that of the upper, except that most mesophytes have many **stomata** in the lower epidermis. (Some have a few stomata in the upper epidermis also.) Stomata are pores in the epidermis through which diffusion of gases occurs. Each stoma is bounded by two sausage-shaped **guard cells** (*figure 2.8*). Changes in the turgidity of these guard cells cause them to change shape so that they open and close the pore. When the guard cells gain water, the pore opens; as they lose water it closes. Guard cells have unevenly thickened cell walls. The wall adjacent to the pore is very thick, whilst the wall furthest from the pore is thin. Bundles of cellulose microfibrils are arranged as hoops around the cells so that, as the cell becomes turgid, these hoops ensure that the cell mostly increases in length and not diameter. Since the ends of the two guard cells are joined and the thin outer wall bends more readily than the thick inner one, the guard cells become curved. This makes the pore between the cells open.

Guard cells gain and lose water by osmosis. A decrease in water potential is needed before water can enter the cells by osmosis. This is achieved by the active removal of hydrogen ions, using energy from ATP, and thence the intake of potassium ions (*figure 2.9*).

The structure of a **palisade cell** is shown in *figure 2.10*. The palisade mesophyll is the main site of photosynthesis, as there are more chloroplasts per cell than in the spongy mesophyll. The cells

stoma
guard cells
(flaccid)
thick cell wall
thin cell wall
guard cells
(turgid)
pore closed

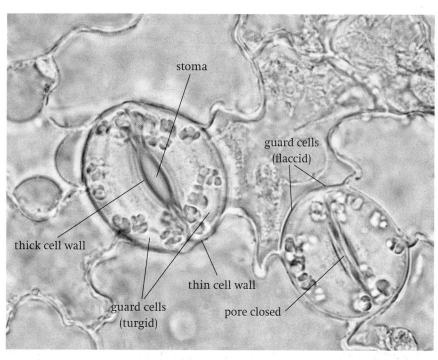

• **Figure 2.8** Photomicrograph of stomata and guard cells in *Tradescantia* leaf epidermis (× 4200).

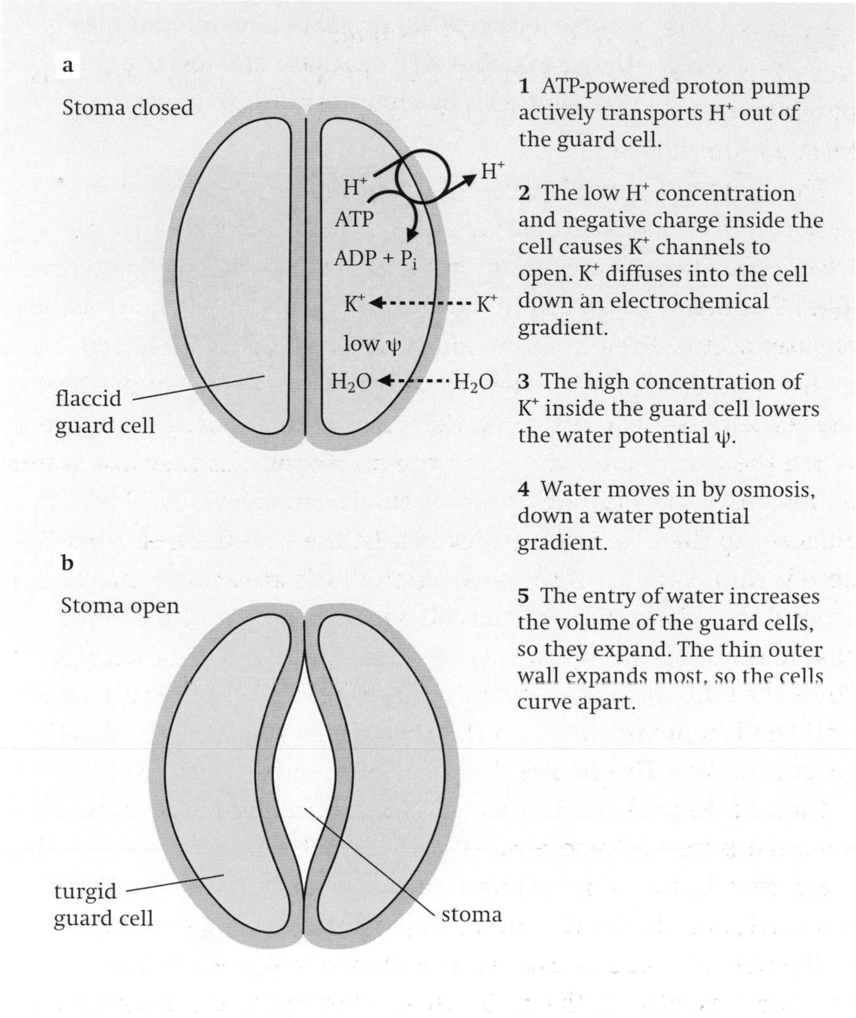

a
Stoma closed
H^+
ATP
ADP + P_i
H^+
K^+ ◄------- K^+
low ψ
H_2O ◄----- H_2O
flaccid
guard cell
1 ATP-powered proton pump actively transports H^+ out of the guard cell.
2 The low H^+ concentration and negative charge inside the cell causes K^+ channels to open. K^+ diffuses into the cell down an electrochemical gradient.
3 The high concentration of K^+ inside the guard cell lowers the water potential ψ.
4 Water moves in by osmosis, down a water potential gradient.
5 The entry of water increases the volume of the guard cells, so they expand. The thin outer wall expands most, so the cells curve apart.
b
Stoma open
turgid
guard cell
stoma

• **Figure 2.9** How a stoma is opened.

show several adaptations for light absorption.

- They are long cylinders arranged at right-angles to the upper epidermis. This reduces the number of light-absorbing cross walls in the upper part of the leaf so that as much light as possible can reach the chloroplasts.
- The cells have a large vacuole with a thin peripheral layer of cytoplasm. This restricts the chloroplasts to a layer near the outside of the cell where light can reach them most easily.
- The chloroplasts can be moved (by proteins in the cytoplasm – they cannot move themselves) within the cells, to absorb the most light or to protect the chloroplasts from excessive light intensities.

The palisade cells also show adaptations for gaseous exchange.

- The cylindrical cells pack together with long, narrow air spaces between them. This gives a large surface area of contact between cell and air.
- The cell walls are thin, so that gases can diffuse through them more easily.

Spongy mesophyll is mainly adapted as a surface for the exchange of carbon dioxide and oxygen. The cells contain chloroplasts, but in smaller numbers than in palisade cells. Photosynthesis occurs in the spongy mesophyll only at high light intensities. The irregular packing of the cells and the large air spaces thus produced provide a large surface area of moist cell wall for gaseous exchange.

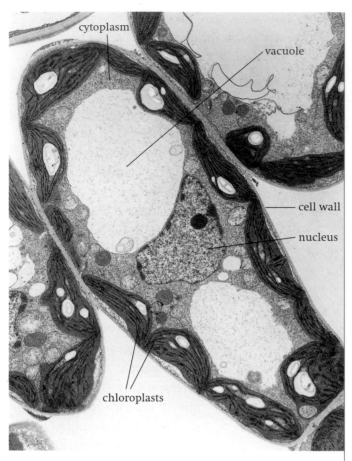

● **Figure 2.10** TEM of a palisade cell from soya bean leaf (× 4200).

surrounded by an envelope of two phospholipid membranes. A system of membranes also runs through the ground substance, or **stroma**. The membrane system is the site of the light-dependent reactions of photosynthesis. It consists of a series of flattened fluid-filled sacs, or **thylakoids**, which in places form stacks, called **grana**, that are joined to one another by membranes. The membranes of the grana provide a large surface area which holds the pigments, enzymes and electron carriers needed for the light-dependent reactions. They make it possible for a large number of pigment molecules to be arranged so that they can absorb as much light as necessary. The pigment molecules are also arranged in particular light-harvesting clusters for efficient light absorption. In each photosystem the different pigments are arranged in the thylakoid in funnel-like structures (*figure 2.3*). Each pigment passes energy to the next member of the cluster, finally 'feeding' it to the chlorophyll *a* reaction centre (either P700 or P680). The membranes of the grana hold ATP synthase and are the site of ATP synthesis by chemiosmosis (page 4).

The veins in the leaf help to support the large surface area of the leaf. They contain xylem, which brings in the water necessary for photosynthesis and for cell turgor, and phloem, which takes the products of photosynthesis to other parts of the plant.

Chloroplast structure and function

In eukaryotic organisms, the photosynthetic organelle is the **chloroplast**. In dicotyledons, chloroplasts can be seen with a light microscope and appear as biconvex discs about 3–10 μm in diameter. There may be only a few chloroplasts in a cell or as many as 100 in some palisade mesophyll cells.

The structure of a chloroplast is shown in *figure 2.11*. Each chloroplast is

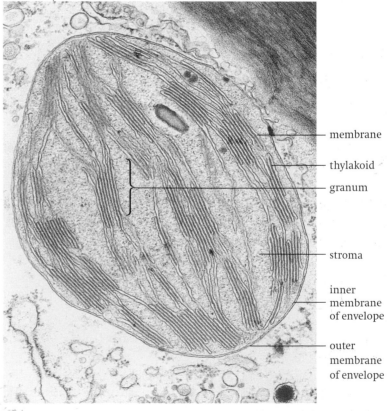

● **Figure 2.11** TEM of a chloroplast from *Potamogeton* leaf (× 27 000).

The stroma is the site of the light-independent reactions. It contains the enzymes of the Calvin cycle, sugars and organic acids. It bathes the membranes of the grana and so can receive the products of the light-dependent reactions. Also within the stroma are small (70 S) ribosomes, a loop of DNA, lipid droplets and starch grains. The loop of DNA codes for some of the chloroplast proteins, which are made by the chloroplast's ribosomes. However, other chloroplast proteins are coded for by the DNA in the plant cell nucleus.

SAQ 2.4

List the features of a chloroplast that aid photosynthesis.

Factors necessary for photosynthesis

You can see from the equation on page 17 that certain factors are necessary for photosynthesis to occur, namely the presence of a suitable photosynthetic pigment, a supply of carbon dioxide, water and light energy.

Factors affecting the rate of photosynthesis

The main external factors affecting the rate of photosynthesis are light intensity, temperature and carbon dioxide concentration.

In the early 1900s F. F. Blackman investigated the effects of light intensity and temperature on the rate of photosynthesis. At constant temperature, the rate of photosynthesis varies with the light intensity, initially increasing as the light intensity increases (*figure 2.12*). However, at higher light intensities this relationship no longer holds and the rate of photosynthesis reaches a plateau.

The effect on the rate of photosynthesis of varying the temperature at constant light intensities can be seen in *figure 2.13*. At high light intensities the rate of photo-

synthesis increases as the temperature is increased over a limited range. At low light intensities, increasing the temperature has little effect on the rate of photosynthesis.

These two experiments illustrate two important points. Firstly, from other research we know that photochemical reactions are not generally affected by temperature. However, these experiments clearly show that temperature affects the rate of photosynthesis, so there must be two sets of reactions in the full process of photosynthesis. These are a light-dependent photochemical stage and a light-independent, temperature-dependent stage. Secondly, Blackman's experiments illustrate the concept of 'limiting factors'.

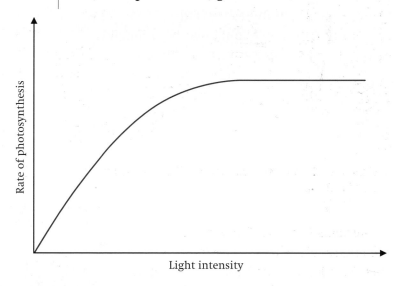

● **Figure 2.12** The rate of photosynthesis at different light intensities and constant temperature.

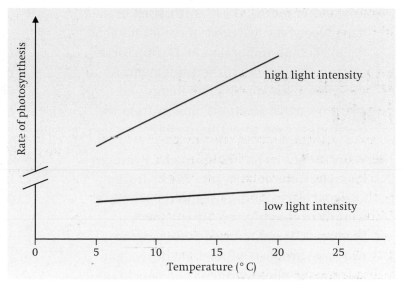

● **Figure 2.13** The rate of photosynthesis at different temperatures and constant light intensities.

Limiting factors

The rate of any process which depends on a series of reactions is limited by the slowest reaction in the series. In biochemistry, if a process is affected by more than one factor, the rate will be limited by the factor which is nearest its lowest value.

Look again at *figure 2.12*. At low light intensities, the limiting factor governing the rate of photosynthesis is the light intensity; as the intensities increase so does the rate. But at high light intensities one or more other factors must be limiting, such as temperature or carbon dioxide supply.

At constant light intensities and temperature, the rate of photosynthesis initially increases with an increasing concentration of carbon dioxide, but again reaches a plateau at higher concentrations. A graph of the rate of photosynthesis at different concentrations of carbon dioxide has the same shape as that for different light intensities (*figure 2.12*). At low concentrations of carbon dioxide, the supply of carbon dioxide is the rate-limiting factor. At higher concentrations of carbon dioxide, other factors are rate-limiting, such as light intensity or temperature.

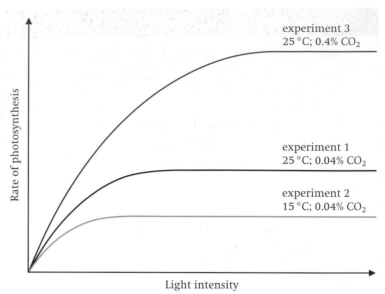

● **Figure 2.14** The rate of photosynthesis at different temperatures and different carbon dioxide concentrations. (0.04% CO_2 is about atmospheric concentration.)

SAQ 2.5

Examine *figure 2.14* which shows the effect of various factors on the rate of photosynthesis and explain the differences in the results of:

a experiments 1 and 2;

b experiments 1 and 3.

SUMMARY

◆ In photosynthesis, ATP is synthesised in the light-dependent reactions of cyclic and non-cyclic photophosphorylation. During these reactions the photosynthetic pigments of the chloroplast absorb light energy and give out excited electrons. Energy from the electrons is used to synthesise ATP.

◆ Water is split by photolysis to give hydrogen ions, electrons and oxygen. The hydrogen ions and electrons are used to reduce NADP and the oxygen is given off as a waste product. ATP and reduced NADP are the two main products of the light-dependent reactions of photosynthesis and pass to the light-independent reactions.

◆ Carbon dioxide is trapped and reduced to carbohydrate in the light-independent reactions of photosynthesis, using ATP and reduced NADP from the light-dependent reactions. This fixation of carbon dioxide requires an acceptor molecule, ribulose bisphosphate, and involves the Calvin cycle.

◆ Chloroplasts, mesophyll cells and whole leaves are all adapted for the process of photosynthesis.

◆ The rate of photosynthesis is subject to various limiting factors.

Questions

1   Discuss the roles of pigments and carrier molecules in the light-dependent stage of photosynthesis.

2   Describe the fixation of carbon dioxide in the light-independent stage of photosynthesis.

3   Explain how
    a   light energy from the Sun, and
    b   carbon dioxide from the air, pass to and are used by the chloroplast during photosynthesis.

4   Give an account of the structure, function and distribution of chloroplasts in leaves.

5   Describe how the light energy of the Sun is converted to chemical energy in green plants.

6   Explain what is meant by the term *limiting factor*. Illustrate your answer by reference to the effects of temperature on photosynthesis.

To answer the following questions you will need to bring together information from other areas of your course as well as from this chapter.

7   a   Compare the structures of chloroplasts and mitochondria with the structure of a typical prokaryotic cell.
    b   Describe the roles of membranes in chloroplast function.

8   a   Describe the functions of xylem and phloem in photosynthesis in a leaf.
    b   Relate these functions to the structure of the two tissues.

9   With reference to enzyme function explain the effect on the rate of photosynthesis of:
    a   increasing the concentration of carbon dioxide;
    b   increasing the temperature.

CHAPTER 3

Populations and interactions

By the end of this chapter you should be able to:

1 describe and explain sigmoidal population growth in a bacterial culture;

2 explain, and give examples of, the significance of limiting factors in determining the final size of a population;

3 explain the meaning of the term *carrying capacity*;

4 describe an example of a predator–prey relationship and its possible effect on the population size of both the predator and the prey;

5 describe, and give examples of, inter- and intraspecific competition;

6 explain the effects of interspecific competition on the distribution and population size of two named species;

7 describe one example of primary succession resulting in a climax community;

8 understand that environmental conditions may limit the distribution of organisms, and describe structural and physiological adaptations of named organisms to their environment;

9 describe techniques you could use to investigate the distribution and abundance of named organisms in a specific habitat, including the use of quadrats, point quadrats and transects;

10 discuss the possible conflicts of interest between production and conservation, with reference to the effects of nitrogen-containing fertilisers, and alternatives to their use;

11 explain how temperate forests and woodland can be sustainably managed for the production of timber.

I n chapter 7 in *Biology 1*, we considered the transfer of energy between the organisms in an ecosystem, and looked briefly at how this can affect the sizes of populations of organisms that feed at different trophic levels. In chapters 1 and 2 in this book, we have now looked in more detail at how organisms obtain the energy that they need. In this chapter, we are going to look at a number of different factors that influence the distribution and sizes of populations, including some aspects of the human activities of farming and forestry.

Population size

You will remember that a population can be defined as a group of organisms of the same species, which live in the same place at the same time, and can interbreed with each other (*Biology 1*, page 92). The number of individuals in a population may remain fairly steady over time, or it may change. Sometimes, populations suddenly rise or fall very dramatically. Sometimes, populations oscillate, rising and falling with a fairly regular pattern – lemmings are famous for this.

The reasons for these changes are often not at all obvious, and although biologists have been collecting data and carrying out laboratory-based experiments since the early part of the twentieth century to find out what controls population sizes, there is still a great deal that we do not understand.

The sigmoid growth curve

In a population of organisms living in the wild, there will usually be a number of different factors influencing its size, and these will probably interact in complex ways. As we cannot control most of these factors, it is extremely difficult to determine just what effects each of them is having. It therefore makes sense to try to investigate the control of population sizes in simple situations that can be set up in a laboratory. One such situation is the growth of a population of microorganisms, such as bacteria, when they are cultured in a flask containing nutrient broth. (Nutrient broth is a solution containing all the nutrients that the bacteria need.)

Figure 3.1 shows the results of such an experiment. At time 0, a few bacteria are introduced into the broth. At first, nothing very much seems to happen; the numbers of bacteria remain almost constant. This is called the **lag phase** of population growth. During this time, the bacteria are adjusting to the conditions in the broth, synthesising the enzymes that they need to be able to

use the nutrients in it (this is described more fully on page 62 in this book). Then, in this case after a few hours, the population begins to grow. The bacterial cells grow and divide, grow and divide, over and over again. This is called the **log phase**. The population grows very rapidly, as one bacterium divides to form two, then four, then eight, then sixteen and so on. The rate at which this happens is limited only by each bacterium's own internal 'machinery', for example how fast it can replicate its DNA and synthesise the proteins that it requires.

After some hours, however, the nutrients in the broth begin to run out. The individuals in the large population of bacteria begin to slow down their rate of growth and division, as they compete with each other for the ever-decreasing quantity of nutrients. Moreover, their own excretory products are now accumulating in the broth, and these may also inhibit their metabolism and slow down their rate of growth and division. The growth curve now begins to level out, and eventually becomes horizontal. This is called the **stationary phase**. During the stationary phase, the overall population size remains constant, although individual bacteria may well be dying or dividing – but the number dying is exactly matched by the number of new individuals being produced.

Eventually, the quantity of nutrients in the broth becomes so low, and the concentration of excretory products so high, that the bacteria can no longer reproduce. Individuals begin to die, and are not replaced by new ones. The population enters the **decline phase** or **death phase**. The population decreases, eventually reaching zero when every bacterium has died.

You can see that the first part of this curve – up to the beginning of the decline phase – makes an S-shape. The curve is said to be **sigmoid**.

Limiting factors and carrying capacity

Anything that stops a population from increasing in size is said to be a **limiting factor**. In the case of the bacteria in the nutrient broth, the limiting factor is the amount of nutrients in the broth. Once these begin to be in short supply, the population can no longer continue to grow at its maximum rate and eventually stops growing completely.

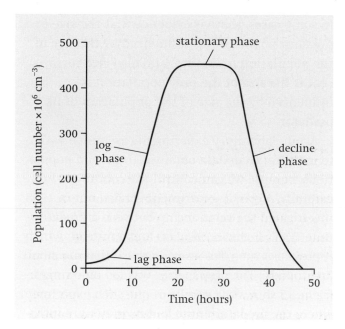

● **Figure 3.1** Growth curve for a population of bacteria in a flask containing nutrient broth.

In a wild population, many different factors may limit population growth at different times and in different ways. Imagine, for example, a population of thrushes in the gardens of a small town (*figure 3.2*). The thrushes feed on snails, slugs and other small invertebrates, so if there is a limited supply of these this may prevent the population from growing beyond a certain level. They need nesting sites, and if these are in limited supply this, too, may act as a limiting factor for their population size. They are predated by cats and birds such as kestrels and sparrow hawks; if the number of predators is high, this may keep the thrush numbers down. Parasites could also affect them. Between them, these factors limiting the size of the thrush population effectively place an upper limit on the number of thrushes that can live in this area. This upper limit on the size of a population that the environment can sustain is known as the **carrying capacity** of the habitat.

You could imagine what might happen if some thrushes were introduced into an area where there had previously been none. Like the bacteria in the flask, their population would probably go through a lag phase and then a log phase, until the limiting factors described above (or perhaps others that we have not thought of) begin to slow down and eventually limit their population growth.

However, unlike the bacteria in their flask, it is unlikely that the thrush population would enter a decline phase, because it is probable that the supply of food and nest sites will never entirely run out – they will just remain in short supply. The thrush population will probably stay in the stationary phase. However, it is unlikely to remain absolutely constant; it will probably fluctuate up and down a little, perhaps in response to particularly cold or wet winters, or summers when snails are in particularly good supply, for example.

Although we have made what seem like sensible suggestions about what factors might be important in limiting a population such as this one, you can imagine how very difficult it would be to obtain experimental evidence to support these ideas. If we thought, for example, that food supply might be limiting the thrush population, we could try supplying lots of extra snails, and then see if this has an effect on the population size. But it would be virtually impossible to control all the other variables, such as size of predator or parasite populations, and we certainly cannot control the weather. So it would be extremely difficult to interpret the results we obtained. We are therefore only very, very rarely sure that one particular factor really does have a significant influence on population size. In most populations that have been studied, the evidence points to many different factors interacting with each other to limit the size of the population.

Predator–prey relationships

In some cases, there is evidence that the size of a predator population is influenced by the size of the population of its prey, and also vice versa – that is the size of the prey population is influenced by the size of the population of its predator.

Again, laboratory experiments are much easier to interpret than data obtained from wild populations, because we can control the conditions more carefully. A classic experiment carried out in 1958 investigated the relationship between a predatory mite *Typhlodromus occidentalis* and a mite on which it preys, *Eotetranychus sexmaculatus*. (Mites are small arthropods.) The prey species was fed on oranges. *Figure 3.3* shows the results of one such experiment, where the predatory mite and its prey were introduced into a complex environment containing a large number of oranges, with partial barriers of

● **Figure 3.2** Song thrushes, *Turdus philomelos*, can break open snail shells by smashing them against a stone.

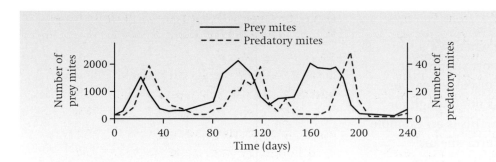

● **Figure 3.3** Changes in population size of a predatory mite (*Typhlodromus occidentalis*) and its prey (*Eotetranychus sexmaculatus*).

Vaseline between the oranges, but also some small upright sticks that allowed the mites to disperse gradually from one orange to the next. You can see that the populations of both mites oscillate.

SAQ 3.1

a At what trophic levels do each of the mites feed?

b From what you know about energy transfer between trophic levels, explain why the size of the population of the predatory mite is always lower than that of its prey.

Closer examination of the graph reveals some other patterns. The population of the prey species rises first, followed by that of the predator. This makes sense, because we would expect the population of the predatory mite to be able to grow only when it has plenty of food – thus the rise in the predator

population *follows* that of the prey. As the predator population rises, this begins to limit the prey population, so that begins to fall. This reduction in food supply limits the predator population, so that then begins to fall. As the predator population decreases, then the prey population can begin to increase again, and so on.

There are a few cases where populations of predator and prey behave like this in 'wild' situations. It only seems to work where the predator specialises in one type of prey. Clearly if the predator eats many different types of prey, then it can just switch to a different one if the population of one particular type begins to fall. For example, dog whelks (predatory snails that live on rocky sea shores) prefer to feed on mussels when these are available, but if the mussel population is not very large then they will feed on barnacles instead. It also only happens where predation is the main limiting factor for the prey population (not disease, or food supply or anything else) and where food supply is the main limiting factor for the predator population. Predator–prey interactions may, for example, be the main factors limiting populations of lynxes (predators) and snowshoe hares (prey) in northern Canada (*figure 3.4*).

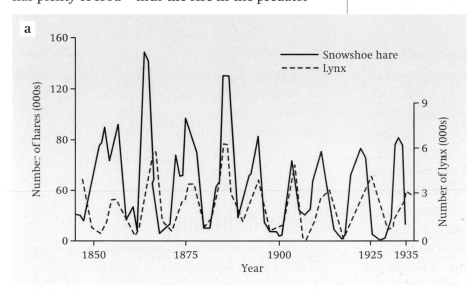

● **Figure 3.4** The relationship between the numbers of lynx (predator) and snowshoe hare (prey) between 1845 and 1935 as shown by the number of animals trapped for the Hudson's Bay Company.

Competition

Organisms are said to **compete** whenever a resource that they need is in short supply. For example, the thrushes that we discussed earlier may compete for food if there is not enough for all of them, or for nesting sites. This is an example of **intraspecific competition**. 'Intra' means 'within', so intraspecific competition occurs between members of the same species. It can be an extremely important factor in limiting population sizes. It can also, as you will see in chapter 5, greatly influence the evolution of species through natural selection.

Competition can also occur between organisms of *different* species. This is known as **interspecific competition**. Interspecific competition will only occur when the niches (*Biology 1*, page 93) of the two species overlap. The more the niches overlap, the more likely competition is to occur. Once again, we have learnt most about this from relatively simple situations set up as laboratory experiments, rather than from trying to unravel the complex situations that occur in the wild.

One such experiment, first carried out in 1948, involved two species of small beetles that live and breed in flour. They have unexciting lives, both the adults and larvae living entirely on and in flour. They are occasionally found in houses, where you might see them as tiny, slow-moving dark insects in bags of flour that have been left around for rather too long.

The two species of flour beetles in this particular experiment were *Tribolium confusum* and *Tribolium castaneum*. If small numbers of both species were placed in some wholemeal flour to which a little yeast had been added, then the population of *T. castaneum* almost always rose and then oscillated, while that of *T. confusum* gradually fell until it died out altogether (*figure 3.5*). Similar results have been found in many other cases when two species with very similar requirements are living and breeding in the same restricted habitat. One very often out-competes the other, so that they cannot coexist. However, in the *Tribolium* experiments, it was found that a very small change in the conditions in which they lived could alter *which* species survived. For example, if the temperature was above 29 °C

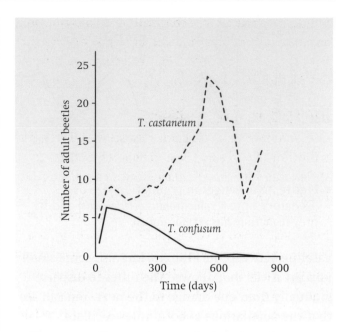

● **Figure 3.5** Changes in population size of two species of flour beetle, *Tribolium castaneum* and *T. confusum*, competing for food and space in a container of wholemeal flour.

then it was *T. castaneum* that survived while, at temperatures below 29 °C, *T. confusum* survived. If a protozoan that parasitised both species was introduced, then *T. castaneum* was almost always the species to die out.

In other similar experiments, however, it is found that two species with very similar niches can survive indefinitely together. For example, two different species of beetles that live and feed in stored wheat grain, *Oryzaephilus* sp. and *Rhizopertha* sp., can coexist in laboratory conditions for long periods of time. Although the adults of both species feed on the outside of the wheat grains and therefore compete directly with one another, the larvae of *Rhizopertha* feed from inside the grains while *Oryzaephilus* larvae feed from the outside. This small difference in their niches seems to be enough to enable the two species to live alongside one another.

Species distribution

In natural populations, interspecific competition can be of great importance in determining the **distribution** of species – that is where they live – as well as the sizes of their populations. Usually, however, interspecific competition is only one of a whole range of factors that influence distribution, and one task of a population biologist or ecologist is to try to sort out just what effects these different factors are having.

Barnacles on a rocky shore

One example that has been well studied is the distribution of two species of barnacles, *Chthamalus stellatus* and *Balanus balanoides*. You can often find these on rocky shores around Britain. Adult barnacles live fixed firmly to rocks, lying on their backs inside their strong outer shells and waving their legs in the water around them to catch food when the tide comes in. Their larvae are planktonic – that is they float in the sea, from which some of them will be washed onto rocks where they settle down to spend the rest of their lives.

Figure 3.6 shows the distribution of these two species of barnacles on a rocky shore in Scotland. The tide comes in twice a day, covering the rocks before retreating again. So each part of the shore is under water for part of each day, and exposed to the air for the rest of the time. The higher up the shore a barnacle lives, the less time it is covered by water. Another problem for barnacles living high up a shore is that temperatures fluctuate much more here than when they are close to, or covered by, the water. It seems that neither *Chthamalus* nor *Balanus* are able to live any higher up the shore than they do, because they cannot cope with the temperature fluctuations or long periods of

exposure to drying air that they would experience there. *Chthamalus*, however, is better than *Balanus* at coping with this, so it is found higher up.

At the bottom end of their range on the shore, *Balanus* is unable to live any further down the shore because here it becomes more likely to be eaten by the predatory dog whelk, *Nucellus*, which is only active when covered by water. Moreover, algae grow on these rocks that spend much of their time covered with water, and *Balanus* is not good at competing with these algae for space on the rocks.

In the middle of the range, there is only a very small area where both *Chthamalus* and *Balanus* are found together. If all the *Balanus* are removed from the region below the bottom of *Chthamalus*'s range, or if rocks with *Chthamalus* on them are placed lower down the shore, then it is found that *Chthamalus* is perfectly capable of surviving here. What normally stops it is competition with *Balanus* – in this part of the shore, *Balanus* grows faster than *Chthamalus*, and so wins the competition for limited space on the rocks.

SAQ 3.2
Summarise the main factors limiting distribution of:

a *Chthamalus* at the top of its range on the shore;

b *Chthamalus* at the bottom of its range on the shore;

c *Balanus* at the top of its range on the shore;

d *Balanus* at the bottom of its range on the shore.

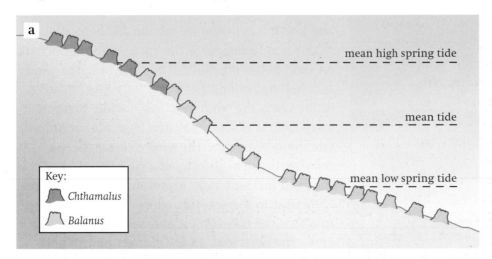

Key:
- *Chthamalus*
- *Balanus*

mean high spring tide

mean tide

mean low spring tide

● **Figure 3.6 a** The distribution of two species of barnacles, *Chthamalus stellatus* and *Balanus balanoides*, on a rocky shore. **b** The barnacle *Balanus balanoides*. When the barnacles are not covered by water, they close the central diamond-shaped opening. *Chthamalus* looks very similar, but has a more kite-shaped opening.

Succession

Species distribution does not necessarily remain constant over long periods of time. Ecosystems are dynamic; they can and do change.

In *Biology 1*, we defined the term 'ecosystem' as a relatively self-contained, interacting community of organisms, and the environment in which they live and with which they interact. Because organisms and their environment interact, a change in one affects the other. A change in the environment affects the organisms, and a change in the organisms affects the environment.

Imagine, for example, a volcanic eruption such as that which occurred from Mount St Helens in the USA in 1980. Huge quantities of lava and ash spread over the mountainside, destroying all forms of life (*figure 3.7*). Ecologists have been studying the recolonisation of one small area since that time. In 1981, there were still no plants growing in it; it was just bare, dry, stony grey ash and rock. By 1990, eleven species of plants had colonised it, though there were not very many of any of them. By 2000, there were more individual plants of more species, and they were covering more of the ground. Instead of just ash, something that is beginning to look like soil is forming.

The first species to colonise bare ground like this are called **pioneer plants**. They are able to survive in very difficult conditions; some, for example wild

● **Figure 3.7** Thick layers of ash covered huge areas following the Mount St Helens eruption, destroying all living things.

lupins, are able to fix nitrogen, which helps them to grow even where there is almost no nitrate in the soil. The presence of the lupins and other pioneer plants gradually changes the environmental conditions; they provide shelter for other seeds to germinate, or for insects to hide. Dead leaves that fall from them provide humus that becomes part of the soil, improving its water-holding capacities and nutrient content. So, over many years, the environmental conditions become suitable for a wider range of plants to live. The number of species increases, and some of the pioneer plants will disappear because they are not good at competing with the newcomers. Eventually, we would expect these devastated mountain slopes to become covered with forests again.

This gradual, directional change in a community over time is called **succession**. In this case, where the starting point was bare ground with no living things present, it is known as **primary succession**. In other cases, such as where a woodland was felled to remove all the trees, but leaving a soil cover and some plants, then you would get a **secondary succession**. In either case, the final community that results – such as the forest on Mount St Helens – is called the **climax community**.

Succession on sand dunes

You may get an opportunity to study succession. You do not necessarily have to stay in one place for years and years to watch the succession happening. In many cases, you can see the early, middle and late stages of the succession all there at once.

One good example is the succession that occurs on sand dunes (*figure 3.8*). On some beaches, sand accumulates inland from the sea's edge. Nearest to the sea is the 'youngest' sand, while furthest away from it is sand that first began to accumulate many years ago. The sand nearest the sea represents the beginning of a succession, while the sand furthest away represents the later stages.

Nearest to the sea, just above the highest point to which the tide comes, only very few plants grow. The ones that do are pioneer plants, and they are adapted to survive the harsh environmental conditions there. The sand has very few nutrients, and it is unstable. The pioneer plants must also be tolerant of salt spray, and they have

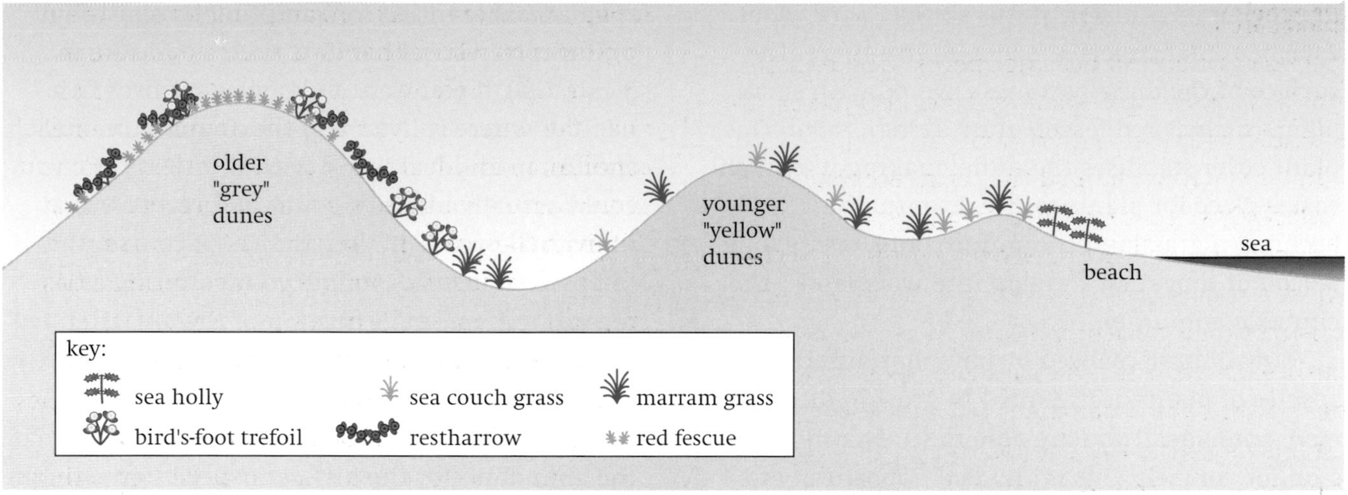

● **Figure 3.8** Succession on sand dunes.

key:
- sea holly
- bird's-foot trefoil
- sea couch grass
- restharrow
- marram grass
- red fescue

xeromorphic features (*Biology 1*, pages 138–9) that help them to cope with the lack of fresh water in the fast-draining sand. Plants that you might find in this area include sea rocket, *Cakile maritima* and sea holly, *Eryngium maritimum*.

As the sand blows in from the shore, it accumulates in little heaps around the bases of these plants. A tiny 'sand dune' forms around them, with most of the sand building up on the side furthest from the sea, in the lee of the onshore wind. This is a slightly more sheltered environment than the open shore, and within it nutrients begin to build up as parts of the plants decay. A little further up the shore, away from the sea, sea couch grass, *Agropyron junceiforme*, may become established. This has underground (or rather undersand) stems that spread out widely, helping to stabilise the sand. Small dunes build up around it.

As these plants trap and stabilise the sand and help nutrients to build up, they alter the conditions so that other plants can grow. Marram grass, *Ammophila arenaria*, is one of these. Water is still in very short supply, so marram grass has xeromorphic adaptations (one of these is shown in *figure 10.14* in *Biology 1*), but here it is more sheltered from the salt spray than it would be if it grew on the most exposed parts of the shore. Once again, dunes build up around the marram plants, but

these can become much higher than the ones that form around sea couch grass, partly because marram is able to produce new shoots higher up its stem, so as the sand builds up the marram plants can 'climb' upwards to keep their leaves above it. The extensive root system of the marram plants stabilises the sand (*figure 3.9*).

When the marram first colonises the 'soil', it is still very low in nutrients and is scarcely more than sand, but gradually humus and nutrients build up in it, and other plants begin to colonise. At the base of the dunes, where most water is available, a wide range of plants can now grow. Quite a few of these are nitrogen-fixers, such as restharrow, *Ononis repens* and bird's-foot trefoil, *Lotus corniculatus*. They add nitrate to the soil,

● **Figure 3.9** These high yellow dunes have built up behind the sea (which is off to the right of this photograph). The vegetation on them is mostly marram grass, which stabilises the sand.

improving its nutrient status so that a yet wider variety of plant species is able to live there. The surface of the dune becomes covered with small plants such as red fescue grass, *Festuca rubra*. This plant cover stabilises the dune, making it a much easier place for plants to live. Eventually, it becomes a grassland community and, over a long period of time, may develop into woodland – the climax community.

You will have realised by now that different species of plants are adapted to grow in different environments. If you are able to study a succession for yourself, this is an ideal opportunity to look closely at the structural and physiological adaptations of different plant species, and to consider how these relate to their environment. In chapter 5, you will see how natural selection is involved in the evolution of these adaptations.

SAQ 3.3

Choose two plant or animal species, and describe the structural and physiological adaptations that help them to survive in a particular environment. You can use the descriptions above, *figure 10.13* in *Biology 1*, your own observations from your fieldwork and other books as sources of information.

Sampling techniques

When ecologists study an ecosystem, they usually want to know what species of organisms live there. They are often also interested in the relative abundance of these different species. In your own ecological fieldwork, you will probably use a variety of different techniques to help you to collect data about the distribution and abundance of organisms in the community you are studying.

Quadrats

You will almost certainly use quadrats in your ecological studies. A **quadrat** (not, notice, a *quadrant*, which is something quite different!) is simply a square frame. Quadrats can be almost any size that you like, and they can be made of almost anything that you like – an old wire coat hanger can be bent into shape to form a square, or you can use specially-made wooden ones, for example.

Quadrats are used for **sampling** in relatively uniform terrestrial habitats such as grassland (*figure 3.10*). If you want to know what lives in a habitat, where it lives, and the abundance of each species, in an ideal world with limitless time you could actually identify, count and record every individual organism. In practice, of course, this is impossible. Instead, you do your counting and recording for a small fraction of the area, defined by your quadrat, that you hope is representative of the whole.

Imagine, for example, that you want to estimate the abundance of the different species growing in a field used for grazing sheep. If the field looks fairly uniform, then you should be able to get a good idea of what grows there, and in what quantity, by sampling a relatively small proportion of it. To ensure that the sample is representative of the whole field, you would normally want to make your sample **random** – that is rather than actually choosing which parts you sample, you would use some system such as a random number generator to make an unbiased decision for you.

The random numbers tell you where to place your quadrat. Think of the area you are sampling as a huge piece of graph paper (you will have to imagine the grid lines!), with you standing on the origin where the *x* and *y* axes meet. Obtain two random numbers, and use the first one as the

● **Figure 3.10** A 0.5 m × 0.5 m quadrat in use, divided into 100 small squares for finding percentage cover.

x coordinate and the second as the *y* coordinate. Place your quadrat on the ground at this point.

The quadrat marks off the area of the ground within which you can make a thorough survey of the species present. You will first need to identify all the plant species, using keys or help from experts. Then you have to decide on the relative abundance of them. You could use some sort of subjective scale for this, such as the ACFOR scale. You simply decide whether each species is Abundant, Common, Frequent, Occasional or Rare. If you want to do something quantitative with these results, such as plotting graphs, you can assign a number to each of these so that A = 5 and R = 1.

Another way of determining the abundance of each species is to estimate their **percentage cover**. If the quadrat is not too large – say with sides of 25 cm or 50 cm – then this is not too difficult to do by eye. You may like to use a quadrat that is divided up into smaller squares to help you to make your estimates. You would usually do it to the nearest 5 or 10% for each species. The total percentage may come to more than 100% if some of the taller plants grow over some of the smaller ones.

To get a reasonably representative sample of the whole field, you will need to estimate percentage cover in a number of quadrats. You can then calculate the mean percentage cover for a particular species in all of the quadrats, to give you the **species cover** for that species in the field. Another

calculation you can do is finding the **species frequency** (sometimes called the **percentage frequency**), which is the percentage of the quadrats in which you found the particular species in question.

SAQ 3.4

A student used random numbers to place a quadrat 12 times in an area of grassland. The results for one species are shown in the table.

quadrat	1	2	3	4	5	6	7	8	9	10	11	12
% cover of species A	25	20	0	10	25	45	0	0	30	15	0	20

a Calculate the species cover for species A in this area of grassland.

b Calculate the species frequency for species A in this area of grassland.

Point quadrats

A point quadrat is a frame with holes in it at regular intervals. You place it randomly in the area you are studying, in just the same way as an ordinary quadrat. You then use it to sample the percentage cover in that area. Point quadrats give a more accurate and consistent estimate of percentage cover than if you try to estimate it by eye.

First, you stand the point quadrat frame on the ground (*figure 3.11*). Now you lower a long pin through the first hole, and identify and record

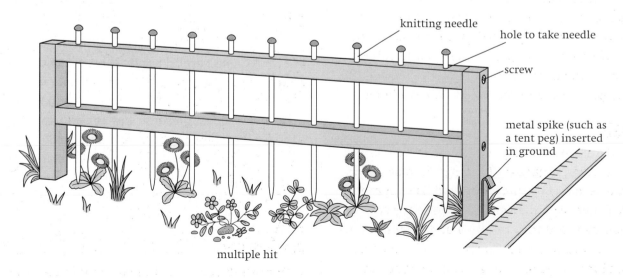

knitting needle

hole to take needle

screw

metal spike (such as a tent peg) inserted in ground

multiple hit

● **Figure 3.11** A point quadrat frame with all ten needles lowered onto the vegetation.

whatever plant or plants the pin touches. Repeat this for each of the holes in the frame. The number of touches for each species is proportional to the percentage cover.

Transects

You do not always want to sample randomly in a habitat. Sometimes, you may be interested in how the community *changes* along a particular line – for example, from the seashore, up and over the dunes and down into the grassland or woodland behind them. In this case, you would sample along a line called a **transect** (*figure 3.12*).

First, you decide where you want your sampling line to run, and fix a measuring tape or piece of string along it. You then have a choice of methods of sampling what lives along your line. You could simply record each organism that touches the line anywhere along its length. This is a good idea if there are not too many organisms there, such as on a rocky seashore, but in a densely vegetated area it could take forever. In those circumstances, it would be better to place a series of quadrats along the line, and then use the techniques described above to estimate abundance of each species. If you place the quadrats in a continuous line along the transect, this is called a **belt transect**. If you place them at intervals along it with gaps in between, this is an **interrupted transect**.

● **Figure 3.12** An interrupted transect is useful for studying the changes in a community going up a rocky shore from the sea, as shown here.

Sustainable production and conservation

Humans, like all living organisms, require nutrients which we obtain from our environment. The first humans were gatherer–hunters, harvesting plants and animals that lived wild. We still do some of this today, sometimes on a very large scale, for example when harvesting fish from the sea. But, about 10 000 years ago, people began systematically to grow crops and to farm animals. Now, the ever-increasing human population largely relies on agriculture to supply its food.

As the human population increases, and expectations of people to have plentiful, high-quality food rise, so agricultural practices have been changing to try to meet these demands. In developed countries, agriculture has become more **intensive**, providing relatively high yields of food from relatively small areas of land. Intensive farming has undoubtedly brought great advantages to many people, ensuring adequate supplies of cheap, safe, nutritious food.

But this increase in food production has a hidden price – the harm it can do to the environment. Increasingly, as people have been able to stop worrying about having enough to eat, they have begun to realise that they are losing many of the things that they value, such as wild flowers and animals. At the beginning of the 21st century, we are seeing in many countries, including those of the EU, a swing away from 'cheap food at all costs', and a gradual increase in 'environmentally friendly' farming practices. With careful use of our increasing understanding of ecology, and careful application of new, energy-efficient technologies, we should be able to prevent further environmental damage being done and, indeed, go some way to restoring habitats that have already been damaged.

In this module, we look at just two examples of the potential conflicts between the use of our environment to produce things that we need, and its conservation. These are the use of nitrate fertilisers in farming, and the use of forests for timber production. If you study the *Environmental Biology* option, you can look at a wider range of such issues in more depth.

Human effects on the nitrogen cycle

The use of nitrogen-containing fertilisers

In most parts of the world, the yield of many crops is limited by the amount of nitrate ions available in the soil. Nitrate gets into the soil naturally when nitrogen gas from the air is **fixed** (see *The nitrogen cycle* in *Biology 1*, pages 97–100) by bacteria or by lightning, or when organic substances such as dead plants or animal droppings are decayed by bacteria. In order to increase production, farmers add nitrogen-containing fertilisers to the soil.

Early farmers would have used **organic** material for this, such as animal dung or seaweed collected from the shore. Such materials are still used, even in relatively intensive farming systems. They have the advantage that, as well as adding nutrients such as nitrate to the soil, they also provide humus which increases the water-holding capacity of sandy soils and improves the drainage of clay soils. Increasingly, however, farmers have been using **inorganic fertilisers** (*figure 3.13*). These are mixtures of chemicals such as ammonium nitrate and potassium nitrate, with nothing to provide humus.

As we shall see, the increased use of nitrate-containing fertilisers, whether these are organic or inorganic, has had some harmful effects on aquatic and terrestrial ecosystems.

Nitrate in water

Figure 3.14 shows the levels of dissolved nitrate in the Great Ouse at Bedford, UK between 1957 and 1982. You can see that there is a long-term trend of increasing nitrate concentrations in the river. The oscillations are caused by seasonal changes in rainfall. Nitrate is highly water-soluble, and is leached from soil and washed into the river from surrounding land in autumn and winter. In 1976, there was a long, hot, dry summer, and the nitrate levels in the Great Ouse fell. However, when it eventually rained in the autumn, there was an especially high peak in these levels.

What has caused this long-term increase in nitrate levels in fresh water? Initially, it was thought to be a direct result of the increasing application of inorganic fertilisers to arable land.

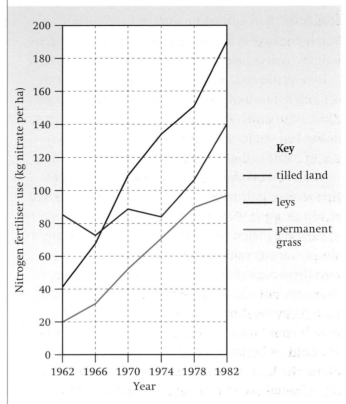

● **Figure 3.13** The use of nitrogen-containing inorganic fertilisers in England and Wales between 1962 and 1982. A ley is a meadow from which grass is harvested each year to make hay or silage.

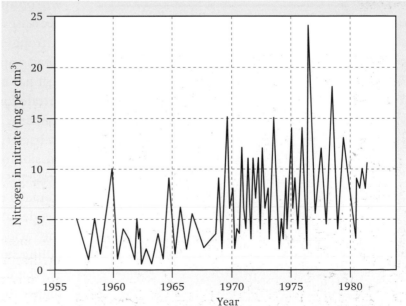

● **Figure 3.14** Nitrate concentrations in the Great Ouse river at Bedford, UK between 1957 and 1982.

It is now known, however, that the picture is not quite that simple. Inorganic fertilisers do contribute to nitrate in fresh water, but so do organic fertilisers such as manure. In fact, spreading animal manure on the land may cause more leaching of nitrate than spreading ammonium nitrate, partly because it is less easy for a farmer to calculate the correct amount to apply.

In a fertile soil, only about 5–8% of the nitrate is likely to have come from recently applied inorganic or organic fertilisers. Over 90% of the nitrate in the soil comes from the breakdown, by bacteria, of organic matter in the soil. A good soil may contain several thousand kilograms of nitrogen per hectare in humus, some of which is converted to nitrate each year by nitrifying bacteria.

Another major cause of the increased nitrate levels in water is the ploughing up of land on which grass has been growing for many years. Grassland on which animals are grazed accumulates large amounts of nitrate in the soil (*figure 3.15*). When this is ploughed up, very significant amounts of nitrate can be washed out. This was done on a large scale in the Second World War, to help to produce more food. The 'half-life' of the store of nitrate in these ploughed soils is around 40 years, so we are still seeing nitrate from these soils washing into rivers.

SAQ 3.5

Suggest why grassland which is grazed by animals accumulates larger amounts of nitrate in the soil than does grassland which is cut to make silage or hay.

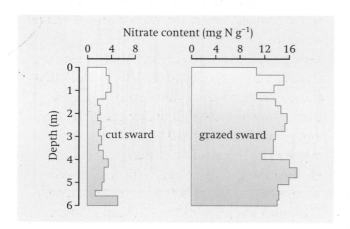

● **Figure 3.15** Nitrate content of soil at different depths beneath grassland that is harvested (cut sward) and grazed by sheep (grazed sward).

Another cause of the increasing quantities of leached nitrate is fixed nitrogen entering the soil from the air. In southern Britain, about 50 kg ha^{-1} year^{-1} of nitrogen is added to the soil in this way. Some of this is from natural sources such as lightning, some as gaseous ammonia from urine from farm animals, and some from nitrogen oxides from car exhausts and power stations.

Problems caused by excess nitrate in fresh water

High nitrate levels increase the growth of aquatic algae and plants. (High phosphate levels, produced by phosphates entering water in untreated sewage and waste from some industrial processes, also cause this to happen.) The rapid algal growth produces green murky water, and prevents light reaching plants growing on or near the bottom of the river or lake. These plants die and are decomposed by bacteria, whose populations rapidly increase. The bacteria respire aerobically, removing dissolved oxygen from the water. Organisms which require high levels of oxygen, such as most fish, and many invertebrates such as dragonfly larvae, must leave or die.

The rate at which dissolved oxygen is removed from water is known as the **biochemical oxygen demand**, or **BOD**. A high BOD is an indication of organic pollution.

The sequence of events described above is called **eutrophication**. Eutrophication generally decreases species diversity. Most people also find eutrophic rivers and lakes less attractive than clear, unpolluted ones.

It has been thought that high concentrations of nitrate ions in drinking water can be harmful to humans. Nitrate ions are converted to nitrite ions by bacteria in the stomach, and there is a possibility that there is a link between the presence of nitrite ions and the development of stomach cancer. However, the evidence for this is slender and controversial, and it is significant that the incidence of stomach cancer in the UK is falling steadily.

Where nitrate concentration is *very* high – much higher than is normally found in any drinking water – small babies drinking it can suffer from 'blue baby syndrome'. There have been a very few cases (in single figures) of this in babies fed on milk

- **Figure 3.16** Hay meadows with a high density of species are now very rare. To create such a meadow, the fertility of the soil must be kept very low, to give the more attractive flowering plants a chance to compete with grasses, which grow vigorously when nitrate and phosphate are in plentiful supply.

made up with water obtained from a heavily-polluted well. The nitrite ions (formed from nitrate as described above) combined with their haemoglobin, stopping the efficient transport of oxygen.

Problems caused by excess nitrate in soil

On agricultural land, the increasing use of fertilisers, especially ammonium nitrate, has reduced species diversity on grassland. Meadows containing a high diversity of flowering plants (figure 3.16) have become increasingly rare. Fertilisers increase the growth of grasses and plants such as nettles and docks. These grow so vigorously that they shade out smaller plants such as orchids. The loss of these species has been speeded up by the use of selective herbicides, which kill most plants other than grasses.

Ammonium nitrate can also break down to form ammonia, which is released into the air. There has been an estimated 50% increase in ammonia emission over Europe since 1950. Although most of this has probably come from animal waste as a result of intensive pig, poultry and cattle rearing systems, some has come from fertilisers. The ammonia in the air increases the rate at which sulphate is deposited, so increasing soil acidity. Acidification of soils is a major cause of damage to forests in many parts of the northern hemisphere.

Measures to reduce problems from excess nitrate

The long half-life of nitrate in the soil means that simply reducing fertiliser inputs now is unlikely to have any *immediate* effect on nitrate levels in water. However, it is generally agreed that we should do our best to make sure that we do not make matters worse.

The major source of nitrate in watercourses in the UK is run-off from agricultural land, and the Ministry of Agriculture, Fisheries and Food produces guidelines for farmers to help them to apply fertilisers safely, with a minimal risk to the environment. In addition, the Government has designated 68 'Nitrate Vulnerable Zones', where the problem of high nitrate levels in watercourses is particularly serious. In these areas, farmers must comply with strict legislation designed to reduce the amount of nitrate they release into the environment.

The guidelines include the following recommendations:

- avoid ploughing up old grassland;
- do not apply excessive amounts of organic manures, as these are even more likely to produce large quantities of leached nitrate than are inorganic fertilisers;
- leave a strip at least 10 metres wide next to water courses, where you do not spread animal wastes;
- before applying inorganic fertilisers, measure the amount of nitrate in the soil, and calculate the probable needs of the crop to be grown, then apply just the right amount of fertiliser;
- apply any fertiliser, whether inorganic or organic, at a time when the crop is actively growing, so that the plants will remove the nitrate from the soil before it can be leached: it is best to apply fertilisers in spring rather than autumn;
- try not to leave land bare for any length of time, especially over winter, because nitrate is

more easily leached from land with no plants growing on it.

Alternatives to the use of nitrogen-containing fertilisers

Although there will never be a complete end to the use of fertilisers, it is possible to reduce their use.

One method, which has been in use for thousands of years, is to use **crop rotation**. Some crops, such as clover, peas, beans and alfalfa, contain nitrogen-fixing bacteria in their root nodules (*Biology 1*, page 98). If these crops are grown one year, and then their roots ploughed back into the soil after harvesting, this can supply nitrate for whatever crop is planted in the next year, for example wheat.

Another possibility is to use **genetic engineering** to introduce genes for nitrogen fixation into crop plants. At the moment, there has been little success with this, but it is very likely that in the future there will be nitrogen-fixing varieties of wheat, for example, that farmers could choose to grow. If so, this could greatly reduce the need to apply nitrogen-containing fertilisers.

Sustainable timber production

For thousands of years woodland and forests have been used as a source of resources such as timber or food. With careful management, it is possible to make use of these resources without destroying the ecosystem. This is in everyone's best interests. It means that we can retain the forests and woodlands that give pleasure to many people, and also that the biodiversity within them can be maintained. It can

also be in the long-term interests of the companies who are making money from harvesting timber, as they can go on using the same forests for this year after year.

In Britain, **coppicing** (*figures 3.17* and *3.18*) has been used for thousands of years to obtain a sustainable supply of wood from forests and woodlands. This traditional woodland management system exploits the fact that most deciduous trees re-grow from the base when their trunks are cut down. The tree – for example oak, ash, lime or hazel – is cut down close to the ground and then left for several years to re-grow. The new growth consists of several stems, so the wood that is harvested from these is normally quite small in diameter, which limits its use. It cannot be used to make large planks, for example, although it is ideal for making items such as garden furniture or fencing, or for use as firewood or for making charcoal.

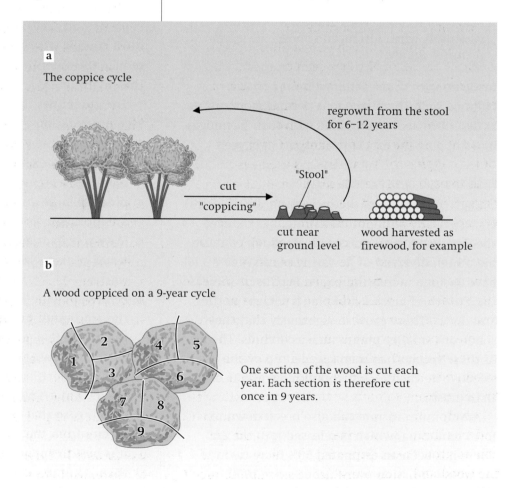

● **Figure 3.17** Coppicing. **a** The coppice cycle. This cycle would be repeated for 100 years or more. **b** How a wood could be coppiced on a 9-year cycle.

● **Figure 3.18** These hazels have regrown after being coppiced several years ago, and are now ready to be harvested again. In the background is an ash tree that has been harvested by cutting off the branches higher up, rather than at ground level, leaving a trunk. This is called **pollarding**.

Within a wood, it is normal to coppice just part of it in any one year. Each year, a different area is coppiced, until all of it has been done and the first area is coppiced again. This is called **rotational** coppicing. The length of the coppice cycle can be varied according to the species involved, and the use that is required of the timber. Often, a system called **coppice with standards** is used, where some trees in each area are not coppiced at all but left to grow into full-sized trees called standards. For example, a wood might contain a mix of hazel, which is regularly coppiced, and oak which is left to grow as standards. The oak trees can be harvested when they are big enough to provide large timber. They may then be left to re-grow from the cut stumps, or new ones can be planted.

Rotational coppicing is an excellent way of maintaining and even increasing biodiversity in woodlands. Left to itself, a deciduous wood in Britain is likely to become thickly vegetated, with relatively little light reaching the woodland floor, and this limits the number of species that are able to grow there. Coppicing opens up parts of the woodland, increasing light levels and so providing conditions in which species such as bluebells and other herbaceous plants can survive. The

fact that different parts of the wood are at different stages of the coppice cycle at any one time helps to maximise species diversity.

While coppicing is a very good way of providing a sustainable supply of timber from a woodland, it is very labour-intensive and is usually done on a relatively small scale, in circumstances where conservation is more important than profit-making. It is more difficult to carry out large-scale forestry in a sustainable way.

'Sustainable forestry' can have different meanings. It may simply mean providing a sustainable timber harvest – in other words, timber is removed from a forest in such a way that similar amounts can be removed year after year for long periods of time. On the other hand, it may mean that the forest *ecosystem* is maintained, with all the different habitats and species able to live in the forest even though timber is being extracted from it.

Maintaining a sustainable forest ecosytem while timber extraction is carried out on a large scale is extremely difficult. However, it is possible to take steps to minimise damage to the ecosystem and still make good profits. For example, rather than **clear-felling**, which is the removal of all the trees in an area at once, **selective cutting** can be used. This involves felling only some of the largest, most commercially valuable trees, while leaving others alone. This does help to leave most habitats largely intact, but it is obviously impossible to do it without considerable disturbance, especially if large machinery is used to fell and drag out the harvested trees. Selective cutting is very useful on steep slopes, where clear felling would leave the soil extremely vulnerable to erosion. Selective cutting helps to maintain nutrients in the forest soil, which is beneficial to the plants growing in the forest, and also reduces the amount of pollution of nearby waterways (*figure 3.19*).

Another practice which increases sustainability is using a **long rotation** time – that is leaving each part of the forest for many years before re-harvesting it. For example, traditional forestry would have left trees to grow for up to 100 years or more, while in some modern forestry industries, such as those which provide wood for making paper, the trees grow for only 10 years

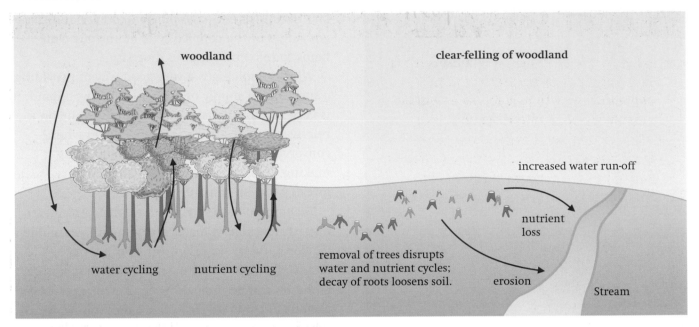

woodland

clear-felling of woodland

increased water run-off

water cycling

nutrient cycling

nutrient loss

removal of trees disrupts
water and nutrient cycles;
decay of roots loosens soil.

erosion

Stream

● **Figure 3.19** Clear-felling of woodland, especially if it is on sloping ground, can increase erosion. This leads to soil and nutrient loss, which means it is less likely that healthy trees will be able to grow in that area in future.

before harvesting. Short rotations do not allow much time for species diversity to build up, and the frequent disturbance by machinery can cause great damage to the soil.

Good forestry practice can increase **efficiency**. This means that the most use is made of each tree that is planted and that there is minimum wastage. Efficiency can be improved in many ways, including:

■ matching the tree species to be grown to the climate, topography and soil type. For example, willow or poplar will grow well on low-lying wet land, whereas oak may not grow so well there;

■ planting trees at the best distance apart. If they are planted too close, they will tend to grow very tall and thin, and competition between them may result in all of the trees producing poor-quality timber. If they are planted too far apart, then a bigger area of land will be used than is necessary to obtain the same amount of timber;

■ controlling pests and pathogens, so that the trees grow well and provide a good-quality harvest of timber.

By increasing efficiency in these ways, the very best use is made of the land, thus reducing the total area of land required. It also means that fewer trees need to be felled, as one well-grown tree may provide as much good-quality timber as two or more poorly grown ones.

SUMMARY

◆ When a small number of organisms is first introduced into a new environment, population growth may follow a sigmoid growth curve. An initial lag phase is followed by a log phase and then a stationary phase. Population growth is limited by environmental factors, which determine the carrying capacity of the habitat for that population.

◆ Usually, a number of different environmental factors interact to affect population size. These factors include predation, food supply, intraspecific competition and interspecific competition.

◆ Predation by one particular predator is only likely to have a significant effect on the population of the prey if no other factors (such as predation by other predators, or food supply) are important. Similarly, availability of a prey species is unlikely to have a significant effect on the population of a predator unless that predator feeds almost exclusively on that prey species. However, in some cases predator and prey populations may follow one another closely, with one oscillating slightly out of step with the other.

◆ Intraspecific (within a species) competition for any resource that is in short supply is usually a very important factor that limits population growth. Interspecific (between different species) competition may also have this effect. It is usually found that two species with very similar niches cannot coexist, as one out-competes the other.

◆ An area of land with no living organisms on it will gradually become populated with pioneer species. These alter the environment, and make it possible for a wider range of species to live there. Over time, the environment and the community gradually changes until it reaches a climax community. This process is called primary succession. Succession can also occur whenever an area of land is greatly disturbed (such as felling a woodland for example) without destroying all the living things. This is called secondary succession.

◆ Ecological investigations usually involve sampling techniques, which provide information about which species live in a habitat, their distribution and their relative abundance. For random sampling, quadrats or point quadrats can be used. Transects are a method of systematic sampling used to investigate changes in a community along a line.

◆ Humans use land for the production of food and other resources such as timber. There are inevitable conflicts between production and conservation, but careful management can reduce these to some extent. For example, careless use of nitrogen-containing fertilisers can cause eutrophication, but the risk of this is much reduced if simple guidelines are followed. Coppicing and selective felling can allow the sustainable use of woodlands and forests for timber production while causing minimal damage to the environment. Coppicing may actually increase species diversity in a woodland.

Questions

1 With reference to a population of a named organism, explain what is meant by the terms *limiting factors* and *carrying capacity*.

2 a Explain what is meant by the term *primary succession*.
   b Describe how you could use transects and quadrats to obtain quantitative information about succession in a sand dune ecosystem such as that shown in *figure 3.8*.

3 Two possible approaches to reducing the adverse effects of agriculture on the environment are:
   ● to farm very intensively on some areas of land, thus maximising rates of production on these areas and freeing other areas for conservation;
   ● to farm 'organically', using low inputs of fertilisers and pesticides.

Discuss the relative merits of these two approaches. Try to consider various points of view, such as those of farmers, conservationists and people buying food in shops. Do not forget that one person may be all of these people at once!

To answer the following question, you will need to bring together information from other areas of your course, as well as from this chapter.

4 Plants obtain nitrate from the soil. In order to maximise productivity, farmers often apply fertilisers containing nitrate to growing crops.
   a Explain why plants require nitrate.
   b Describe how nitrate ions are absorbed into the roots of plants.
   c Explain why farmers do not usually apply nitrogen-containing fertilisers close to watercourses or when it is likely to rain.

CHAPTER 4

Meiosis, genetics and gene control

By the end of this chapter you should be able to:

1 understand the roles of meiosis and fertilisation in sexual reproduction;

2 describe, with the aid of diagrams, the behaviour of chromosomes during meiosis, and the associated behaviour of the nuclear envelope, plasma (cell surface) membrane and centrioles;

3 explain how meiosis and fertilisation can lead to variation;

4 explain the terms *gene*, *allele*, *locus*, *phenotype*, *genotype*, *dominant*, *recessive* and *codominant*;

5 use genetic diagrams to solve problems involving monohybrid and dihybrid crosses, including those involving sex linkage, codominance and multiple alleles;

6 understand the use of the test cross, and use genetic diagrams to solve problems involving such crosses;

7 use the chi-squared (χ^2) test to test the significance of the difference between observed and expected results in genetic crosses;

8 explain, using sickle cell anaemia and other examples, how mutation may affect phenotype;

9 explain, with examples, how environment may affect phenotype;

10 outline the regulation of protein synthesis in bacteria, with reference to the *lac* operon;

11 outline the implications of the Human Genome Project.

All species of living organisms are able to reproduce. Reproduction may be **asexual** or **sexual**. In asexual reproduction, a single organism produces offspring that are genetically identical to itself (*Biology 1, figure 6.13*). The cells of the new organisms are formed as a result of mitosis in eukaryotes or binary fission in prokaryotes. However, in sexual reproduction, the offspring that are produced are genetically different from each other and from their parent or parents. Each parent produces specialised reproductive cells, known as **gametes**, that fuse together in **fertilisation** to produce the first cell of the new organism – a **zygote**.

You saw in *Biology 1* (page 83) that if a life cycle involves sexual reproduction, then it is necessary for the number of chromosomes to be halved at some point (*figure 4.1*). This is done by a special type of cell division called **meiosis**. In animals such as humans, for example, meiosis occurs as gametes are formed inside the testes and ovaries. The cells from which the gametes will be produced are normal **diploid** (2n) cells, each containing two complete sets of chromosomes. As a result of

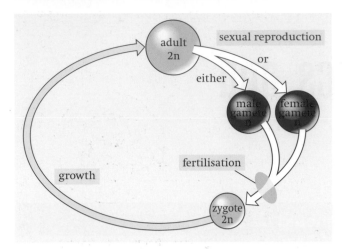

● **Figure 4.1** Outline of the life cycle of an animal.

meiosis, the gametes contain only half the normal number of chromosomes, and they are said to be **haploid** (n) cells. Thus, when two gametes fuse together at fertilisation, the zygote that is formed obtains two complete sets of chromosomes, returning to the diploid condition.

As you will see in this chapter, meiosis does more than halve the number of chromosomes in a cell. Meiosis also introduces **genetic variation** into the gametes and therefore the zygotes that are produced. Genetic variation may also arise as a result of **mutation**, which can occur at any stage in a life cycle. Such variation is the raw material on which natural selection has worked to produce the huge range of species that live on Earth, and we will look at this in chapter 5.

Meiosis

The process of meiosis is best described by means of annotated diagrams (*figure 4.2*). An animal cell is shown where 2n = 4, and different colours represent maternal and paternal chromosomes.

Unlike mitosis (*Biology 1*, page 84), meiosis involves two divisions, called meiosis I and meiosis II. **Meiosis I** is a reduction division, resulting in two daughter nuclei with *half* the number of chromosomes of the parent nucleus. In **meiosis II**, the chromosomes behave as in mitosis, so that each of the two haploid daughter nuclei divides again. Meiosis therefore results in a total of four haploid nuclei. Note that it is the behaviour of the chromosomes in *meiosis I* that is particularly important and contrasts with mitosis.

Figure 4.2 summarises the process of meiosis diagrammatically. *Figure 4.3* shows photographs of the process as seen with a light microscope.

SAQ 4.1

Name the stage of meiosis at which each of the following occurs. Remember to state whether the stage you name is during division I or division II.
a Homologous chromosomes pair to form bivalents.
b Crossing over between chromatids of homologous chromosomes takes place.
c Homologous chromosomes separate.
d Centromeres split and chromatids separate.
e Haploid nuclei are first formed.

SAQ 4.2

A cell with 3 sets of chromosomes is said to be triploid, 3n. A cell with 4 sets of chromosomes is said to be tetraploid, 4n. Could meiosis take place in a 3n or a 4n cell? Explain your answer.

Two of the events that take place during meiosis help to produce genetic variation between the daughter cells that are produced. These are **independent assortment** of the homologous chromosomes, and **crossing over**, which happens between the chromatids of homologous chromosomes. When these genetically different gametes fuse, randomly, at fertilisation, yet more variation is produced amongst the offspring. In order to understand how these events produce variation, we first need to consider the **genes** that are carried on the chromosomes, and the way in which these are passed on from parents to offspring. This branch of biology is known as **genetics**.

Genetics

You will remember that a **gene** is a length of DNA that codes for the production of a polypeptide molecule. The code is held in the sequence of bases in the DNA. A triplet of three bases 'stands for' one amino acid in the protein that will be constructed on the ribosomes in the cell (*Biology 1*, chapter 5). One chromosome contains enough DNA to code for many polypeptides.

Meiosis I

1 Early prophase I – as mitosis early prophase

2 Middle prophase I

Homologous chromosomes pair up. This process is called **synapsis**. Each pair is called a **bivalent**.

centrioles moving to opposite ends of nucleus as in mitosis

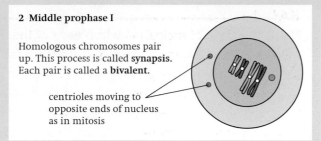

3 Late prophase I

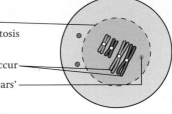

nuclear envelope breaks up as in mitosis

crossing over of chromatids may occur

nucleolus 'disappears' as in mitosis

Bivalent showing crossing over:

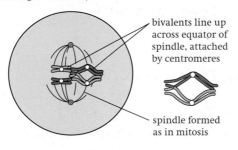

chromatids may break and may reconnect to another chromatid

centromere

chiasma=point where crossing over occurs (plural,chiasmata)

one or more chiasmata may form, anywhere along length

At the end of prophase I a spindle is formed.

4 Metaphase I (showing crossing over of long chromatids)

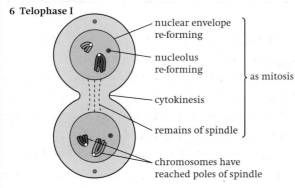

bivalents line up across equator of spindle, attached by centromeres

spindle formed as in mitosis

5 Anaphase I

Centromeres do not divide, unlike mitosis.

Whole chromosomes move towards opposite ends of spindle, centromeres first, pulled by microtubules.

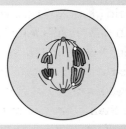

6 Telophase I

nuclear envelope re-forming

nucleolus re-forming

cytokinesis

remains of spindle

as mitosis

chromosomes have reached poles of spindle

Animal cells usually divide before entering Meiosis II. Many plant cells go straight into Meiosis II with no reformation of nuclear envelopes or nucleoli. During Meiosis II chromatids separate as in mitosis.

Meiosis II

7 Prophase II

nuclear envelope and nucleolus disperse

centrioles replicate and move to opposite poles of the cell

8 Metaphase II

chromosomes line up separately across equator of spindle

9 Anaphase II

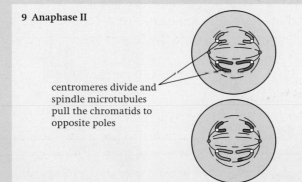

centromeres divide and spindle microtubules pull the chromatids to opposite poles

10 Telophase II

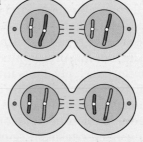

Telophase II as mitosis telophase but four haploid daughter cells formed

● **Figure 4.2** Meiosis and cytokinesis in an animal cell. Compare this process with nuclear division by mitosis, shown in *figure 6.10* in *Biology 1*.

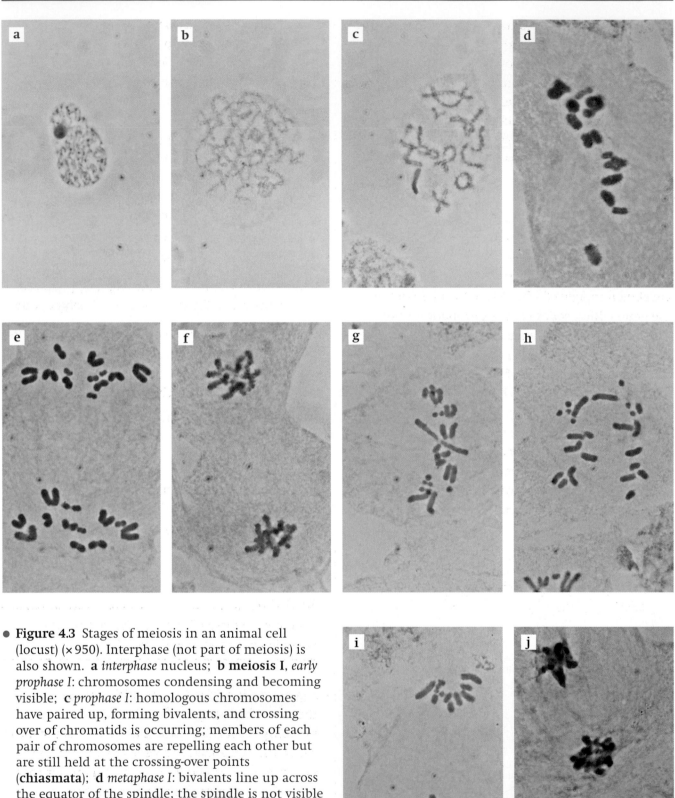

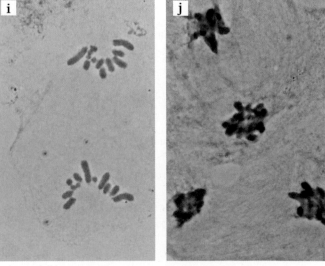

● **Figure 4.3** Stages of meiosis in an animal cell (locust) (× 950). Interphase (not part of meiosis) is also shown. **a** *interphase* nucleus; **b meiosis I**, *early prophase I*: chromosomes condensing and becoming visible; **c** *prophase I*: homologous chromosomes have paired up, forming bivalents, and crossing over of chromatids is occurring; members of each pair of chromosomes are repelling each other but are still held at the crossing-over points (**chiasmata**); **d** *metaphase I*: bivalents line up across the equator of the spindle; the spindle is not visible in the photo; **e** *anaphase I*; homologous chromosomes move to opposite poles of the spindle; **f** *telophase I* and *cytokinesis*; **g meiosis II**, *metaphase II*; single chromosomes line up across the equator of a new spindle; **h** *anaphase II*: chromatids separate and move to opposite poles of the new spindle; **i** *late anaphase II*; **j** *telophase II*.

Chromosomes that contain DNA for making the same polypeptides are said to be **homologous**. A diploid cell contains two of each type of chromosome, one homologue from the mother and one homologue from the father. So, in a diploid cell, there are two copies of each gene. The two copies lie in the same position, or **locus**, on the two homologous chromosomes (*figure 4.4*).

Alleles

The number of chromosomes per cell is characteristic for each species. Human cells contain 46 chromosomes, two each of 23 types. Each type is numbered and has its own particular genes. (They are shown in *figure 6.3* in *Biology 1*.) For example, the gene which codes for the production of the β polypeptide of the haemoglobin molecule (see *Biology 1*, pages 34–5) is on chromosome 11. Each cell contains two copies of this gene, one maternal in origin (from the mother) and one paternal (from the father).

There are several forms or varieties of this gene. One variety contains the base sequence CCTGAGGAG, and codes for the normal β polypeptide. Another variety contains the base sequence CCTGTGGAG, and codes for a different

sequence of amino acids which forms a variant of the β polypeptide know as the **sickle cell** β polypeptide. These different varieties of the same gene are called **alleles**.

Genotype

Most genes, including the β polypeptide gene, have several different alleles. For the moment, we will consider only the above two alleles of the β polypeptide gene.

For simplicity, the different alleles of a gene can be represented by symbols. In this case, they can be represented as follows:

H^N = the allele for the normal β polypeptide;
H^S = the allele for the sickle cell β polypeptide.

The letter H stands for the locus of the haemoglobin gene, while the superscripts N and S stand for particular alleles of the gene.

In a human cell, which is diploid, there are two copies of the β polypeptide gene. The two copies might be:

H^NH^N or H^SH^S or H^NH^S.

The alleles that an organism has form its **genotype**. In this case, where we are considering just two different alleles, there are three possible genotypes.

SAQ 4.3

If there were three different alleles, how many possible genotypes would there be?

A genotype in which the two alleles of a gene are the same, for example H^NH^N, is said to be **homozygous** for that particular gene. A genotype in which the two alleles of a gene are different, for example H^NH^S, is said to be **heterozygous** for that gene. The organism can also be described as homozygous or heterozygous for that characteristic.

SAQ 4.4

How many of the genotypes in your answer to SAQ 4.3 are homozygous, and how many are heterozygous?

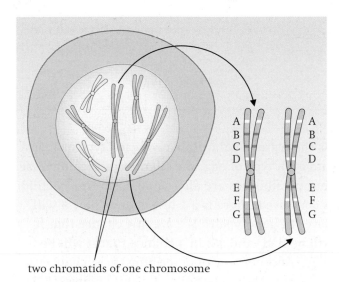

two chromatids of one chromosome

● **Figure 4.4** Homologous chromosomes carry the same genes at the same loci. Just seven genes, labelled A–G, are shown on these chromosomes, but in reality there are often hundreds or thousands of genes on each chromosome. This is a diploid cell as there are two complete sets of chromosomes (2n = 6).

Genotype affects phenotype

A person with the genotype $H^N H^N$ has two copies of the gene in each cell coding for the production of the normal β polypeptide. All of their haemoglobin will be normal.

A person with the genotype $H^S H^S$ has two copies of the gene in each cell coding for the production of the sickle cell β polypeptide. All of their haemoglobin will be sickle cell haemoglobin, which is inefficient at transporting oxygen. The person will have **sickle cell anaemia**. This is a very dangerous disease, in which great care has to be taken not to allow the blood to become short of oxygen, or death may occur (page 74). A person with the genotype $H^N H^S$ has one allele of the haemoglobin gene in each cell coding for the production of the normal β polypeptide, and one coding for the production of the sickle cell β polypeptide. Half of their haemoglobin will be normal, and half will be sickle cell haemoglobin. They will have **sickle cell trait**, and are sometimes referred to as **carriers**. They will probably be completely unaware of this, because they have enough normal haemoglobin to carry enough oxygen, and so will have no problems at all. They will appear to be perfectly healthy. Difficulties arise only very occasionally, for example if a person with sickle cell trait does strenuous exercise at high altitudes, when oxygen concentrations in the blood might become very low (*Biology 1*, page 117).

The observable characteristics of an individual are called their **phenotype**. We will normally use the word 'phenotype' to describe just the one or two particular characteristics that we are interested in. In this case, we are considering the characteristic of having, or not having, sickle cell anaemia (*table 4.1*).

Genotype	Phenotype
$H^N H^N$	normal
$H^N H^S$	normal, but with sickle cell trait
$H^S H^S$	sickle cell anaemia

● **Table 4.1** Genotypes and phenotypes for sickle cell anaemia.

Inheriting genes

In sexual reproduction, haploid gametes are made, following meiosis, from diploid body cells. Each gamete contains one of each pair of chromosomes. Therefore, each gamete contains only one copy of each gene.

Think about what will happen when sperm are made in the testes of a man who has the genotype $H^N H^S$. Each time a cell divides during meiosis, four gametes will be made, two of them with the H^N allele and two with the H^S allele. Of all the millions of sperm that are made in his lifetime, half will have the genotype H^N and half will have the genotype H^S (*figure 4.5*).

Similarly, a heterozygous woman will produce eggs of which half have the genotype H^N and half have the genotype H^S.

This information can be used to predict the possible genotypes of children born to a couple who are both heterozygous. Each time fertilisation occurs, either a H^N sperm or a H^S sperm may fertilise either a H^N egg or a H^S egg. The possible results can be shown like this:

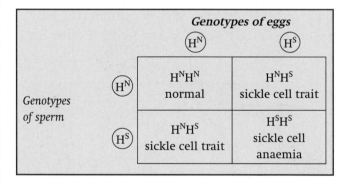

As there are equal numbers of each type of sperm and each type of egg, the chances of each of these four possibilities are also equal. Each time a child is conceived, there is a 1 in 4 chance that it will have the genotype $H^N H^N$, a 1 in 4 chance that it will be $H^S H^S$ and a 2 in 4 chance that it will be $H^N H^S$. Another way of describing these chances is to say that the probability of a child being $H^S H^S$ is 0.25, the probability of being $H^N H^N$ is 0.25, and the probability of being $H^N H^S$ is 0.5. It is important to realise that these are only *probabilities*. It would not be surprising if this couple had two children, both of whom had the genotype $H^S H^S$ and so suffered from sickle cell anaemia.

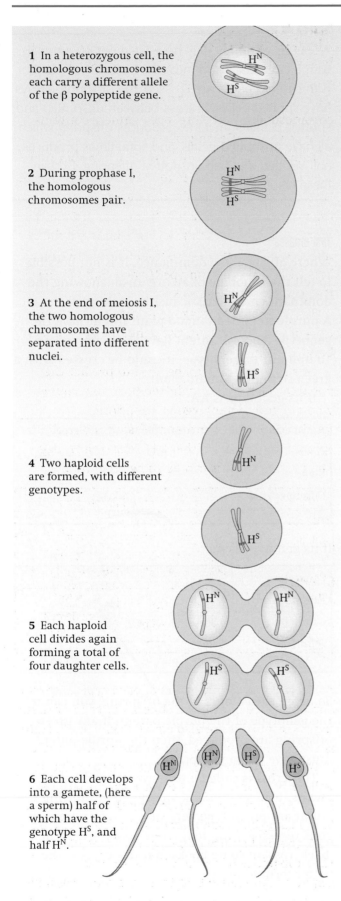

1 In a heterozygous cell, the homologous chromosomes each carry a different allele of the β polypeptide gene.

2 During prophase I, the homologous chromosomes pair.

3 At the end of meiosis I, the two homologous chromosomes have separated into different nuclei.

4 Two haploid cells are formed, with different genotypes.

5 Each haploid cell divides again forming a total of four daughter cells.

6 Each cell develops into a gamete, (here a sperm) half of which have the genotype H^S, and half H^N.

Figure 4.5 Meiosis of a heterozygous cell produces gametes of two different genotypes. Only one pair of homologous chromosomes is shown.

Genetic diagrams

A genetic diagram is the standard way of showing the genotypes of offspring that might be expected from two parents. To illustrate this, let us consider a different example: flower colour in snapdragons (*Antirrhinum*).

One of the genes for flower colour has two alleles, namely C^R which gives red flowers, and C^W which gives white flowers. The phenotypes produced by each genotype are:

Genotype	Phenotype
C^{R}C^R	red
C^{R}C^W	pink
C^{W}C^W	white

What colour flowers would be expected in the offspring from a red and a pink snapdragon?

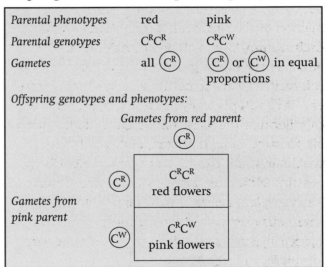

Parental phenotypes	red	pink
Parental genotypes	C^{R}C^R	C^{R}C^W
Gametes	all C^R	C^R or C^W in equal proportions

Offspring genotypes and phenotypes:

Gametes from red parent

C^R

Gametes from pink parent

	C^R
C^R	C^{R}C^R red flowers
C^W	C^{R}C^W pink flowers

Thus, you would expect about half of the offspring to have red flowers and half to have pink flowers.

SAQ 4.5

Red Poll cattle are homozygous for an allele which gives red coat colour. White Shorthorn are homozygous for an allele which gives white coat colour. When crossed, the offspring all have a mixture of red and white hairs in their coats, producing a colour called roan.

a Suggest suitable symbols for the two alleles of the coat colour gene.

b List the three possible genotypes for the coat colour gene and their phenotypes.

c Draw genetic diagrams to show the offspring expected from the following matings:
(i) a Red Poll with a roan; (ii) two roans.

Dominance

In the examples used so far, both of the alleles in a heterozygous organism have an effect on the phenotype. A person with the genotype $H^N H^S$ has some normal haemoglobin and some sickle haemoglobin. A snapdragon with the genotype $C^R C^W$ has some red colour and some white colour, so that the flowers appear pink. Alleles which behave like this are said to be **codominant** alleles.

Frequently, however, only one allele has an effect in a heterozygous organism. This allele is said to be the **dominant** allele, while the one which has no effect is **recessive**. An example is stem colour in tomatoes. There are two alleles for stem colour, one of which produces green stems, and the other purple stems. In a tomato plant which has one allele for purple stems and one allele for green stems, the stems are exactly the same shade of purple as in a plant which has two alleles for purple stems. The allele for purple stems is dominant, and the allele for green stems is recessive.

When alleles of a gene behave like this, their symbols are written using a capital letter for the dominant allele and a small letter for the recessive allele. You are often free to choose the symbols you will use. In this case, the symbols could be **A** for the purple allele and **a** for the green allele. The possible genotypes and phenotypes for stem colour are:

Genotype	Phenotype
AA	purple stem
Aa	purple stem
aa	green stem

It is a good idea, when choosing symbols to use for alleles, to use letters where the capital looks very different from the small one. If you use symbols such as S and s or P and p, it can become difficult to tell them apart if they are written down quickly.

SAQ 4.6

In mice, the gene for eye colour has two alleles. The allele for black eyes is dominant, while the allele for red eyes is recessive.

Choose suitable symbols for these alleles, and then draw a genetic diagram to show the probable results of a cross between a heterozygous black-eyed mouse and a red-eyed mouse.

SAQ 4.7

A species of poppy may have plain petals, or petals with a large black spot near the base. If two plants with spotted petals are crossed, the offspring always have spotted petals. A cross between unspotted and spotted plants sometimes produces offspring which all have unspotted petals, and sometimes produces half spotted and half unspotted offspring. Explain these results.

Test crosses

Where alleles show dominance, it is not possible to tell the genotype of an organism showing the dominant characteristic just by looking at it. A purple-stemmed tomato plant might have the genotype AA, or it might have the genotype Aa. To find out its genotype, it could be crossed with a green-stemmed tomato plant.

If its genotype is AA:

Parental phenotypes	purple	green
Parental genotypes	AA	aa
Gametes	Ⓐ	ⓐ
Offspring	all Aa purple	

If its genotype is Aa:

Parental phenotypes	purple		green
Parental genotypes	Aa		aa
Gametes	Ⓐ or ⓐ		ⓐ
Offspring	Aa purple	or	aa green

So, from the colours of the offspring, you can tell the genotype of the purple parent. If any green offspring are produced, then the purple parent must have the genotype Aa.

This cross is called a **test cross**. A test cross always involves crossing an organism showing the dominant phenotype with one which is homozygous recessive. (You may come across the term 'backcross' in some books, but test cross is the better term to use.)

SAQ 4.8

In dalmatian dogs, the colour of the spots is determined by a gene which has two alleles. The allele for black spots is dominant, and the allele for brown spots is recessive.

A breeder wanted to know the genotype of a black-spotted bitch. She crossed her with a brown-spotted dog, and a litter of three puppies was produced, all of which were black. The breeder concluded that her bitch was homozygous for the allele for black spots. Was she right? Explain your answer.

Multiple alleles

So far, we have considered just two alleles, or varieties, of any one gene. Most genes, however, have more than two alleles. An example of this situation, known as **multiple alleles**, is the gene for human blood groups.

The four blood groups A, B, AB and O are all determined by a single gene. Three alleles of this gene exist, I^A, I^B, and I^O. Of these, I^A and I^B are codominant, while I^O is recessive to both I^A and I^B. As a diploid cell can carry only two alleles, the possible genotypes and phenotypes are as shown in *table 4.2*.

SAQ 4.9

A man of blood group B and a woman of blood group A have three children. One is group A, one group B and one group O. What are the genotypes of these five people?

Genotype	Blood group
$I^A I^A$	A
$I^A I^B$	AB
$I^A I^O$	A
$I^B I^B$	B
$I^B I^O$	B
$I^O I^O$	O

● **Table 4.2** Genotypes and phenotypes for blood groups.

● **Figure 4.6** Colour variations in rabbits, caused by multiple alleles of a single gene: **a** agouti; **b** albino; **c** chinchilla; **d** Himalayan.

SAQ 4.10

Coat colour in rabbits is determined by a gene with four alleles. The allele for agouti (normal) coat is dominant to all of the other three alleles. The allele for albino coat is recessive to the other three alleles. The allele for chinchilla (grey) coat is dominant to the allele for Himalayan (white with black ears, nose, feet and tail) (*figure 4.6*).

a Write down the ten possible genotypes for coat colour, and their phenotypes.

b Draw genetic diagrams to explain each of the following.

  (i) An albino rabbit is crossed with a chinchilla rabbit, producing offspring which are all chinchilla. Two of these chinchilla offspring are then crossed, producing 4 chinchilla offspring and 2 albino.

  (ii) An agouti rabbit is crossed with a Himalayan rabbit, producing 3 agouti offspring and 3 Himalayan.

  (iii) Two agouti rabbits produce a litter of 5 young, three of whom are agouti and two chinchilla. The two chinchilla young are then crossed, producing 4 chinchilla offspring and 1 Himalayan.

Sex inheritance

In humans, sex is determined by one of the 23 pairs of chromosomes. These chromosomes are called the **sex chromosomes**. The other 22 pairs are called **autosomes**.

The sex chromosomes differ from the autosomes in that the two sex chromosomes in a cell are not always alike. They do not always have the same genes in the same position, and so they are not always homologous. This is because there are two types of sex chromosome, known as the X and Y chromosomes, because of their shapes. The Y chromosome is much shorter than the X, and carries fewer genes. A person with two X chromosomes is female, while a person with one X and one Y chromosome is male.

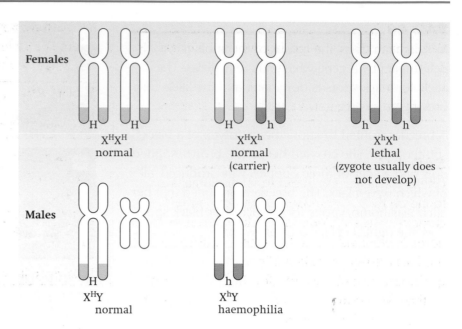

● **Figure 4.7** The possible genotypes and phenotypes for haemophilia.

SAQ 4.11

Draw a genetic diagram to explain why there is always an equal chance that a child will be male or female. (You can do this in just the same way as the other genetic diagrams you have drawn, but using symbols to represent whole chromosomes, not genes.)

Sex linkage

The X chromosome contains many different genes. (You can see some of these in *figure 6.5* in *Biology 1*.) One of them is a gene that codes for the production of a protein needed for blood clotting, called **factor VIII**. There are two alleles of this gene, the dominant one **H** producing normal factor VIII, and the recessive one **h** resulting in lack of it. People who are homozygous for the recessive allele suffer from the disease haemophilia, in which the blood fails to clot properly.

The fact that this gene is on the X chromosome, and not on an autosome, affects the way that it is inherited. Females, who have two X chromosomes, have two copies of the gene. Males, however, who have only one X chromosome, have only one copy of the gene. Therefore, the possible genotypes for men and women are different. They are shown in *figure 4.7*.

The factor VIII gene is said to be **sex-linked**. A sex-linked gene is one which is found on a part of the X chromosome not matched by the Y, and therefore not found on the Y chromosome.

Genotypes including sex-linked genes are always represented by symbols which show that they are on an X chromosome. Thus the genotype of a woman who has the allele H on one of her X chromosomes and the allele h on the other is written as $X^H X^h$.

You can draw genetic diagrams to show how sex-linked genes are inherited in exactly the same way as for other genes. For example, the following diagram shows the children that could be born to a couple where the man does not have haemophilia, while the woman is a carrier for the disease.

Parental phenotypes	normal man	carrier woman
Parental genotypes	$X^H Y$	$X^H X^h$
Gametes	X^H or Y	X^H or X^h

Offspring genotypes and phenotypes:

		Gametes from woman	
		X^H	X^h
Gametes from man	X^H	$X^H X^H$ normal female	$X^H X^h$ carrier female
	Y	$X^H Y$ normal male	$X^h Y$ haemophiliac male

Each time this couple have a child, therefore, there is a 0.25 probability that it will be a normal girl, a 0.25 probability that it will be a normal boy, a 0.25 probability that it will be a carrier girl and a 0.25 probability that it will be a boy with haemophilia.

SAQ 4.12

Can a man with haemophilia pass on the disease to:

a his son?

b his grandson?

Draw genetic diagrams to explain your answers.

SAQ 4.13

One of the genes for colour vision in humans is found on the X chromosome, but not on the Y chromosome. The dominant allele of this gene gives normal colour vision, while a recessive allele produces red-green colour blindness.

a Choose suitable symbols for these alleles, and then write down all of the possible genotypes for a man and for a woman.

b A couple who both have normal colour vision have a child with colour blindness. Explain how this may happen, and state what the sex of the colour blind child must be.

c Is it possible for a colour blind girl to be born? Explain your answer.

SAQ 4.14

One of the genes for coat colour in cats is sex-linked. The allele C^O gives orange fur, while C^B gives black fur. The two alleles are codominant, and when both are present the cat has patches of orange and black, which is known as tortoiseshell.

a Explain why male cats cannot be tortoiseshell.

b Draw a genetic diagram to show the expected genotypes and phenotypes of the offspring from a cross between an orange male and a tortoise-shell female cat. (Remember to show the X and Y chromosomes, as well as the symbols for the alleles.)

Dihybrid crosses

So far, we have considered the inheritance of just one gene. Such examples are called **monohybrid crosses**. **Dihybrid crosses** look at the inheritance of two genes at once.

You have already seen that, in tomato plants, there is a gene which codes for stem colour. This gene has two alleles:

stem colour gene   **A** = allele for purple stem and
a = allele for green stem
where A is dominant and a is recessive.

A different gene, at a different locus on a different chromosome, codes for leaf shape. Again, there are two alleles:

leaf shape gene   **D** = allele for cut leaves (jagged edges)
d = allele for potato leaves (smooth edges)
where D is dominant and d is recessive.

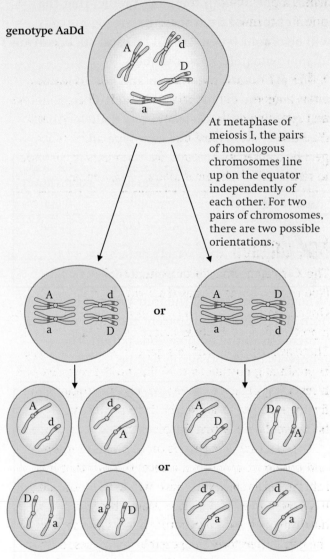

At the end of meiosis II each orientation gives two types of gamete. There are therefore four types of gamete altogether.

● **Figure 4.8** Independent assortment of homologous chromosomes during meiosis I results in a variety of genotypes in the gametes formed.

What will happen if a plant which is heterozygous for both of these genes is crossed with a plant with green stem and potato leaves?

Figure 4.8 shows the alleles in a cell of the plant which is heterozygous for both genes. When this cell undergoes meiosis to produce gametes, the pairs of homologous chromosomes line up independently of each other on the equator during metaphase I. There are two ways in which the two pairs of chromosomes can do this. If there are many such cells undergoing meiosis, then the chromosomes in roughly half of them will probably line up one way, and the other half will line up the other way. This is **independent assortment**. We can therefore predict that the gametes formed from these heterozygous cells will be of four types, **AD**, **Ad**, **aD** and **ad**, occurring in approximately equal numbers.

The plant with green stem and potato leaves must have the genotype **aadd**. Each of its gametes will contain one **a** allele and one **d** allele. All of the gametes will have the genotype **ad**.

Parental phenotypes	purple stem, cut leaves	green stem, potato leaves
Parental genotypes	AaDd	aadd
Gametes	(AD) or (Ad)	all (ad)
	or (aD) or (ad)	
	in equal proportions	

At fertilisation, any of the four types of gamete from the heterozygous parent may fuse with the gametes from the homozygous parent. The genotypes of the offspring will be:

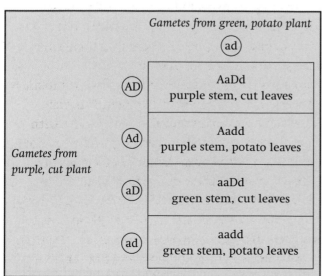

From this cross, therefore, we would expect approximately equal numbers of the four possible phenotypes. This 1:1:1:1 ratio is typical of a dihybrid cross between a heterozygous organism and a homozygous recessive organism, where the alleles show complete dominance.

If *both* parents are heterozygous, then things become a little more complicated, because both of them will produce four kinds of gametes.

Parental phenotypes	purple stem, cut leaves	purple stem, cut leaves
Parental genotypes	AaDd	AaDd
Gametes	(AD) or (Ad)	(AD) or (Ad)
	or (aD) or (ad)	or (aD) or (ad)
	in equal proportions	in equal proportions

Offspring genotypes and phenotypes:

		Gametes from one parent			
		(AD)	(Ad)	(aD)	(ad)
Gametes from other parent	(AD)	AADD purple, cut	AADd purple, cut	AaDD purple, cut	AaDd purple, cut
	(Ad)	AADd purple, cut	AAdd purple, potato	AaDd purple, cut	Aadd purple, potato
	(aD)	AaDD purple, cut	AaDd purple, cut	aaDD green, cut	aaDd green, cut
	(ad)	AaDd purple, cut	Aadd purple, potato	aaDd green, cut	aadd green, potato

If you sort out the numbers of each phenotype amongst these sixteen possibilities, you will find that the offspring would be expected to occur in the following ratio:

9 purple, cut : 3 purple, potato : 3 green, cut : 1 green, potato.

This 9:3:3:1 ratio is typical of a dihybrid cross between two heterozygous organisms, where the two alleles show complete dominance and where the genes are on different chromosomes.

SAQ 4.15
Explain the contribution made to the variation amongst the offspring of this cross by:
a independent assortment;
b random fertilisation.

SAQ 4.16

Draw genetic diagrams to show the genotypes of the offspring from each of the following crosses.

a AABb × aabb

b GgHh × gghh

c TTyy × ttYY

d eeFf × Eeff

SAQ 4.17

The allele for grey fur in a species of animal is dominant to white, and the allele for long tail is dominant to short.

a Using the symbols G and g for coat colour, and T and t for tail length, draw a genetic diagram to show the genotypes and phenotypes of the off-spring you would expect from a cross between a pure-breeding grey animal with a long tail and a pure-breeding white animal with a short tail.

b If this first generation of offspring were bred together, what would be the expected pheno-types in the second generation of offspring, and in what ratios would they occur?

SAQ 4.18

In a species of plant, the allele for tall stem is dominant to short. The two alleles for leaf colour, giving green or white in the homozygous condition, are codominant, producing variegated leaves in the heterozygote.

A plant with tall stems and green leaves was crossed with a plant with short stems and variegated leaves. The offspring from this cross consisted of plants with tall stems and green leaves and plants with tall stems and variegated leaves in the ratio of 1:1. Construct a genetic diagram to explain this cross.

SAQ 4.19

In a species of animal, it is known that the allele for black eyes is dominant to the allele for red eyes, and that the allele for long fur is dominant to the allele for short fur.

a What are the possible genotypes for an animal with black eyes and long fur?

b How could you find out which genotype this animal had?

The χ^2 (chi-squared) test

If you look back at the cross between the two heterozygous tomato plants, on page 58, you will see that we would expect to see a 9:3:3:1 ratio of phenotypes in the offspring. It is important to remember that this ratio represents the *probability* of getting these phenotypes, and we would proba-bly be rather surprised if the numbers came out absolutely precisely to this ratio.

But just how much difference might we be happy with, before we began to worry that perhaps the situation was not quite what we had thought? For example, let us imagine that the two plants produced a total of 144 offspring. If the parents really were both heterozygous, and if the purple stem and cut leaf alleles really are dominant, and if the alleles really do assort independently, then we would expect the follow-ing numbers of each genotype to be present in the offspring:

$$\text{purple, cut} = \tfrac{9}{16} \times 144 = 81$$

$$\text{purple, potato} = \tfrac{3}{16} \times 144 = 27$$

$$\text{green, cut} = \tfrac{3}{16} \times 144 = 27$$

$$\text{green, potato} = \tfrac{1}{16} \times 144 = 9$$

But imagine that, amongst these 144 offspring, the results we actually observed were as follows:

purple, cut	86	green, cut	24
purple, potato	26	green, potato	8

We might ask: are these results sufficiently close to the ones we expected that the differences between them have probably just arisen by chance, or are they so different that something unexpected must be going on?

To answer this question, we can use a statistical test called the χ^2 (**chi-squared**) **test**. This test allows us to compare our observed results with the expected results, and decide whether or not there is a significant difference between them.

The first stage in carrying out this test is to work out the expected results, as we have already done. These, and the observed results, are then recorded in a table like the one overleaf. We then calculate the difference between each set of results, and square each difference. (Squaring it gets rid of any minus signs – it is irrelevant whether the differences are negative or positive.) Then we divide each squared difference by the expected value, and add up all of these answers:

$$\chi^2 = \Sigma \frac{(O - E)^2}{E}$$

where Σ = the sum of
O = the observed value
E = the expected value

Phenotypes of plants	purple stems, cut leaves		purple stems, potato leaves		green stems, cut leaves		green stems, potato leaves
Observed number (O)	86		26		24		8
Expected ratio	9	:	3	:	3	:	1
Expected number (E)	81		27		27		9
O – E	+5		−1		−3		−1
(O −E)^2	25		1		9		1
(O − E)^2/E	0.31		0.04		0.33		0.11

$\Sigma(O - E)^2/E = 0.79$
$\chi^2 = 0.79$

So now we have our value of χ^2. Next we have to work out what it means.

To do this, we look in a table that relates χ^2 values to probabilities (*table 4.3*). The probabilities given in the table are

the probability that the differences between our expected and observed results are due to chance.

For example, a probability of 0.05 means that we would expect these differences to occur in 5 out of every hundred experiments, or 1 in 20, just by chance. A probability of 0.01 means that we would expect them to occur in 1 out of every hundred experiments, just by chance. In biological experiments, we usually take a probability of 0.05 as being the critical one. If our χ^2 value represents a probability of 0.05 or larger, then we can be fairly certain that the differences between our observed and expected results are due to chance – the differences between them are not **significant**. However, if the probability is smaller than this, then it is likely that the difference *is* significant, and we must reconsider our assumptions about what was going on in this cross.

There is one more aspect of our results to consider, before we can look up our value of χ^2 in the table. This is the number of **degrees of freedom** in our results. This takes into account the number of comparisons made. (Remember that to get our value of χ^2, we added up all our calculated values, so obviously the larger the number of observed and expected values we have, the larger χ^2 is likely to be. We need to compensate for this.) To work out the number of degrees of freedom, simply calculate the (number of classes of data – 1). Here we have four classes of data (the four possible sets of phenotypes), so the degrees of freedom = (4 – 1) = 3.

Now, at last, we can look at the table to determine whether our results show a significant deviation from what we expected. The numbers in the body of the table are χ^2 values. We look at the third row in the table (because that is the one relevant to 3 degrees of freedom), and find the χ^2 value that represents a probability of 0.05. You can see that this is 7.82. Our calculated value of χ^2 was 0.79. So our value is a much, much smaller value than the one we have read from the table. In fact, we cannot find anything like this number in the table – it would be way off the left hand side, representing a probability of much more than 0.1 (1 in 10) that the difference in our results is just due to chance. So we can say that the difference between our observed and expected results is almost certainly due to chance, and there is **no significant difference** between what we expected, and what we actually got.

Degrees of freedom	Probability greater than			
	0.1	0.05	0.01	0.001
1	2.71	3.84	6.64	10.83
2	4.60	5.99	9.21	13.82
3	6.25	7.82	11.34	16.27
4	7.78	9.49	13.28	18.46

● **Table 4.3** Table of χ^2 values.

SAQ 4.20

Look back at your answer to SAQ 4.17b. In the actual crosses between the animals in this generation, the numbers of each phenotype obtained in the offspring were:

grey, long 54
grey, short 4
white, long 4
white, short 18

Use a χ^2 test to determine whether or not the difference between these observed results and the expected results is significant.

Mutations

You have seen that most genes have several different variants, called alleles. A gene is a made up of a sequence of nucleotides, each with its own base. The different alleles of a gene contain slightly different sequences of bases.

These different alleles originally arose by a process called **mutation**. Mutation is an unpredictable change in the genetic material of an organism. A change in the structure of a DNA molecule, producing a different allele of a gene, is a **gene mutation**. Mutations may also cause changes in the structure or number of whole chromosomes in a cell, in which case they are known as **chromosome mutations**.

Mutations may occur completely randomly, with no obvious cause. However, there are several environmental factors that significantly increase the chances of a mutation occurring. All types of **ionising radiation** (alpha, beta and gamma radiation) can damage DNA molecules, altering the structure of the bases within them. **Ultraviolet radiation** has a similar effect, as do many chemicals, for example mustard gas. A substance that increases the chances of mutation occurring is said to be a **mutagen**.

In gene mutations, there are three different ways in which the sequence of bases in a gene may be altered. These are:

- **base substitution**, where one base simply takes the place of another. For example:
  CCT GAG GAG may change to CCT GTG GAG;

- **base addition**, where one or more extra bases are added to the sequence. For example:
  CCT GAG GAG may change to CCA TGA GGA G;

- **base deletion**, where one or more bases are lost from the sequence. For example:
  CCT GAG GAG may change to CCG AGG AG.

Base additions or deletions usually have a very significant effect on the structure, and therefore the function, of the polypeptide that the allele codes for. If you look up the amino acids that are coded for by the 'normal' sequence shown above in the appendix, you will see that it is Gly Leu Leu. But the new sequence resulting from the base addition codes for Gly Thr Pro, and that resulting from the base deletion is Gly Ser. Base additions or deletions always have large effects, because they alter every set of three bases that 'follows' them in the DNA molecule. They are said to cause **frame shifts** in the code. Often, the effects are so large that the protein that is made is totally useless. Or they may introduce a 'stop' triplet part way through a gene, so that a complete protein is never made at all.

Base substitutions, on the other hand, often have no effect at all. A mutation that has no apparent effect on an organism is said to be a **silent mutation**. Base substitutions are often silent mutations because many amino acids have more than one triplet code (see the appendix again), so even if one base is changed the same amino acid is still coded for. You have seen above that a change from CCT to CCA or CCG makes no difference – the amino acid that will be slotted into the chain at that point will still be Gly.

However, base substitutions *can* have very large effects. If, for example, the base sequence ATG (coding for Tyr) mutated to ATT, this has produced a 'stop' triplet, so the synthesis of the protein would stop at this point.

Sickle cell anaemia

One example of a base substitution that has a significant effect on the phenotype is the one involved in the inherited blood disorder sickle cell anaemia. (We have already looked at the inheritance of this disease, on pages 52–53.)

Haemoglobin is the red pigment in red blood cells which carries oxygen around the body. A haemoglobin molecule is made up of four polypeptide chains, each with one iron-containing haem group in the centre. Two of these polypeptide chains are called α chains, and the other two β chains. (The structure of haemoglobin is described in *Biology 1* on page 34.)

The gene which codes for the amino acid sequence in the β chains is not the same in everyone. In most people, the β chains begin with the amino acid sequence:

Val-His-Leu-Thr-Pro-Glu-Glu-Lys-

But in some people, the base sequence CTT is replaced by CAT, and the amino acid sequence becomes:

Val-His-Leu-Thr-Pro-Val-Glu-Lys-

This small difference in the amino acid sequence makes little difference to the haemoglobin molecule when it is combined with oxygen. But when it is not combined with oxygen, the 'unusual' β chains make the haemoglobin molecule much less soluble. The molecules tend to stick to each other, forming long fibres inside the red blood cells. The red cells are pulled out of shape, into a half-moon or sickle shape. When this happens, the distorted cells become quite useless at transporting oxygen. They also get stuck in small capillaries, stopping any unaffected cells from getting through (*figure 4.9*).

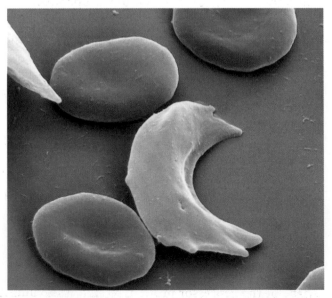

● **Figure 4.9** A scanning electron micrograph of red blood cells from a person with sickle cell anaemia. You can see both normal and sickled cells. (× 12 200)

A person with these unusual β chains can suffer severe anaemia (lack of oxygen transported to the cells) and may die. It is especially common in some parts of Africa, and in India. You can read about the reasons for this distribution on pages 74–75.

Phenylketonuria

Phenylketonuria, or **PKU**, is another disease caused by an abnormal base sequence in part of a DNA molecule. However, in PKU the affected gene codes for an enzyme, not for an oxygen-carrying pigment.

The enzyme affected in PKU is phenylalanine hydroxylase. People with the disease lack this enzyme because their DNA does not carry the correct code for making it. Phenylalanine hydroxylase helps to catalyse the conversion of the amino acid phenylalanine to tyrosine, which can then be converted into melanin.

$$\text{phenylalanine} \xrightarrow{\text{phenylalanine hydroxylase}} \text{tyrosine} \longrightarrow \text{melanin}$$

Phenylalanine is found in many different kinds of foods. Melanin is the brown pigment in skin and hair. If phenylalanine cannot be converted to tyrosine, then little melanin is formed, so people with PKU frequently have a lighter skin and hair colour than normal.

However, a far more important problem which arises is that phenylalanine accumulates in the blood and tissue fluid. This causes severe brain damage in young children. Children with untreated PKU become severely mentally retarded.

All babies born in the UK are tested for PKU at birth, simply by testing the phenylalanine levels in their blood. This testing is very important because brain damage can be completely prevented if a child with PKU is, at birth, put on to a diet which does not contain phenylalanine.

The Human Genome Project is providing us with considerable amounts of information about the genes involved in diseases such as sickle cell anaemia and PKU. You can read about this project, and some of its implications, in the *box* on page 151 in *Biology 1*.

SAQ 4.21

A man and woman who have a history of an inherited disease in one or both of their families might worry that any children they might have could inherit this disease. How may the results from the Human Genome Project help such people? Might there be any negative consequences?

Environment and phenotype

In all the examples in this chapter, we have so far assumed that the genotype of the organism will always affect its phenotype in the same way. This is not always true.

Consider human height. If you have inherited a number of alleles for tallness from your parents, you have the *potential* to grow tall. However, if your diet is poor while you are growing, your cells might not be supplied with sufficient nutrients to allow you to develop this potential. You will not grow as tall as you could. Part of your environment, your diet, has also affected your height. Many characteristics of organisms are affected in this way by both genes and environment.

Another example is the development of the dark tips to ears, nose, paws and tail in the Himalayan colouring of rabbits (*figure 4.6*). This colouring is caused by an allele which allows the formation of the dark pigment only at low temperature. The parts of the rabbit which grow dark fur are the coldest parts. If an area somewhere else on its body is plucked of fur and kept cold, the new fur growing in this region will be dark.

The *lac* operon in *Escherichia coli*

A third example of the interaction between genes and environment concerns the bacterium *Escherichia coli*. This bacterium can be grown on nutrient agar jelly, where it secretes enzymes to digest the various nutrients in the jelly. The enzymes are synthesised by following the codes on the bacterium's genes. *E. coli* has genes that code for the synthesis of the enzymes **lactose permease**, which enables the cell to take up lactose, and **β galactosidase**, which hydrolyses lactose to glucose and galactose. If the bacterium is grown on a medium containing only glucose, it does not produce either of these enzymes. If it is then transferred to a medium containing only lactose, the genes are 'switched on', and both lactose permease and β galactosidase are synthesised. The genes are said to be **expressed**.

SAQ 4.22

What advantage is it to *E. coli* to switch on its lactose permease and β galactosidase genes only when it is growing on a lactose-containing medium?

The genes involved in this regulatory process are part of a stretch of DNA known as the *lac* operon. (An operon is a length of DNA containing the base sequence that actually codes for the production of the proteins, known as the **structural genes**, and also other base sequences that determine whether or not mRNA will be transcribed from the structural genes.) *Figure 4.10* shows the structure of the *lac* operon in *E. coli*.

You can see that the longest length of DNA in the operon makes up the structural genes, which code for the production of lactose permease and β galactosidase. Close to this section (on its left in the diagram) is a short length of DNA containing a **promoter**. This is the part of the DNA to which the enzyme **RNA polymerase** must bind before it can begin to catalyse the transcription of mRNA from the structural genes.

Next to the promoter is a region called the **operator**. If nothing is bound to the operator, then the promoter is available for mRNA polymerase to bind to, and the structural genes can be expressed. However, in another part of the molecule lies yet another stretch of DNA, a **regulator** gene. The regulator DNA codes for a protein called a **repressor**.

The repressor protein molecule has two binding sites. One of these fits the operator DNA, and so binds with it. When this is happening, the promoter is blocked, RNA polymerase cannot bind to it and the structural genes cannot be expressed. This is the normal situation in the *E. coli* cell.

The repressor protein can also bind with the sugar lactose. When this happens, it changes the shape of the repressor protein, so that it no longer fits onto the operator DNA. So, if you grow *E. coli* on agar jelly containing lactose, the repressor protein leaves the operator, which frees the promoter site, so mRNA polymerase can bind and start transcribing the structural genes. Within a very short time, lactose permease and β galactosidase have been synthesised, and the bacterium can begin to make use of the lactose on which it is growing.

a Structure of the *lac* operon

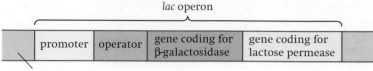

part of the bacterium's DNA molecule

b How activity of the *lac* operon is controlled

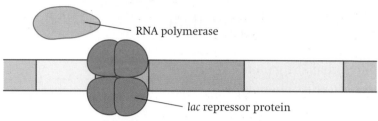

Normally, a protein called *lac* repressor is bound to the operator gene. This prevents RNA polymerase binding to the promoter.

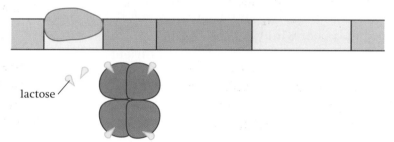

When lactose is present, it binds to the *lac* repressor protein and changes its shape. The repressor protein can no longer bind to DNA. This allows RNA polymerase to bind to the promoter gene, and begin to transcribe the β-galactosidase and lactose permease genes.

● **Figure 4.10** The *lac* operon in *E. coli*.

SUMMARY

♦ Diploid organisms contain two copies of each gene in each of their cells. In sexual reproduction, gametes are formed containing one copy of each gene. Each offspring receives two copies of each gene, one from each of its parents.

♦ Gametes are haploid cells, and they are formed from diploid cells by meiosis. Meiosis consists of two divisions. The first division, meiosis I, separates the homologous chromosomes, so that each cell now has only one of each pair. The second division, meiosis II, separates the chromatids of each chromosome. Meiotic division therefore produces four cells, each with one complete set of chromosomes.

♦ The cells produced by meiosis are genetically different from each other and from their parent cell. This results from independent assortment of the chromosomes as the bivalents line up on the equator during metaphase I, and also from crossing over between the chromatids of homologous chromosomes during prophase I.

♦ Genetic variation also results from random fertilisation, as gametes containing different varieties of genes fuse together to form a zygote.

♦ Different varieties of a gene are called alleles. Alleles may show dominance or codominance. An organism possessing two identical alleles of a gene is homozygous; an organism possessing two different alleles of a gene is heterozygous. If a gene has several different alleles, such as the gene for human blood groups, these are known as multiple alleles.

♦ The genotype of an organism showing dominant characteristics can be determined by looking at the offspring produced when it is crossed with an organism showing recessive characteristics. This is called a test cross.

♦ A gene found on the X chromosome but not on the Y chromosome is known as a sex-linked gene.

♦ Monohybrid crosses consider the inheritance of one gene. Dihybrid crosses consider the inheritance of two different genes.

♦ The χ^2 test can be used to find out whether any differences between expected results and observed results of a genetic cross are due to chance, or whether the difference is significant.

♦ Mutation can be defined as an unpredictable change in the base sequence in a DNA molecule (gene mutation) or in the structure or number of chromosomes (chromosome mutation). New alleles arise by gene mutation. Gene mutations include base substitutions, deletions or additions. The sickle cell allele arose by base substitution.

♦ The genotype of an organism gives it the potential to show a particular characteristic. In many cases, the degree to which this characteristic is shown is also affected by the organism's environment.

♦ An operon is an operational unit on a DNA molecule containing genes that each code for the production of a polypeptide, plus other genes that control whether or not these genes are expressed. The *lac* operon in *Escherichia coli* controls the production of proteins that allow the bacterium to metabolise lactose, and ensures that these proteins are only synthesised when lactose is present in the environment.

♦ The Human Genome Project has mapped most of the DNA sequences in each human chromosome. This information may eventually help with the diagnosis and treatment of genetic diseases.

Questions

1 Explain the difference between each of the following pairs of terms:
   a genotype and phenotype;
   b dominance and codominance;
   c gene and allele;
   d homologous and homozygous.

2 For each of the following, discuss whether genotype or environment is more important in determining the phenotype of: a height; b blood group; c shoe size; d athletic ability; e how good you are at maths.

3 Describe the ways in which sexual reproduction can bring about variation between individuals.

4 When mutation produces a new allele of a gene, it is usually recessive and harmful. Explain why:
   a it is advantageous for organisms to be diploid rather than haploid;
   b mutations do not usually appear in the phenotype of organisms until many generations after the mutation occurred;
   c inbreeding (breeding between close relatives) in humans is discouraged.

5 a Describe how the *lac* operon in *Escherichia coli* functions.
   b Discuss the advantages to organisms of controlling gene expression in this way.

To answer the following questions, you will need to bring together information from other areas of your course, as well as from this chapter.

6 a Compare and contrast nuclear division by mitosis and meiosis.
   b Discuss the biological significance of the differences between these two types of cell division.

7 a With reference to examples, explain the differences between an infectious disease and an inherited disease.
   b Duchenne muscular dystrophy is caused by a faulty recessive allele of a gene that is carried on the X chromosome. With the aid of a genetic diagram, calculate the probability that a woman who is heterozygous for this condition could pass it on to her son.

8 a Haemoglobin is a globular protein with quaternary structure. Explain the meaning of this statement.
   b Explain how gene mutation can affect the solubility of haemoglobin, and therefore its oxygen-carrying properties.

CHAPTER 5

Classification, selection and evolution

By the end of this chapter you should be able to:

1 explain how variation is produced in sexually reproducing organisms;

2 explain why variation caused by genes can be inherited, but variation caused by the environment cannot;

3 explain how all organisms can potentially overproduce;

4 describe how different selection pressures may act on individual organisms with different alleles, so affecting allele frequencies in a population;

5 explain, with examples, how environmental factors can act as stabilising or evolutionary forces of natural selection;

6 describe one example of artificial selection;

7 explain the meaning of the term *species*, and explain the roles of natural selection and isolating mechanisms in the evolution of new species;

8 describe the classification of species into taxonomic groups (genus, family, order, class, phylum, kingdom);

9 explain the relationship between classification and phylogeny;

10 describe the important features of the five kingdoms.

Variation

In chapter 4, you have seen how sexual reproduction produces **genetic variation** amongst the individuals in a population. Genetic variation is caused by:

■ independent assortment of chromosomes, and therefore alleles, during meiosis,

■ crossing over between chromatids of homologous chromosomes during meiosis;

■ random mating between organisms within a species;

■ random fertilisation of gametes;

■ mutation.

The first four of these processes reshuffle alleles in the population. Offspring have combinations of alleles which differ from those of their parents,

and from each other. This genetic variation produces phenotypic variation.

Mutation, however, does more than reshuffle alleles that are already present. Mutation can produce completely new alleles. This may happen, for example, if a mistake occurs in DNA replication, so that a new base sequence occurs in a gene. This is probably how the sickle cell allele of the gene for the production of the β polypeptide of haemoglobin first arose. Such a change in a gene, which is quite unpredictable, is called a **gene mutation**. The new allele is very often recessive, so it frequently does not show up in the population until some generations after the mutation actually occurred, when by chance two descendants of the organism in which the mutation happened mate and produce offspring.

Mutations that occur in body, or **somatic**, cells often have no effects at all on the organism. A malfunctioning cell in a tissue is only one of thousands of similar cells, and it is very unlikely that this cell would cause any problems. Most mutated cells are recognised as foreign by the body's immune systems and are destroyed (*Biology 1*, page 88 and chapter 16). Occasionally the mutation may affect the regulation of cell division. If a cell with such a mutation escapes the attack of the immune system, it can produce a lump of cells called a tumour. Tumours often cause little harm, but sometimes the tumour cells are able to spread around the body and invade other tissues. This type of tumour is described as **malignant**, and the diseases caused by such tumours are **cancers**.

Mutations in somatic cells cannot be passed on to offspring by sexual reproduction. However, mutations in cells in the ovaries or testes of an animal, or in the ovaries or anthers of a plant, may be inherited by offspring. If a cell containing a mutation divides to form gametes, then the gametes may also contain the mutated gene. If such a gamete is one of the two which fuse to form a zygote, then the mutated gene will also be in the zygote. This single cell then divides repeatedly to form a new organism, in which all the cells will contain the mutated gene.

Genetic variation, whether caused by the reshuffling of alleles during meiosis and sexual reproduction or by the introduction of new alleles by mutation, can be passed on by parents to their offspring giving differences in phenotype. Variation in phenotype is also caused by the *environment* in which organisms live. For example, some organisms might be larger than others because they had access to better quality food while they were growing. This type of variation is *not* passed on by parents to their offspring.

SAQ 5.1

Explain why variation caused by the environment cannot be passed from an organism to its offspring.

Overproduction

All organisms have the reproductive potential to increase their populations. Rabbits, for example, produce several young in a litter, and each female may produce several litters each year. If all the young rabbits survived to adulthood and reproduced, then the rabbit population would increase rapidly. *Figure 5.1* shows what might happen.

This sort of population growth actually did happen in Australia in the nineteenth century. In 1859, twelve pairs of rabbits from Britain were released on a ranch in Victoria, as a source of food. The rabbits found conditions to their liking. Rabbits feed on low-growing vegetation, especially grasses, of which there was an abundance. There were very few predators to feed on them, so the number of rabbits soared. Their numbers became so great that they seriously affected the availability of grazing for sheep (*figure 5.2*).

Such population explosions are rare in normal circumstances. Although rabbit populations have the potential to increase at such a tremendous rate, they do not usually do so.

As a population of rabbits increases, various **environmental factors** come into play to keep down their numbers. These factors may be **biotic**, that is caused by other living organisms such as predation, competition for food, or infection by pathogens, or they may be **abiotic**, that is caused by non-living components of the environment such as water supply or nutrient levels in the soil.

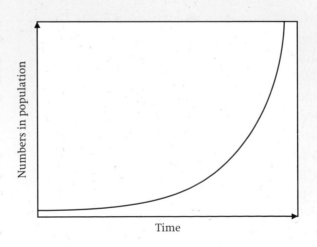

● **Figure 5.1** If left unchecked by environmental factors, numbers in a population may increase exponentially.

- **Figure 5.2** Attempts to control the rabbit population explosion in Australia in the mid to late nineteenth century included 'rabbit drives', in which huge numbers were rounded up and killed. Eventually, myxomatosis brought numbers down.

For example, the increasing number of rabbits eats an increasing amount of vegetation, until food is in short supply. The larger population may allow the populations of predators, such as foxes, stoats and weasels, to increase. Overcrowding may occur, increasing the ease with which diseases such as myxomatosis (*figure 5.3*) may spread. This disease is caused by a virus which is transmitted by fleas. The closer together the rabbits live, the more easily fleas, and therefore viruses, will pass from one rabbit to another.

These environmental factors act to reduce the rate of growth of the rabbit population. Of all the rabbits born, many will die from lack of food, or be killed by predators, or die from myxomatosis. Only a small proportion of young will grow to adulthood and reproduce, so population growth slows.

If the pressure of the environmental factors is sufficiently great, then the population size will decrease. Only when the numbers of rabbits have fallen considerably will the numbers be able to grow again. Over a period of time, the population will oscillate about a mean level. *Figure 5.4* overleaf shows this kind of pattern in a lemming population over eleven years. The oscillations in lemming populations are particularly marked; in others, they are usually less spectacular!

This type of pattern is shown by the populations of many organisms. The number of young produced is far greater than the number which will survive to adulthood. Many young die before reaching reproductive age.

- **Figure 5.3** Rabbits living in dense populations are more likely to get myxomatosis than those in less crowded conditions.

Natural selection

What determines which will be the few rabbits to survive, and which will die? It may be just luck.

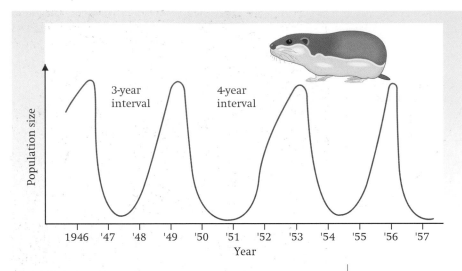

● **Figure 5.4** Lemming populations are famous for their large increases and decreases. In some years, populations become so large that lemmings may emigrate 'en masse' from overcrowded areas. The reason for the oscillating population size is not known for certain, although it has been suggested that food supply or food quality may be the main cause. As the population size rises, food supplies run out, so the population size 'crashes'. Once the population size has decreased, food supplies begin to recover, and the population size rises again.

However, some rabbits will be born with a better chance of survival than others. Variation within a population of rabbits means that some will have features which give them an advantage in the 'struggle for existence'.

One feature that may vary is coat colour. Most rabbits have alleles which give the normal agouti (brown) colour. A few, however, may be homozygous for the recessive allele which gives white coat. Such white rabbits will stand out distinctly from the others, and are more likely to be picked out by a predator such as a fox. They are less likely to survive than agouti rabbits. The chances of a white rabbit reproducing and passing on its alleles for white coat to its offspring are very small, so the allele for white coat will remain very rare in the population.

Predation by foxes is an example of a **selection pressure**. Selection pressures increase the chances of some alleles being passed on to the next generation, and decrease the chances of others. In this case, the alleles for agouti coat have a selective advantage over the alleles for white. The alleles for agouti will remain the commoner alleles in the population, while the alleles for white will remain very rare. The alleles for white coat may even disappear completely.

The effects of such selection pressures on the frequency of alleles in a population is called **natural selection**. Natural selection raises the frequency of alleles conferring an advantage, and reduces the frequency of alleles conferring a disadvantage.

SAQ 5.2

Skomer is a small island off the coast of Wales. Rabbits have been living on the island for many years. There are no predators on the island.

a Rabbits on Skomer are not all agouti. There are quite large numbers of rabbits of different colours, such as black and white. Suggest why this is so.

b What do you think might be important selection pressures acting on rabbits on Skomer?

Evolution

Usually, natural selection keeps things the way they are. This is **stabilising selection**. Agouti rabbits are best adapted to survive predation, so the agouti allele remains the most common coat colour allele in rabbit populations. Unless something changes, then natural selection will ensure that this continues to be the case.

However, if a *new environmental factor*, or a *new allele* appears, then allele frequencies may also change. This is called **directional selection** (*figures 5.5* and *5.6*).

A new environmental factor

Imagine that we are plunged into a new Ice Age. The climate becomes much colder, so that snow covers the ground for almost all of the year. Assuming that rabbits can cope with these conditions, white rabbits now have a selective advantage during seasons when snow lies on the ground, as they are better camouflaged (*figure 5.7*). Rabbits with white fur are more likely to survive

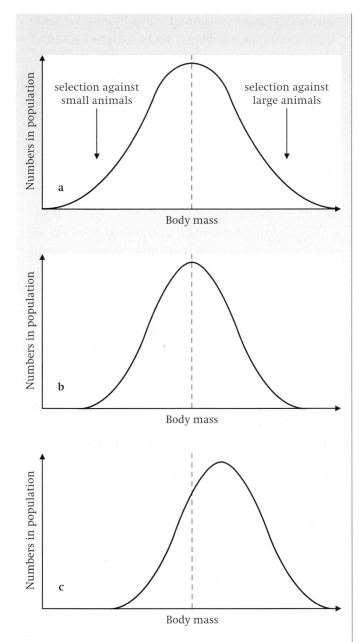

● **Figure 5.6** The tuatara, *Sphenodon punctatus*, is a lizard-like reptile that lives in New Zealand. Fossils of a virtually identical animal have been found in rocks 200 million years old. Natural selection has acted to keep the features of this organism the same over all this time.

and reproduce, passing on their alleles for white fur to their offspring. The frequency of the allele for white coat increases, at the expense of the allele for agouti. Over many generations, almost all rabbits will come to have white coats rather than agouti.

A new allele

Because they are random events, most mutations that occur produce features that are harmful. That is, they produce organisms that are less well

● **Figure 5.5** If a characteristic in a population, such as body mass, shows wide variation, selection pressures often act against the two extremes (graph **a**). Very small or very large individuals are less likely to survive and reproduce than those whose size lies nearer the centre of the range. This results in a population with a narrower range of body size (graph **b**). This type of selection, which tends to keep the variation in a characteristic centred around the same mean value, is called **stabilising selection**. Graph **c** shows what would happen if selection acted against smaller individuals but not larger ones. In this case, the range of variation shifts towards larger size. This type of selection, which results in a change in a characteristic in a particular direction, is called **directional selection**.

● **Figure 5.7** The white winter coat of a mountain hare provides excellent camouflage from predators when viewed against snow.

adapted to their environment than 'normal' organisms. Other mutations may be 'neutral', conferring neither an advantage nor a disadvantage on the organisms within which they occur. Occasionally mutations may produce useful features.

Imagine that a mutation occurs in the coat colour gene of a rabbit, producing a new allele which gives a better camouflaged coat colour than agouti. Rabbits possessing this new allele will have a selective advantage. They will be more likely to survive and reproduce than agouti rabbits, so the new allele will become more common in the population. Over many generations, almost all rabbits will come to have the new allele.

Such changes in allele frequency in a population are the basis of **evolution**. Evolution occurs because natural selection gives some alleles a better chance of survival than others. Over many generations, populations may gradually change, becoming better adapted to their environments. Examples of such change are the development of antibiotic resistance in bacteria and industrial melanism in the peppered moth *Biston betularia*.

Antibiotic resistance

Antibiotics are chemicals produced by living organisms, which inhibit or kill bacteria, but do not normally harm human tissue. Most antibiotics are produced by fungi. The first antibiotic to be discovered was penicillin, which was first used during the Second World War to treat a wide range of diseases caused by bacteria. Penicillin stops cell wall formation in bacteria, so preventing cell reproduction.

If someone takes penicillin to treat a bacterial infection, bacteria which are sensitive to penicillin will die. In most cases, this will be the entire population of the disease-causing bacteria. However, by chance, there may be among them one or more individual bacteria with an allele giving resistance to penicillin. One example of such an allele occurs in some populations of the bacterium *Staphylococcus*, where some individual bacteria produce an enzyme, penicillinase, which inactivates penicillin.

As bacteria have only a single loop of DNA, they have only one copy of each gene, so the mutant allele will have an immediate effect on the phenotype of any bacterium possessing it. These individuals have a tremendous selective advantage. The bacteria without this allele will be killed, while those bacteria with resistance to penicillin can survive and reproduce. Bacteria reproduce very rapidly in ideal conditions, and even if there was initially only one resistant bacterium, it might produce ten thousand million descendants within 24 hours. A large population of a penicillin-resistant strain of *Staphylococcus* would result.

Such antibiotic-resistant strains of bacteria are continually appearing (*figure 5.8*). By using antibiotics, we change the environmental factors which exert selection pressures on bacteria. A constant 'arms race' is on to find new antibiotics against new resistant strains of bacteria.

Alleles for antibiotic resistance often occur on plasmids (*Biology 1*, pages 16 and 77). Plasmids are quite frequently transferred from one bacterium to another, even between different species. Thus it is even possible for resistance to a particular antibiotic to arise in one species of bacterium, and be passed on to another. The more we use

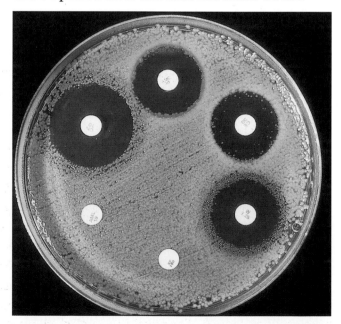

● **Figure 5.8** The grey areas on the agar jelly in this petri dish are colonies of the bacterium *Escherichia coli*. The white discs are pieces of card impregnated with different antibiotics. Where there are clear areas around the disc, the antibiotic has prevented the bacteria from growing. However, you can see that this strain of *E. coli* is resistant to the antibiotics on the discs at the bottom left and has been able to grow right up to the discs.

antibiotics, the greater the selection pressure we exert on bacteria to evolve resistance to them.

SAQ 5.3

Suggest how each of the following might decrease the chances of an antibiotic-resistant strain of bacteria developing:

a limiting the use of antibiotics to cases where there is a real need;

b regularly changing the type of antibiotic which is prescribed for a particular disease;

c using two or more antibiotics together to treat a bacterial infection.

Industrial melanism

One well-documented case of the way in which changing environmental factors may produce changes in allele frequencies is that of the peppered moth *Biston betularia* (*figure 5.9*). This is a night-flying moth, which spends the day resting underneath the branches of trees. It relies on camouflage to protect it from insect-eating birds which hunt by sight. Until 1849, all specimens of this moth in collections had pale wings with dark markings, giving a speckled appearance. In 1849, however, a black (melanic) individual was caught near Manchester. During the rest of the nineteenth century, the numbers of black *Biston betularia* increased dramatically in some areas, while in other parts of the country the speckled form remained the more common.

The difference in the black and speckled forms of the moth is caused by a single gene. The normal speckled colouring is produced by a recessive allele of this gene, c, while the black colour is produced by a dominant allele, C. Up until the late 1960s, the frequency of the allele C increased in areas near to industrial cities. In non-industrial areas, the allele c remained the more common allele (*figure 5.10*).

The selection pressure causing the change of allele frequency in industrial areas was predation by birds. In areas with unpolluted air, tree branches are often covered with grey, brown and green lichen. On such tree branches, speckled moths are superbly camouflaged.

However, lichens are very sensitive to pollutants such as sulphur dioxide, and do not grow on trees near to or downwind of industries releasing pollutants into the air. Trees in these areas therefore have much darker bark, against which the dark moths are better camouflaged. Experiments have shown that light moths have a much higher chance of survival in unpolluted areas than dark moths, while in polluted areas the dark moths have the selective advantage. As air pollution from industry is reduced, the selective advantage swings back in favour of the speckled variety. So we would expect the proportion of speckled moths to increase if we succeeded in reducing the output of certain pollutants. This is, in fact, what has happened since the 1970s. It is predicted that by 2005 there will be hardly any dark individuals left.

It is important to realise that the C allele has probably been present in *B. betularia* populations for a very long time. It has not been produced by pollution. Until the nineteenth century there was such a strong selection pressure against the C allele that it remained exceedingly rare. Mutations of the c allele to the C allele may have occurred quite frequently, but moths with

● **Figure 5.9** Light and melanic forms of peppered moths on light and dark tree bark.

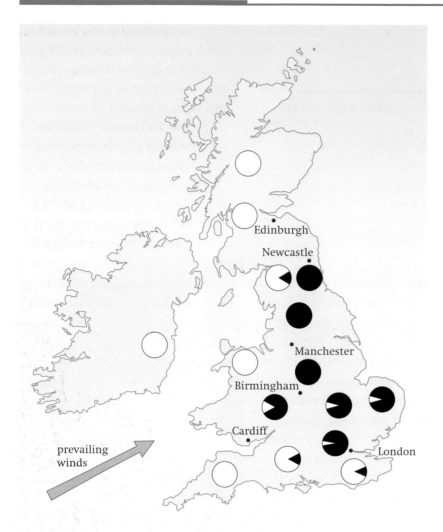

prevailing winds

● **Figure 5.10** The distribution of the pale and dark forms of the peppered moth, *Biston betularia*, in the early 1960s. The ratio of dark to light areas in each circle shows the ratio of dark to light moths in that part of the country.

this allele would almost certainly have been eaten by birds before they could reproduce. Changes in environmental factors only affect the likelihood of an allele surviving in a population; they do not affect the likelihood of such an allele arising by mutation.

Sickle cell anaemia

In chapter 4, we saw how an allele, H^S, of the gene which codes for the production of the β polypeptides of the haemoglobin molecule can produce sickling of red blood cells. People who are homozygous for this allele have sickle cell anaemia. This is a severe form of anaemia which is often lethal.

The possession of two copies of this allele obviously puts a person at a great selective disadvantage. People who are homozygous for the sickle cell allele are less likely to survive and reproduce. Until recently, almost everyone with sickle cell anaemia died before reaching reproductive age. Yet the frequency of the sickle cell allele is very high in some parts of the world. In some parts of East Africa, almost 50% of babies born are carriers for this allele, and 14% are homozygous, suffering from sickle cell anaemia. How can this be explained?

The parts of the world where the sickle cell allele is most common are also the parts of the world where malaria is found (*figure 5.12*). Malaria is caused by a protoctist parasite, *Plasmodium*, which can be introduced into a person's blood when an infected mosquito bites (*figure 5.11* and *Biology 1* pages 205–208)). The parasites enter the red blood cells and multiply inside them. Malaria is the major source of illness and death in many parts of the world.

In studies carried out in some African states, it has been found that people who are heterozygous for the sickle cell allele are much less likely to suffer from a serious attack of malaria than

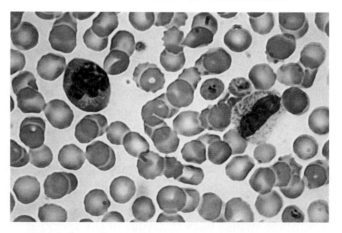

● **Figure 5.11** The purple structure in this micrograph of human blood is a *Plasmodium*, the protoctist which causes malaria (× 1400). At an earlier stage in the life cycle of *Plasmodium*, the organism reproduces inside the red blood cells.

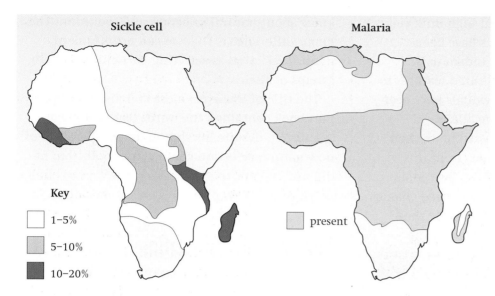

Sickle cell Malaria

Key

☐ 1–5%

▨ 5–10%

▧ 10–20%

☐ present

● **Figure 5.12** The distribution of people with at least one copy of the sickle cell allele, and the distribution of malaria, in Africa.

people who are homozygous for the normal allele. Heterozygous people with malaria only have about one third the number of *Plasmodium* in their blood as normal homozygotes. In one study, of a sample of 100 children who died from malaria, all except one were normal homozygotes, although within the population as a whole 20% of people were heterozygotes.

There are, therefore, two strong selection pressures acting on these two alleles. Selection against people who are homozygous for the sickle cell allele, $H^S H^S$, is very strong, because they become seriously anaemic. Selection against people who are homozygous for the normal allele, $H^N H^N$, is also very strong, because they are more likely to die from malaria. In areas where malaria is common, heterozygotes, $H^N H^S$, have a strong selective advantage; they do not suffer from sickle cell anaemia and are much less likely to suffer badly from malaria. So both alleles remain in populations where malaria is an important environmental factor. In places where malaria was never present, selection against people with the genotype $H^S H^S$ has almost completely removed the H^S allele from the population.

Artificial selection

Sometimes, the most important selection pressures on organisms are those applied by humans.

When humans purposefully apply selection pressures to populations, the process is known as **artificial selection**.

Consider, for example, the development of modern breeds of cattle. Cattle have been domesticated for a very long time (*figure 5.13*). For thousands of years, people have tried to 'improve' their cattle. Desired features include docility (making the animal easier

● **Figure 5.13** The original wild cattle from which individuals were first domesticated are thought to have looked very much like **a**, the modern Chillingham White breed. Selective breeding over many centuries has produced many different breeds, such as **b**, the Guernsey. Guernseys have been bred for the production of large quantities of fat-rich milk. Notice the large udder compared with the Chillingham.

to control), fast growth rates and high milk yields. Increases in these characteristics have been achieved by **selective breeding**. Individuals showing one or more of these desired features to a larger degree than other individuals have been chosen for breeding. Some of the alleles conferring these features are passed on to their offspring. Again, the 'best' animals from this generation are chosen for breeding. Over many generations, alleles conferring the desired characteristics will increase in frequency, while those conferring characteristics not desired by the breeder will decrease in frequency. In many cases, such 'disadvantageous' alleles are lost entirely.

The Darwin–Wallace theory of evolution by natural selection

The original theory that natural selection might be a mechanism by which evolution could occur was put forward independently by both Charles Darwin and Alfred Russel Wallace in 1856. They knew nothing of genes or mutations, so did not understand how natural variation could arise or be inherited. Nevertheless, they realised the significance of variation. Their observations and deductions can be summarised briefly as follows:

Observation 1 Organisms produce more offspring than are needed to replace the parents.

Observation 2 Natural populations tend to remain stable in size over long periods.

Deduction 1 There is competition for survival (a 'struggle for existence').

Observation 3 There is variation among the individuals of a given species.

Deduction 2 The best adapted variants will be selected for by the natural conditions operating at the time. In other words, natural selection will occur. The 'best' variants have a selective advantage; 'survival of the fittest' occurs.

As you can see, this theory, put forward well over a century ago, hardly differs from what we now know about natural selection and evolution. The major difference is that we can now think of natural selection as selecting particular *alleles* or groups of alleles.

The title of Darwin's most famous and important book contained the words *On the Origin of Species*. Yet, despite his thorough consideration of how natural selection could cause evolution, he did not attempt to explain how *new species* could be produced. This process is called **speciation**.

Species and speciation

In this chapter, you have seen how natural selection can act on variation within a population to bring about changes in allele frequencies. Biologists believe that natural selection is the force which has produced all of the different species of organisms on Earth. Yet in the examples of directional selection described on pages 72–74, that is the evolution of antibiotic resistance in bacteria, and changes in the frequency of wing colour in peppered moths, no *new* species have been produced. How can natural selection produce new species? Before we can begin to answer this question, we must answer another: exactly what is a species? This proves to be an extremely difficult question, with no neat answer.

The definition of a species which is most widely accepted by biologists is:

> a group of organisms, with similar morphological, physiological, biochemical and behavioural features, which can interbreed to produce fertile offspring, and are reproductively isolated from other species.

'Morphological' features are structural features, while 'physiological' features are the way that the body works. 'Biochemical' features include the sequence of bases in DNA molecules and the sequence of amino acids in proteins.

Thus all donkeys look and work like donkeys, and can breed with other donkeys to produce more donkeys which themselves can interbreed. All donkeys belong to the same species. Donkeys can interbreed with organisms of another similar species, horses, to produce offspring called mules.

However, mules are infertile, that is they cannot breed and are effectively a 'dead-end'. Thus donkeys and horses belong to different species.

When a decision needs to be made as to whether two organisms belong to the same species or to two different species, they should ideally be tested to find out if they can interbreed successfully, producing fertile offspring. However, as you can imagine, this is not always possible. Perhaps the organisms are dead; they may even be museum specimens or fossils. Perhaps they are both of the same sex. Perhaps the biologist making the decision does not have the time or the facilities to attempt to interbreed them. Perhaps the organisms will not breed in captivity. Perhaps they are not organisms which reproduce sexually, but only asexually. Perhaps they are immature, and not yet able to breed.

As a result of all of these problems, it is quite rare to test the ability of two organisms to interbreed. Biologists frequently rely only on morphological, biochemical, physiological and behavioural differences to decide whether they are looking at specimens from one or two species. In practice, it may only be morphological features which are considered, because physiological and biochemical, and to some extent behavioural, ones are more time-consuming to investigate. Sometimes, however, detailed studies of DNA sequences may be used to assess how similar two organisms are to each other.

It can be extremely difficult to decide when these features are sufficiently similar or different to decide whether two organisms should belong to the same or a different species. This leads to great uncertainties and disagreements about whether to lump many slightly different variations of organisms together into one species, or whether to split them up into many different species.

Despite the problems described above, most biologists would agree that the feature which really decides whether or not two organisms belong to different species is their inability to interbreed successfully. In explaining how natural selection can produce new species, therefore, we must consider how a group of interbreeding organisms, and so all of the same species, can produce another group of organisms which cannot interbreed successfully with the first group. The two groups must become **reproductively isolated**.

Once again, this is not a question with a neat and straightforward answer. The main difficulty is that this process *takes time*. You cannot, at least not easily, set up a speciation experiment in a laboratory because it would have to run for many years. The evidence which we have for the ways in which speciation can occur is almost all circumstantial evidence. We can look at populations of organisms at one moment in time, that is now, and use the patterns we can see to suggest what might have happened, and might still be happening, over long periods of time.

Allopatric speciation

One picture which emerges from this kind of observation is that **geographical isolation** has played a major role in the evolution of many species. This is suggested by the fact that many islands have their own unique groups of species. The Hawaiian and Galapagos islands, for example, are famous for their spectacular array of species of all kinds of animals and plants found nowhere else in the world.

Geographical isolation requires a barrier of some kind to arise between two populations of the same species, preventing them from mixing. This barrier might be a stretch of water. We can imagine that a group of organisms, perhaps a population of a species of bird, somehow arrived on one of the Hawaiian islands from mainland America; they might have been blown off course by a storm. Here, separated by hundreds of miles of ocean from the rest of their species on mainland America, the group interbred. The selection pressures on the island were very different from those on the mainland, resulting in different alleles being selected for. Over time, the morphological, physiological and behavioural features of the island population became so different from the mainland population that they could no longer interbreed. A new species had evolved.

You can probably think of many other ways in which two populations of a species could be physically separated. A species living in dense forest, for example, could become split if large areas of forest are cut down, leaving 'islands' of forest in a 'sea' of agricultural land. Very small or immobile organisms can be isolated by even smaller-scale barriers.

Speciation which happens like this, when two populations are separated from each other geographically, is called **allopatric speciation**. 'Allopatric' means 'in different places'. However, it is also possible for new species to arise without the original populations being separated by a geographical barrier. This is known as **sympatric speciation**.

Sympatric speciation

Perhaps the commonest way in which sympatric speciation can occur is through **polyploidy**.

A polyploid organism is one with more than two complete sets of chromosomes in its cells. This can happen if, for example, meiosis goes wrong when gametes are being formed, so that a gamete ends up with two sets of chromosomes instead of one set. If two such gametes fuse, then the zygote gets four complete sets of chromosomes. It is said to be **tetraploid**.

Tetraploids formed in this way are often sterile. As there are four of each kind of chromosome, all four try to 'pair' up during meiosis I, and get in a terrible muddle. It is very difficult for the cell to divide by meiosis and produce new cells each with complete sets of chromosomes.

However, it may well be able to grow perfectly well, and to reproduce asexually. There is nothing to stop mitosis happening absolutely normally. (Remember that chromosomes do not need to pair up in mitosis – they each behave quite independently.) This does quite often happen in plants but only rarely in animals, largely because most animals do not reproduce asexually anyway.

Just occasionally, this tetraploid plant may manage to produce gametes. They will be diploid gametes. If one of these should fuse with a gamete from the normal, diploid, plant, then the resulting zygote will be triploid. Once again, it may be able to grow normally, but it will certainly be sterile. There is no way in which it can produce gametes, because it cannot share the three sets of chromosomes out evenly between the daughter cells.

So, the original diploid plant and the tetraploid that was produced from it cannot interbreed successfully. They can be considered to be

different species. A new species has arisen in just one generation!

The kind of polyploid described here contained four sets of chromosomes all from the same species. It is said to be an **autopolyploid**. ('Auto' means 'self'.) Polyploids can also be formed that contain, say, two sets of chromosomes from one species and two sets from another closely-related species. They are called **allopolyploids**. ('Allo' means 'other' or 'different'.) Meiosis actually happens more easily in an allotetraploid than in an autotetraploid, because the chromosomes from each species are not quite identical. So the two chromosomes from one species pair up with each other, whilst the two chromosomes from the other species pair up. This produces a much less muddled situation than in an autopolyploid where the chromosomes try to get together in fours, so it is much more likely that meiosis can come to a successful conclusion. The allopolyploid may well be able to produce plenty of gametes. It is fertile.

Once again, however, the allopolyploid cannot interbreed with individuals from its parent species, for the same reasons as for the autopolyploid. It is a new species.

One well-documented instance of speciation through allopolyploidy is the cord grass *Spartina anglica*. This is a vigorous grass that grows in salt marshes.

Before 1830, the species of *Spartina* that grew in these places was *S. maritima*. Then, in 1829, a different species called *S. alterniflora* was imported from America. *S. maritima* and *S. alterniflora* hybridised, producing a new species called *S. townsendii*. This is a diploid plant, with one set of chromosomes from *S. maritima* and one set from *S. alterniflora*. It is sterile, because the two sets of chromosomes from its parents cannot pair up, so it cannot undergo meiosis successfully. Nor can it interbreed with either of its two parents, which is what makes it a different species. Although it is sterile, it has been able to spread rapidly, reproducing asexually by producing long underground stems called rhizomes, from which new plants can grow.

At some later time, probably around 1892, faulty cell division in *S. townsendii* somehow produced cells with double the number of chromosomes. A tetraploid plant was produced, probably from the fusion of two diploid gametes from *S. townsendii*. So this tetraploid has two sets of chromosomes that originally came from *S. maritima*, and two sets from *S. alterniflora*. It is an allotetraploid. These chromosomes can pair up with each other, two and two, during meiosis, so this tetraploid plant is fertile. It has been named *S. anglica*. It is more vigorous than any of the other three species, and has spread so widely and so successfully that it has practically replaced them in England.

Classification

Biologists not only classify organisms into species, but also classify species into larger groups. The study of the classification of organisms is called **taxonomy**.

Organisms can be classified according to their evolutionary relationships. In order to do this, taxonomists look for shared **homologous features** between different organisms. These are features which appear to have similar underlying designs, and so have almost certainly evolved from the same 'original' design that

existed in a particular organism at one stage. A classic example of homologous features is the limb bones of vertebrates. In all birds and mammals, for example, these limb bones take the same general pattern, with a single bone in the upper limb and two bones in the lower limb (*figure 5.14*). You can always pick out this pattern, despite great variations in the way the pattern has been modified in the course of evolution. Such features supply strong evidence that all organisms possessing them had a common ancestor.

You have already seen the criteria which are used (or not used!) to classify organisms into a

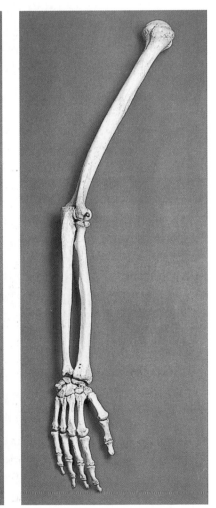

● **Figure 5.14** These three vertebrate limb skeletons are from a bird, a sheep and a human. They are homologous structures; each has the same basic design of a single bone in the upper part of the limb, and two bones in the lower part. This indicates that these three very different species shared a common ancestor, and so are related. Try to identify the different bones in each limb, and consider how the different relative shapes and sizes of these bones in each animal may adapt them to their way of life.

particular **species**. Species which share many homologous features, suggesting that they may have evolved from a common ancestor, are grouped into the same **genus**. Thus horses, donkeys and zebras all belong to the genus *Equus*. They have probably all evolved from what was a single species a long time ago.

Every species is given a two-word Latin name, called a **binomial**. This system was invented by Carl Linnaeus, a Swedish naturalist, in the early eighteenth century, when Latin was a language widely used by educated people all over Europe. Although some people find Latin names awkward, they are extremely useful to biologists, because their use is very precise and universal. Thus a biologist in Malaysia and another in Britain both know exactly what organism they are talking about when they use the name *Equus burchelli*. (It is a particular species of zebra.)

The binomial is made up of the name of the organism's genus, followed by that of its species. The generic name is always given a capital letter, while that of the species has a small letter. Both are written in italics. When you are writing by hand, and cannot use italics, you should underline the binomial. To be really scientifically correct, a binomial should also include the name of the person who first named the organism, written in brackets. However, there is no need for you to do this, as it is of no use to anyone other than a professional taxonomist!

Genera (the plural of genus) are in turn grouped into **families**. Families are grouped into **orders**, orders into **classes**, classes into **phyla** (singular phylum) and phyla into **kingdoms**. Thus, a full classification of the common zebra is:

Kingdom	Animalia (non-photosynthetic, multicellular organisms)
Phylum	Chordata (animals with a stiffening rod along the back)
Class	Mammalia (chordates with hair and mammary glands)
Order	Perissodactyla (mammals with hooves made up of an odd number of toes)
Family	Equidae (horse-like perissodactyls)
Genus	*Equus* (horses, zebras and asses)
Species	*burchelli* (common zebra)

This classification reflects the evolutionary history of the zebra and its relationship with other organisms. A common zebra is extremely closely related to all other common zebras, and all common zebras are believed to share a common ancestor. The common zebra is closely related to all other organisms belonging to the genus *Equus* – they, too, almost certainly share a common ancestor, but this goes much further back than the ancestor giving rise to the species *Equus burchelli*. Going even further back, all of the organisms in the family Equidae probably had a common ancestor, and long before that so, perhaps, did all of the organisms in the order Perissodactyla.

The evolutionary history of living organisms is known as **phylogeny**, and the biological classification system attempts to classify organisms according to what we think this history may be. However, you have seen that we cannot even be sure about classifying organisms into species, so it is not surprising that the higher up the classification hierarchy we go – and the further back in time as regards when groups split apart from one another – then the less certain we become about the real relationships between these groups. Quite often, new evidence shows that we have got it wrong, and so the classification of particular species, genera or families is changed. As you will see, there are even problems and uncertainties with what you might expect to be a totally secure and correct classification – that of the five kingdoms.

The five kingdoms

Traditionally, all living organisms were divided into animals and plants. 'Plants' included anything that was not an animal – so not only green plants but also fungi and bacteria were included in this group. However, as microscopy allowed us to see more detail of cellular structure, and as investigations of physiology, biochemistry and molecular biology provided us with more detail of what organisms are made of and how they function, it became very clear that the 'plant' grouping contained several very distinct types of organisms.

In 1988, Margulis and Schwartz proposed that the living world should be divided into five

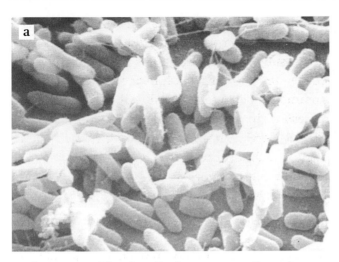

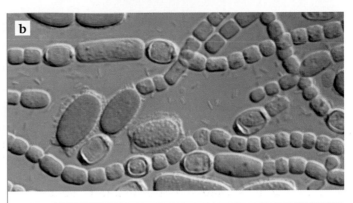

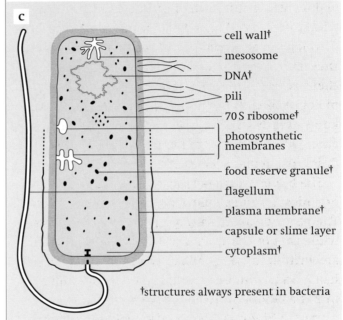

• **Figure 5.15** Kingdom Prokaryota. **a** Scanning electron micrograph (SEM) of the rod-shaped Gram-negative bacterium *Escherichia coli* (× 12 100); **b** light micrograph of the filamentous cyanobacterium *Cylindrospermum* sp. (× 1200), which is photosynthetic and can fix nitrogen; **c** generalised rod-shaped bacterial cell.

kingdoms. These are the **Prokaryotae**, **Protoctista**, **Fungi**, **Plantae** and **Animalia**.

Prokaryotes (*figure 5.15*) are organisms made up of prokaryotic cells, that is the bacteria. *Table 5.1* lists the main differences between the cells of prokaryotes and those of organisms in the other four kingdoms. Prokaryotic cells have no membrane-bound organelles. Their ribosomes are smaller than those found in eukaryotic cells (bacterial ribosomes are said to be 70 S and those of eukaryotes 80 S). Prokaryotes have a single loop of DNA, sometimes referred to as a bacterial chromosome, containing nucleic acid but no histones, and this is free in the cytoplasm rather than contained within a nucleus. They may be autotrophic or heterotrophic.

Prokaryotes	Eukaryotes
Average diameter of cell 0.5–5 μm	Cells commonly up to 40 μm diameter and commonly 1000–10 000 times the volume of prokaryotic cells
DNA is circular and lies free in the cytoplasm	DNA is not circular and is contained in a nucleus. The nucleus is surrounded by an envelope of two membranes
DNA is naked	DNA is associated with protein, forming structures called chromosomes
Slightly smaller ribosomes (about 18 nm diameter; 70 S)	Slightly larger ribosomes (about 22 nm diameter; 80 S)
No ER present	ER present, to which ribosomes may be attached
Very few cell organelles; none are surrounded by an envelope of two membranes	Many types of cell organelle present (extensive compartmentalisation and division of labour). Some organelles are bounded by a single membrane, e.g. lysosomes, Golgi apparatus, vacuoles; some are bounded by two membranes (an envelope), e.g. nucleus, mitochondrion; some have no membrane, e.g. ribosomes
Cell wall present	Cell wall sometimes present, e.g. in plants

• **Table 5.1** A comparison of prokaryotic and eukaryotic cells.

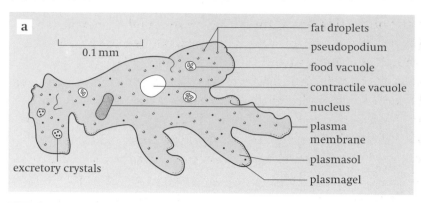

a

0.1 mm

fat droplets
pseudopodium
food vacuole
contractile vacuole
nucleus
plasma membrane
plasmasol
plasmagel
excretory crystals

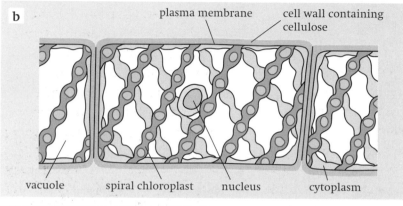

b

plasma membrane
cell wall containing cellulose
vacuole
spiral chloroplast
nucleus
cytoplasm

c

● **Figure 5.16** Kingdom Protoctista. **a** *Amoeba* is a heterotrophic unicellular protoctist. Different species live in freshwater or marine environments, and in the soil. Some are parasites. **b** *Spirogyra* is a multicellular, filamentous, photosynthetic protoctist that lives in freshwater ponds and slow-moving streams. **c** *Fucus vesiculosus* is a multicellular, thalloid, photosynthetic protoctist – a common seaweed found on rocky shores.

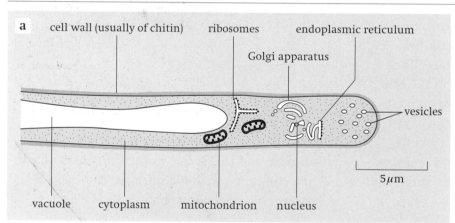

a

cell wall (usually of chitin)
ribosomes
endoplasmic reticulum
Golgi apparatus
vesicles
5 μm
vacuole
cytoplasm
mitochondrion
nucleus

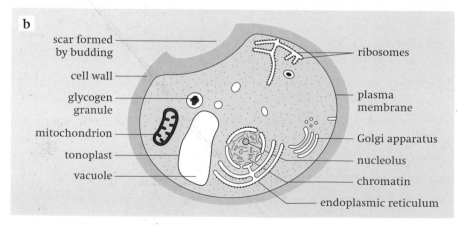

b

scar formed by budding
ribosomes
cell wall
glycogen granule
plasma membrane
mitochondrion
tonoplast
Golgi apparatus
nucleolus
vacuole
chromatin
endoplasmic reticulum

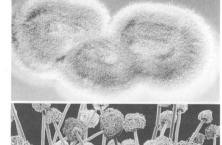

c

● **Figure 5.17** Kingdom Fungi. **a** Diagram of the tip of a typical fungal hypha (based on electron micrographs). **b** Section through *Saccharomyces* cell (based on electron micrographs × 10 000). **c** Some examples of fungi: *Saccharomyces cerevisiae*, *Boletus* sp., *Penicillium chrysogenum*, *Aspergillus niger*.

Protoctists (*figure 5.16*) are simple eukaryotic organisms. Many are unicellular, while others are filamentous (made up of chains of single cells joined end to end), colonial (for example made up of balls of cells) or thalloid (made up of sheets of cells, such as those found in seaweed fronds). They may be autotrophic or heterotrophic. Most protoctists are aquatic or live in moist conditions such as the soil.

Fungi (*figure 5.17*) are eukaryotic organisms that feed heterotrophically. They have cells with cell walls, but unlike those of plants their cell walls contain materials such as chitin, never cellulose. Fungi are saprotrophs or parasites. Some, such as yeasts, are unicellular. Others have bodies made of threads called hyphae, forming a mass called a mycelium.

Plants (*figure 5.18*) are multicellular eukaryotic organisms that feed by photosynthesis. They have cells with walls made of cellulose. Some cells contain chloroplasts, and many contain large sap-filled vacuoles. Mosses, liverworts and ferns belong in this kingdom, as well as conifers and flowering plants.

Animals (*figure 5.19*) are multicellular eukaryotic organisms that feed heterotrophically. Their cells do not have cell walls, and never contain chloroplasts or large, sap-filled vacuoles. Animals include relatively simple organisms such as jellyfish and flatworms, as well as more complex ones such as arthropods and mammals.

Although this five-kingdom system is now widely used, most biologists have serious reservations about it. In particular, all would agree that the wide variety of organisms currently classified in the kingdom Protoctista are not all related to each other; the protoctists are really put in that group because they do not fit in any other. Another difficulty with the system is that it is now widely recognised that the kingdom

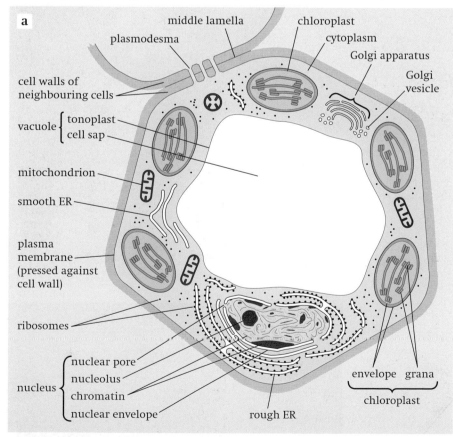

● **Figure 5.18** Kingdom Plantae.
a A plant cell.
b A moss, *Eurhychium crassinervium*.
c A fern, *Polystichum setiferum*.
d A flowering plant, *Ranunculus ficaria*.

Prokaryotae contains two distinct groups of organisms – the true bacteria and the 'ancient' bacteria – that are probably as different from one another as plants are from animals. It is likely that one day this kingdom will be divided into two.

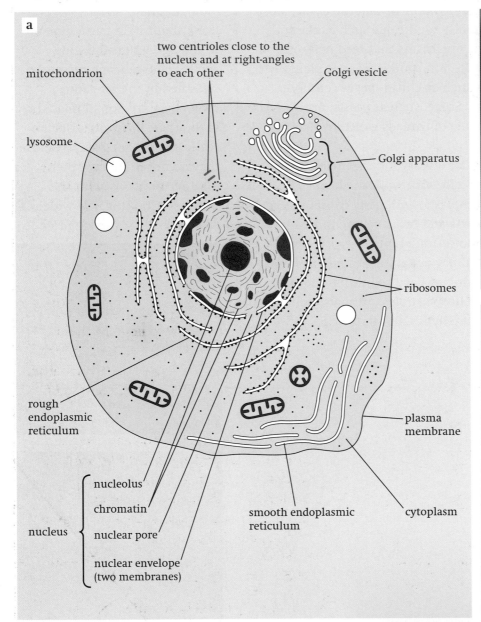

● **Figure 5.19** Kingdom Animalia.
a An animal cell.
b A cnidarian, the Pacific sea nettle jellyfish, *Chrysarora fuscescens*.
c A mammal, the orang-utan, *Pongo pygmaeus*.
d An arthropod, the common house spider *Tegenaria domestica*.

SUMMARY

◆ Meiosis, random mating and the random fusion of gametes produce variation amongst populations of sexually reproducing organisms. Variation is also caused by the interaction of the environment with genetic factors, but such environmentally induced variation is not passed on to an organism's offspring. The only source of new alleles is mutation.

◆ All species of organisms have the reproductive potential to increase the sizes of their populations, but, in the long term, this rarely happens. This is because environmental factors come into play to limit population growth. Such factors decrease the rate of reproduction, or increase the rate of mortality so that many individuals die before reaching reproductive age.

◆ Within a population, certain alleles may increase the chance that an individual will survive long enough to be able to reproduce successfully. These alleles are therefore more likely to be passed on to the next generation than others. This is known as natural selection. Normally, natural selection keeps allele frequencies as they are; this is stabilising selection. However, if environmental factors which exert selection pressures change, or if new alleles appear in a population, then natural selection may cause a change in the frequencies of alleles; this is directional selection.

◆ Over many generations, directional selection may produce large changes in allele frequencies. This is how evolution occurs.

◆ Artificial selection involves the choice by humans of which organisms to allow to breed together, in order to bring about a desirable change in characteristics. Thus artificial selection, like natural selection, can affect allele frequencies in a population.

◆ A species can be defined as a group of organisms with similar morphology, behaviour, physiology and biochemistry that are capable of interbreeding to produce fertile offspring. In practice, however, it is not always possible to determine whether or not organisms can interbreed.

◆ New species arise by a process called speciation. In allopatric speciation, two populations become isolated from one another, perhaps by some geographical feature, and then evolve along different lines until they become so different that they can no longer interbreed. In sympatric speciation, new species may arise through polyploidy.

◆ Biologists classify living organisms into groups according to what can be deduced about their phylogeny (evolutionary history). The taxonomic groups are arranged in a hierarchy: the smallest group containing the most closely-related organisms is species, then genus, family, order, class, phylum and kingdom.

◆ One widely used classification system includes five kingdoms: Prokaryotae, Protoctista, Fungi, Plantae and Animalia.

Questions

1 'Artificial selection of crop plants and farm animals has tended to reduce variety within their populations.' Discuss the validity of this statement, with reference to specific examples (you will need to research these), and consider the possible disadvantages of such a reduction in variation.

2 It is frequently found that individuals within populations of small mammals, such as mice or voles, which live on islands are larger than those living on the mainland; while those of large mammals, such as elephants and bears, tend to be smaller than those on the mainland. Suggest reasons for this.

3 The table shows the results of an experiment carried out to investigate the selection pressures acting on the dark and light forms of the moth *Biston betularia*. Dark and light moths were marked, and then released in two different areas. They were then recaptured by attracting them to a light at night.

   a What percentage of dark moths were recaptured in (i) the unpolluted area and (ii) the polluted area?

Area		Dark form	Light form
unpolluted	released	473	496
	recaptured	30	62
polluted	released	601	201
	recaptured	205	32

   b What percentage of light moths were recaptured in (i) the unpolluted area and (ii) the polluted area?
   c The main selection pressure on these two forms of the moth is thought to be predation by birds. Suggest a way in which you could investigate whether this is true.

   d From these results, in which of the two areas does the selection pressure appear to be greater? Suggest what this might mean in terms of the rate of change of allele frequencies in polluted and unpolluted areas.
   e There is some evidence that other selection pressures act on *Biston betularia*. Outline an experiment you could carry out to test the hypothesis that caterpillars that will develop into dark moths are more resistant to pollutants on the leaves that they eat than caterpillars that will develop into light moths.

4 Construct a table summarising the important features of the five kingdoms. Your headings could include: type of cells, presence or absence of cell wall, cell wall material (if present), uni- or multicellular and method of feeding.

To answer the following questions, you will need to bring together information from other areas of your course, as well as from this chapter.

5 a With reference to the structure of haemoglobin, explain the importance of R groups in determining the structure and function of a protein.
   b Discuss the reasons for the continued existence of the sickle cell allele of the gene that codes for the β polypeptide in haemoglobin, despite the fact that this allele produces haemoglobin that is inefficient at carrying oxygen.

6 a Explain how the structure of cellulose molecules is related to their functions in the cell walls of organisms belonging to the plant kingdom.
   b Name the other kingdoms in which organisms also possess cell walls, and describe the properties that you would expect to find in the molecules from which these walls are constructed.

Control, coordination and homeostasis

Most animals and plants are complex organisms, made up of many millions of cells. Different parts of the organism perform different functions. It is essential that information can pass between these different parts, so that their activities are coordinated. Sometimes, the purpose of this information transfer is to regulate the levels of some substance within the organism, such as the control of blood sugar levels in mammals. Sometimes, the purpose may be to change the activity of some part of the organism in response to some external stimulus, such as moving away from an unpleasant stimulus.

In both animals and plants, chemical messengers called **hormones** (in plants they are sometimes known as **plant growth regulators**) help to transfer information from one part to another and so achieve coordination. In many animals, including mammals, **nerves** transfer information in the form of electrical impulses. We will look at both of these methods of information transfer in this chapter.

First, however, we will look at the need for mammals to maintain a stable environment, and consider how **excretion** (especially by the kidneys) helps to achieve this.

Homeostasis

A vital function of control systems in mammals is to maintain a stable internal environment. This is called **homeostasis**. 'Internal environment' means the conditions inside the body, in which cells function. For a cell, its immediate environment is the tissue fluid that surrounds it. Many features of the environment affect the functioning of the cell. Three such features are:

■ **temperature** – low temperatures slow metabolic reactions, while high temperatures cause denaturation of proteins, including enzymes;

■ **amount of water** – lack of water in the tissue fluid causes water to be drawn out of cells by osmosis, causing metabolic reactions in the cell to slow or stop, while too much water entering the cell may cause it to swell and burst;

■ **amount of glucose** – glucose is the fuel for respiration, so lack of it causes respiration to slow or stop, depriving the cell of an energy source, while too much glucose may draw water out of the cell by osmosis.

In general, homeostatic mechanisms work by controlling the composition of blood, which therefore controls the composition of tissue fluid.

Most control mechanisms in living organisms use a **negative feedback** control loop (*figure 6.1*). This involves a **receptor** (or **sensor**) and an **effector**. The receptor picks up information about the parameter being regulated. This is known as the **input**. This sets off a series of events culminating in some action, by the effector, which is called the **output**. Continuous monitoring of the parameter by the receptor produces continuous adjustments of the output, which keep the parameter oscillating around a particular 'ideal' level, or set point. In negative feedback such as this, a rise in the parameter results in something happening that makes the parameter fall.

There are a few instances of the opposite thing happening in living organisms. For example, if a person breathes air that has a very high carbon dioxide content, this produces a high concentration of carbon dioxide in the blood. This is sensed by carbon dioxide receptors, which cause the breathing rate to increase. So the person breathes faster, taking in even more carbon dioxide, which stimulates the receptors even more, so they breathe faster and faster... This is an example of **positive feedback**. You can see that it cannot play any role in keeping things constant!

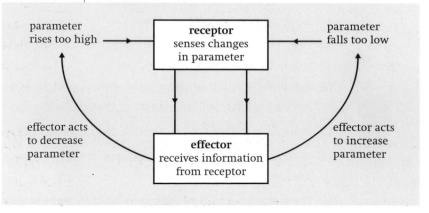

● **Figure 6.1** A negative feedback control loop.

Excretion

Many of the metabolic reactions occurring within the body produce unwanted substances. Some of these are toxic (poisonous). The removal of these unwanted products of metabolism is known as **excretion**.

Many excretory products are formed in humans, but two are made in much greater amounts than the others. These are **carbon dioxide** and **urea**. Carbon dioxide is produced virtually continuously by almost every cell in the body, by the reactions of aerobic respiration. The waste carbon dioxide is transported from the respiring cells to the lungs, in the bloodstream (*Biology 1*, page 115). It diffuses from the blood into the alveoli of the lungs, and is excreted in the air we breathe out (*Biology 1*, page 61 and chapter 13).

In contrast, urea is produced in only one organ in the body, that is the **liver**. It is produced from excess amino acids (as described in the next section) and is transported from the liver to the kidneys, in solution in blood plasma. The kidneys remove urea from the blood and excrete it, dissolved in water, as **urine**. Here, we will look more fully at the production and excretion of urea.

Deamination

If more protein is eaten than is needed, the excess cannot be stored in the body. It would be wasteful, however, simply to get rid of all the excess, because the amino acids contain useful energy. The liver salvages this energy by removing the nitrogen atoms from the amino acids, excreting these in the form of urea, and keeping the rest of each amino acid molecule. The process by which urea is made from excess amino acids is called **deamination**.

Figure 6.2 shows how deamination takes place. In the liver cells, the amino (NH_2) group of an amino acid is removed, together with an extra hydrogen atom. These combine to produce ammonia. The keto acid that remains may become a carbohydrate, which can be used in respiration, or may be converted to fat and stored.

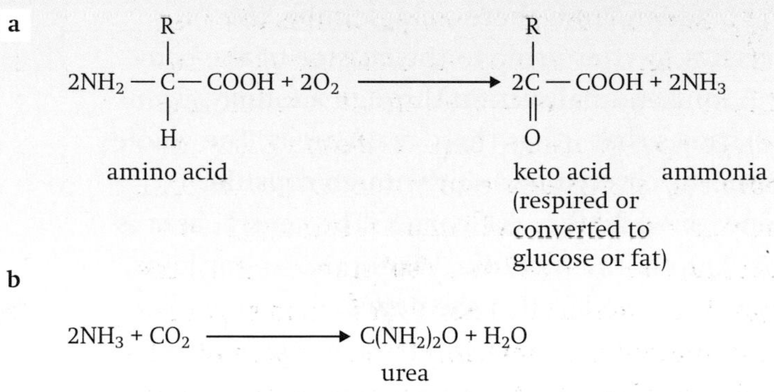

Ammonia is a very soluble and highly toxic compound. In aquatic animals, such as fish, this poses

$$\text{a} \qquad 2NH_2 - \underset{\underset{H}{|}}{\overset{\overset{R}{|}}{C}} - COOH + 2O_2 \longrightarrow 2\underset{\underset{O}{\|}}{\overset{\overset{R}{|}}{C}} - COOH + 2NH_3$$

amino acid   keto acid   ammonia
(respired or converted to glucose or fat)

$$\text{b} \qquad 2NH_3 + CO_2 \longrightarrow C(NH_2)_2O + H_2O$$

urea

● **Figure 6.2 a** Deamination and **b** urea formation.

no danger as the ammonia can simply dissolve into the water around them. However, in terrestrial animals, such as humans, ammonia would rapidly build up in the blood and cause immense damage. So the ammonia produced in the liver is instantly converted to the less soluble and less toxic compound, **urea**. Urea is made by combining ammonia with carbon dioxide (*figure 6.2b*). An adult produces around 25–30 g of urea per day.

Urea is the main **nitrogenous excretory product** of humans. We also produce small quantities of other nitrogenous excretory products, mainly **creatinine** and **uric acid**. Creatine is made in the liver, from certain amino acids. Much of this creatine is used in the muscles, in the form of creatine phosphate, where it acts as an energy store (see page 5 in chapter 1). However, some is converted to creatinine and excreted. Uric acid is made from the breakdown of nucleic acids, not from amino acids.

The urea made in the liver passes from the liver cells into the blood plasma. All of the urea made each day must be excreted, or its concentration in the blood would build up and become dangerous. As the blood passes through the kidneys, the urea is extracted and excreted. To explain how this happens, we must first look at the structure of a kidney.

The structure of the kidney

Figure 6.3 shows the position of the kidneys in the body together with their associated structures. Each kidney receives blood from a **renal artery**, and returns blood via a **renal vein**. A narrow tube, called the **ureter**, carries urine from the kidney to the bladder. From there a single tube, the **urethra**, carries urine to the outside of the body.

A longitudinal section through a kidney (*figure 6.4*) shows that it has three main areas. The whole kidney is covered by a fairly tough **capsule**, beneath which lies the **cortex**. The central area is made up of the **medulla**. Where the ureter joins, there is an area called the **pelvis**.

A section through a kidney seen through a microscope (*figure 6.6*), shows it to be made up of thousands of tiny tubes that are called **nephrons**. *Figure 6.5* shows the position and structure of a single nephron. One end of the tube forms a cup-shaped structure called a **renal (Bowman's) capsule**. The renal capsules of all nephrons are in the cortex of the kidney. From the renal capsule, the tube runs towards the centre of the kidney, first forming a twisted region called the **proximal convoluted tubule**, and then a long hairpin loop in the medulla, the **loop of Henle**. The tubule then runs back upwards into the cortex, where it forms another twisted region called the **distal convoluted tubule**, before finally joining a **collecting duct** which leads down through the medulla and into the pelvis of the kidney. Here the collecting ducts join the ureter.

Blood vessels are closely associated with the nephrons (*figure 6.5c*). Each renal capsule is supplied with blood by a branch of the renal

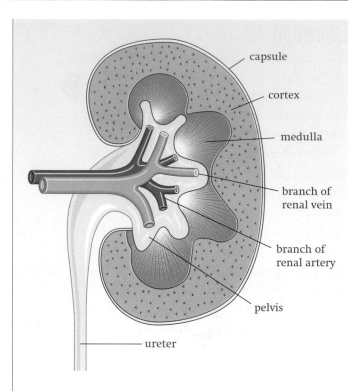

● **Figure 6.4** A kidney, cut in half vertically (LS).

artery, called an **afferent arteriole**, which splits into a tangle of capillaries in the 'cup' of the capsule, called a **glomerulus**. The capillaries of the glomerulus rejoin to form an **efferent arteriole**. This leads off to form a network of capillaries running closely alongside the rest of the nephron, before linking up with other capillaries to feed into a branch of the renal vein.

Ultrafiltration

The kidney makes urine in a two-stage process. The first stage, **ultrafiltration**, involves filtering small molecules, including urea, out of the blood and into the renal capsule. From here they flow along the nephron towards the ureter. The second stage, **reabsorption**, involves taking back any useful molecules from the fluid in the nephron as it flows along.

Figure 6.7 shows a section through part of a glomerulus and renal capsule. The blood in the glomerular capillaries is separated from the lumen of the renal capsule by two cell layers and a basement membrane. The first cell layer is the lining, or **endothelium**, of the capillary. Like the endothelium of most capillaries, this has gaps in it, but there are far more gaps than in other capillaries:

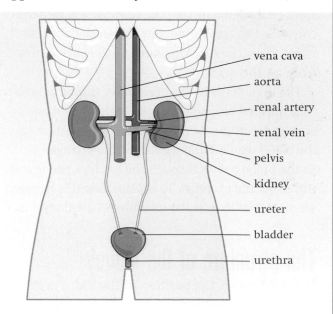

● **Figure 6.3** Position of the kidneys and associated structures in the human body.

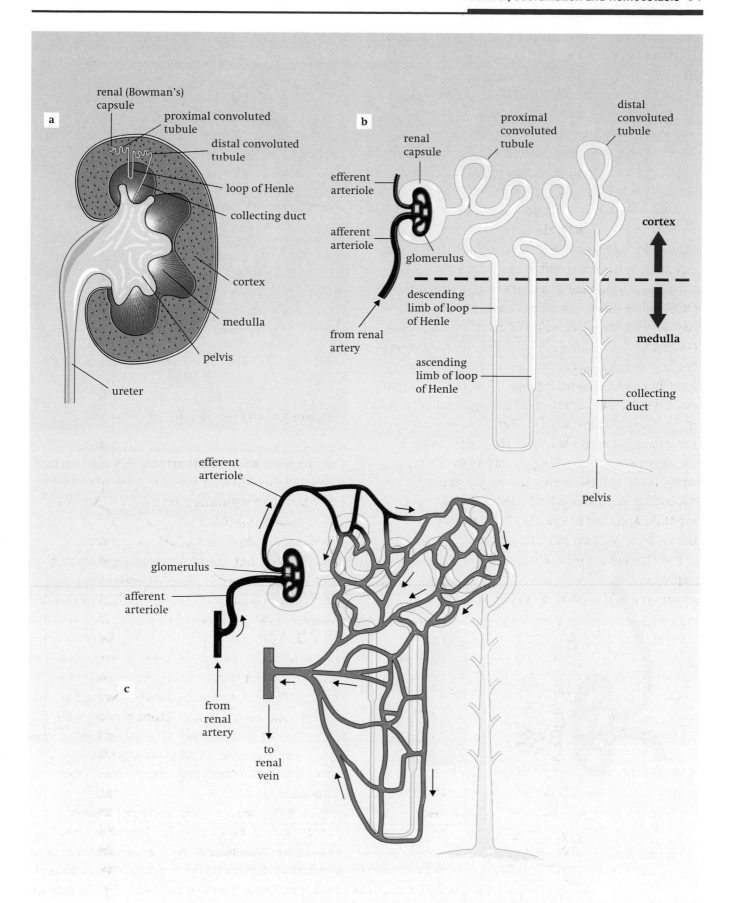

● **Figure 6.5 a** Section through the kidney to show the position of a nephron. **b** A nephron. **c** The blood supply associated with a nephron.

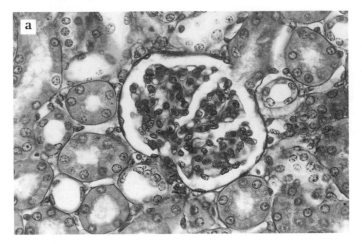

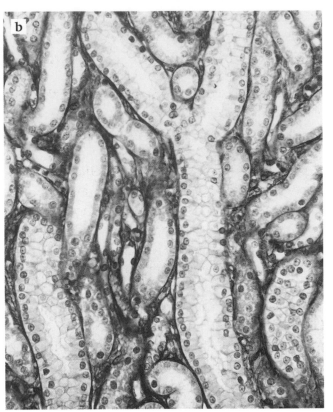

● **Figure 6.6**

a Light micrograph of a section through the cortex of a kidney. The white circular area in the centre is the lumen of a renal capsule. The darkly stained area in the centre of the capsule contains the blood capillaries of the glomerulus. There are also several proximal convoluted tubules and distal convoluted tubules in transverse section.

b Light micrograph of a longitudinal section through the medulla of a kidney. This section cuts through several loops of Henle (relatively narrow) and collecting ducts (relatively wide, with almost cubical cells making up their walls).

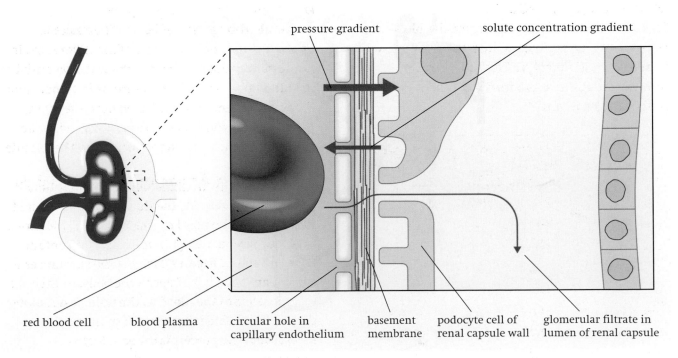

● **Figure 6.7** Detail of the wall of a glomerular capillary and renal capsule. The arrows show how the net effect of higher pressure in the capillary and lower solute concentration in the renal capsule is that fluid moves out of the capillary and into the lumen of the capsule. The basement membrane acts as a molecular filter.

each endothelial cell has thousands of tiny holes in it. Next comes the **basement membrane** which is made up of a network of collagen and glycoproteins. The second cell layer is formed from **epithelial cells** which make up the wall of the renal capsule. These cells have many tiny finger-like projections, with gaps in between them and are called **podocytes**.

The holes in the capillary endothelium, and the gaps in the renal capsule epithelium, are quite large, and make it easy for any substances dissolved in the blood plasma to get through from the blood into the capsule. However, the basement membrane stops large protein molecules from getting through. Any protein molecule with a relative molecular mass of around 69 000 or more cannot pass through the basement membrane, and so cannot escape from the glomerular capillaries. This basement membrane therefore acts as a filter. Blood cells, both red and white, are also too large to pass through this barrier, and so remain in the blood. *Table 6.1* shows the relative concentrations of substances in the blood and in the glomerular filtrate. You will see that glomerular filtrate is identical to blood plasma minus plasma proteins.

Factors affecting glomerular filtration rate

The rate at which fluid seeps from the blood in the glomerular capillaries, into the renal capsule, is called the **glomerular filtration rate**. In a human, for all the glomeruli in both kidneys, this is about $125 \, cm^3 \, min^{-1}$.

Substance	Concentration in blood plasma (g dm^{-3})	Concentration in glomerular filtrate (g dm^{-3})
water	900	900
proteins	80.0	0.05
amino acids	0.5	0.5
glucose	1.0	1.0
urea	0.3	0.3
uric acid	0.04	0.04
creatinine	0.01	0.01
inorganic ions (mainly Na$^+$, K$^+$ and Cl$^-$)	7.2	7.2

● **Table 6.1** Relative concentrations of substances in the blood and in the glomerular filtrate.

What makes the fluid filter through so quickly? This is determined by the differences in **water potential** between the contents of the glomerular capillaries and the renal capsule. You will remember from *Biology 1* (page 56) that water moves from a region of high water potential to a region of low water potential, down a water potential gradient. Water potential is lowered by the presence of solutes, and raised by high pressures.

Inside the capillaries in the glomerulus, the blood pressure is relatively high, because the diameter of the afferent arteriole is wider than that of the efferent arteriole, causing a 'traffic jam' inside the glomerulus. This therefore tends to raise the water potential of the blood plasma above the water potential of the contents of the renal capsule (*figure 6.7* again).

However, the concentration of solutes in the blood plasma in the capillaries is *higher* than the concentration of solutes inside the renal capsule. This is because, while most of the contents of the blood plasma filter through the basement membrane and into the renal capsule, the plasma protein molecules are too big to get through, and so stay in the blood. This difference in solute concentration tends to make the water potential in the blood capillaries *lower* than that in the renal capsule.

Overall, though, the effect of differences in pressure outweighs the effect of the differences in solute concentration. Overall, the water potential of the blood plasma in the glomerulus is higher than the water potential of the liquid in the renal capsule. So water continues to move down this water potential gradient, from the blood into the capsule.

Reabsorption in the proximal convoluted tubule

As you saw in *table 6.1*, the fluid which has filtered through into the renal capsule is virtually identical to blood plasma, except that it does not contain large protein molecules. Many of the substances in the filtrate need to be kept in the body, so they are reabsorbed into the blood as the fluid passes along the nephron. Since only certain substances are reabsorbed, the process is called **selective reabsorption**. Most of the reabsorption takes place in the proximal convoluted tubule.

The basal membranes (the ones nearest the blood and furthest from the lumen) of the cells lining the proximal convoluted tubule actively transport sodium ions out of the cell (*figure 6.8*). The sodium ions are carried away in the blood. This lowers the concentration of sodium ions inside the cell, so that they passively diffuse into it, down their concentration gradient, from the fluid in the lumen of the tubule. However, they do not just diffuse freely through the membrane; they can only enter through special transporter (carrier) proteins in the membrane. There are several different kinds of these, each of which transports something else, such as glucose, at the same time as the sodium. The concentration gradient for the sodium provides enough energy to pull in glucose molecules. Thus glucose is taken up by the cell, and into the blood.

All of the **glucose** in the glomerular filtrate is transported out of the proximal convoluted tubule and into the blood. Normally, no glucose is left in the tubule, so no glucose is present in urine. Similarly, **amino acids**, **vitamins**, and many **sodium** and **chloride ions** are actively reabsorbed here.

The uptake of these substances would decrease the solute concentration of the filtrate. However, **water** can (and does) move freely out of the filtrate, through the walls of the tubule and into the blood. As the substances listed above move into the cells surrounding the tubule, water follows by osmosis. Thus the overall concentration of the filtrate remains about the same. About 65% of the water in the filtrate is reabsorbed here.

SAQ 6.1

Look back at *figure 6.6*.
a Where has the blood in the capillaries surrounding the proximal convoluted tubule come from?
b What solutes will this blood contain that are *not* present in the glomerular filtrate?
c How might this help in the reabsorption of water from the proximal convoluted tubule?

Surprisingly, quite a lot of urea is reabsorbed too. Urea is a small molecule, which passes easily through cell membranes. Its concentration in the glomerular filtrate is considerably higher than that in the capillaries, so it diffuses passively through the wall of the proximal convoluted tubule and into the blood. About half of the urea in the filtrate is reabsorbed in this way.

The other two nitrogenous excretory products, uric acid and creatinine, are not reabsorbed. Indeed, creatinine is actively **secreted** by the cells of the proximal convoluted tubule into its lumen.

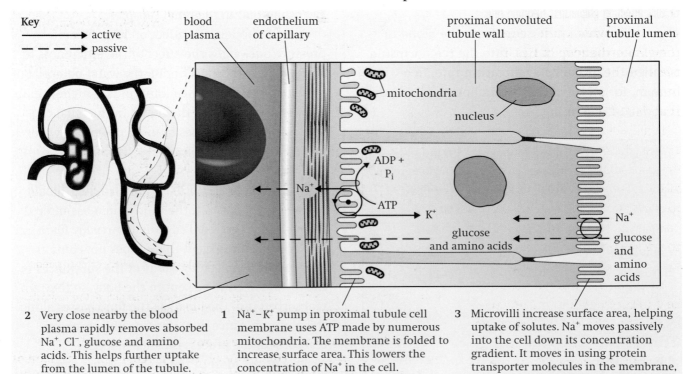

Key
→ active
--→ passive

blood plasma · endothelium of capillary · proximal convoluted tubule wall · proximal tubule lumen

mitochondria

nucleus

ADP + P$_i$

Na$^+$

ATP

K$^+$

glucose and amino acids

Na$^+$

glucose and amino acids

2 Very close nearby the blood plasma rapidly removes absorbed Na$^+$, Cl$^-$, glucose and amino acids. This helps further uptake from the lumen of the tubule.

1 Na$^+$–K$^+$ pump in proximal tubule cell membrane uses ATP made by numerous mitochondria. The membrane is folded to increase surface area. This lowers the concentration of Na$^+$ in the cell.

3 Microvilli increase surface area, helping uptake of solutes. Na$^+$ moves passively into the cell down its concentration gradient. It moves in using protein transporter molecules in the membrane, which bring in glucose and amino acids at the same time.

● **Figure 6.8** Reabsorption in the proximal convoluted tubule.

The reabsorption of so much water and solutes from the filtrate in the proximal convoluted tubule greatly reduces the volume of liquid remaining. In an adult human, around 125 cm³ of fluid enter the proximal tubules every minute, but only 45 cm³ per minute are passed on to the next region, the loop of Henle.

SAQ 6.2

Although almost half of the urea in the glomerular filtrate is reabsorbed from the proximal convoluted tubule, the *concentration* of urea in the fluid in the nephron actually increases as it passes through the proximal convoluted tubule. Explain why this is so.

Reabsorption in the loop of Henle and collecting duct

The function of the loop of Henle is to create a very high concentration of salts in the tissue fluid in the medulla of the kidney. As you will see, this allows a lot of water to be reabsorbed from the fluid in the collecting duct, as it flows through the medulla. As a result, very concentrated urine can be produced. The loop of Henle therefore allows water to be conserved in the body, rather than lost in urine.

Figure 6.9a shows the loop of Henle. The hairpin loop runs deep down into the medulla of the kidney, before turning back towards the cortex again. The first part of the loop is therefore called the **descending limb**, and the *second* part the **ascending limb**.

To explain how it works, it is best to begin by looking at what happens in the *second* part of the loop, the ascending limb. The walls of the upper parts of the ascending limb are *impermeable* to water. The cells in the walls of this area actively transport

sodium and chloride ions out of the fluid in the tube, into the tissue fluid between the cells filling the space between the two limbs. This produces a high concentration of sodium and chloride ions around the descending limb. This concentration can be as much as four times greater than the normal concentration of tissue fluid.

The walls of the descending limb are *permeable* to water, and also to sodium and chloride ions. As the fluid flows down this tube, water from it is drawn *out*, by osmosis, into the tissue fluid, because of the high concentration of sodium and chloride ions there. At the same time, sodium and

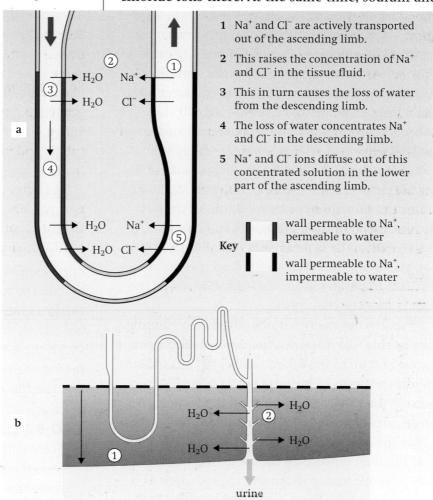

1 Na⁺ and Cl⁻ are actively transported out of the ascending limb.

2 This raises the concentration of Na⁺ and Cl⁻ in the tissue fluid.

3 This in turn causes the loss of water from the descending limb.

4 The loss of water concentrates Na⁺ and Cl⁻ in the descending limb.

5 Na⁺ and Cl⁻ ions diffuse out of this concentrated solution in the lower part of the ascending limb.

Key: wall permeable to Na⁺, permeable to water

wall permeable to Na⁺, impermeable to water

1 The tissue in the deeper layers of the medulla contains a very concentrated solution of Na⁺, Cl⁻ and urea.

2 As urine passes down the collecting duct, water can pass out of it by osmosis. The reabsorbed water is carried away by the blood in the capillaries.

● **Figure 6.9** How the loop of Henle allows the production of concentrated urine.   **a** The counter-current mechanism in the loop of Henle builds up a high sodium ion and chloride ion concentration in the tissue fluid of the medulla.   **b** Water can be drawn out of the collecting duct by the high salt concentration in the surrounding tissue fluid.

chloride ions diffuse *into* the tube, down their concentration gradient. So, by the time the fluid has reached the very bottom of the hairpin, it contains much less water and many more sodium and chloride ions than it did at the top. The fluid becomes more concentrated towards the bottom of the loop. The longer the loop, the more concentrated it can become.

This concentrated fluid now turns the corner and begins to flow up the ascending limb. Because the fluid inside the loop is so concentrated, it is relatively easy for sodium and chloride ions to leave it and pass into the tissue fluid, even though the concentration in the tissue fluid is also very great. Thus, especially high concentrations of sodium and chloride can be built up in the tissue cells between the two limbs near the bottom of the loop. As the fluid continues up the ascending limb, losing sodium and chloride ions all the time, it becomes gradually less concentrated. However, it is still relatively easy for sodium and chloride to be actively removed, because these higher parts of the ascending loop are next to less concentrated regions of tissue fluid. All the way up, the concentration of sodium and chloride inside the tubule is never very different from the concentration in the tissue fluid, so it is never too difficult to pump sodium and chloride out of the tubule into the tissue fluid.

Thus, having the two limbs of the loop running side by side like this, with the fluid flowing down in one and up in the other, enables the maximum concentration to be built up both inside and outside the tube at the bottom of the loop. This mechanism is called a **counter-current multiplier**.

But the story is not yet complete! You have seen that the fluid flowing up the ascending limb of the loop of Henle loses sodium and chloride ions as it goes, so becoming more dilute and having a high water potential. However, in *figure 6.9b* you can see that the fluid continues round through the distal convoluted tubule into the **collecting duct**, which runs down into the medulla again. It therefore passes once again through the regions where the solute concentration of the tissue fluid is very high, with a very low water potential. Water therefore moves out of the collecting duct, by osmosis, until the water potential of urine is the same as the

water potential of the tissue fluid in the medulla, which may be much greater than the water potential of the blood. The degree to which this happens is controlled by **antidiuretic hormone, ADH**, and is explained later in this chapter.

The longer the loop of Henle, the greater the concentration that can be built up in the medulla, and the greater the concentration of the urine which can be produced. Desert animals such as kangaroo rats, which need to conserve as much water as they possibly can, have especially long loops of Henle. Humans, however, only have long loops of Henle in about one third of their nephrons, the other two thirds hardly dipping into the medulla at all.

Reabsorption in the distal convoluted tubule and collecting duct

The first part of the distal convoluted tubule behaves in the same way as the ascending limb of the loop of Henle. The second part behaves in the same way as the collecting duct, so the functions of this part of the distal convoluted tubule and the collecting duct will be described together.

In the distal convoluted tubule and collecting duct, **sodium ions** are actively pumped from the fluid in the tubule into the tissue fluid, from where they pass into the blood. **Potassium ions**, however, are actively transported *into* the tubule. The rate at which these two ions are moved into and out of the fluid in the nephron can be varied, and helps to regulate the amount of these ions in the blood.

SAQ 6.3

a *Figure 6.10* shows the relative rate at which fluid flows through each part of a nephron. If water flows into an impermeable tube, such as a hosepipe, it will flow *out* of the far end at the same rate that it flows *in*. However, this clearly does not happen in a nephron. Consider what happens in each region, and suggest an explanation for the shape of the graph.

b *Figure 6.11* shows the relative concentrations of four substances in each part of a nephron. Explain the shapes of the curves for (i) glucose, (ii) urea, (iii) sodium ions, and (iv) potassium ions.

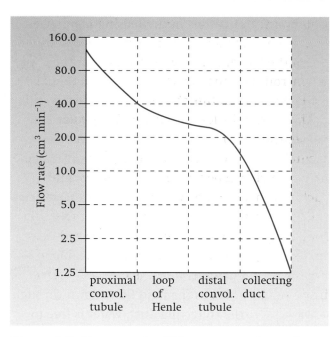

Figure 6.10 Flow rates in different parts of a nephron.

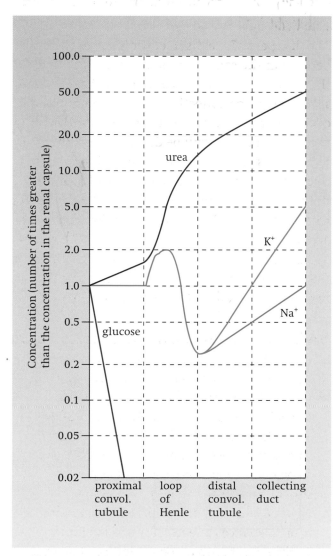

● **Figure 6.11** Relative concentrations of four substances in different parts of a nephron.

Control of water content

Osmoreceptors, the hypothalamus and ADH

At the beginning of this chapter, we saw that mammals maintain a relatively stable environment in which their cells can function – a process known as **homeostasis**. The kidneys play an important role in homeostasis by regulating the concentration of water in the body fluids. This is known as **osmoregulation**.

If you look back to *figure 6.1*, you will remember that control mechanisms that keep something relatively constant usually work by a **negative feedback mechanism**. There needs to be a **receptor** that monitors whatever it is that is being controlled, and an **effector** that does something to bring it back to normal if it deviates too far. In the osmoregulation mechanism in mammals, the receptor is cells in the **hypothalamus**, and the effectors are the **pituitary gland** and the walls of the distal convoluted tubules.

The amount of water in the blood is constantly monitored by cells, called **osmoreceptors**, within the hypothalamus (*figure 6.12*). It is not known exactly how these work, but it is probable that differences in water content of the blood cause water to move either into them or out of them by osmosis. When water content of the blood is low, the loss of water from the osmoreceptor cells reduces their volume, which triggers stimulation of nerve cells in the hypothalamus.

These nerve cells are rather different from other nerve cells that will be described later in this chapter, because they produce a chemical called **antidiuretic hormone**, or **ADH**. ADH is a polypeptide made up of just nine amino acids. It is made in the cell bodies of the nerve cells, and passes along them to their endings in the posterior lobe of the pituitary gland. When the nerve cells are stimulated by the osmoreceptor cells, electrical impulses called **action potentials** travel down them (page 110). This causes ADH to be released from their endings into the blood in capillaries in the posterior pituitary gland. From here, it is then carried all over the body.

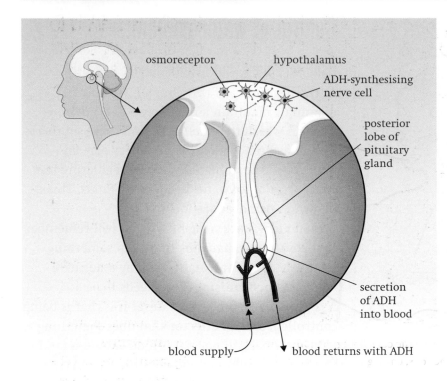

● **Figure 6.12** The secretion of ADH.

How ADH affects the kidneys

ADH acts on the plasma membranes of the cells making up the walls of the collecting ducts in the kidneys. It makes these membranes more permeable to water than usual (*figure 6.13*).

This change in permeability is brought about by increasing the number of water-permeable channels in the plasma membrane (*figure 6.14*). The ADH molecule is picked up by a receptor on the plasma membrane, which then activates an enzyme inside the cell. Inside the cell are ready-made vesicles surrounded by pieces of membrane full of water-permeable channels. The activation of the enzyme by ADH causes these vesicles to move to, and fuse with, the plasma membrane of the cell, so adding many water-permeable channels to it.

So, as the fluid flows down through the collecting duct, water is free to move out of the tubule and into the tissue fluid, and it does so because this region of the kidney contains a high concentration of salts. Thus, the fluid in the collecting duct loses water and becomes more concentrated. The secretion of ADH has caused the increased reabsorption of water into the blood. The amount of urine which flows from the kidneys into the bladder will be smaller, and the urine will be more concentrated (*figure 6.15*).

The word 'diuresis' means the production of dilute urine. Antidiuretic hormone gets its name because it stops dilute urine being produced.

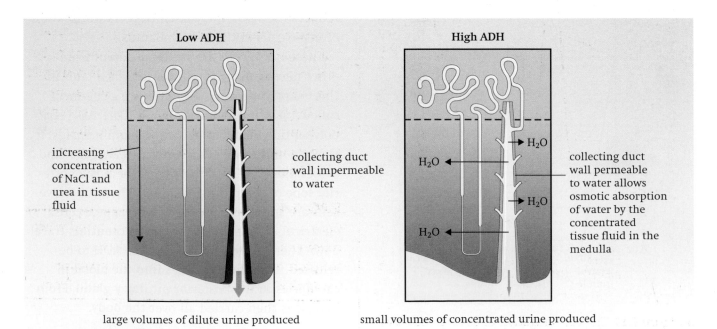

● **Figure 6.13** The effects of ADH on water reabsorption from the collecting duct.

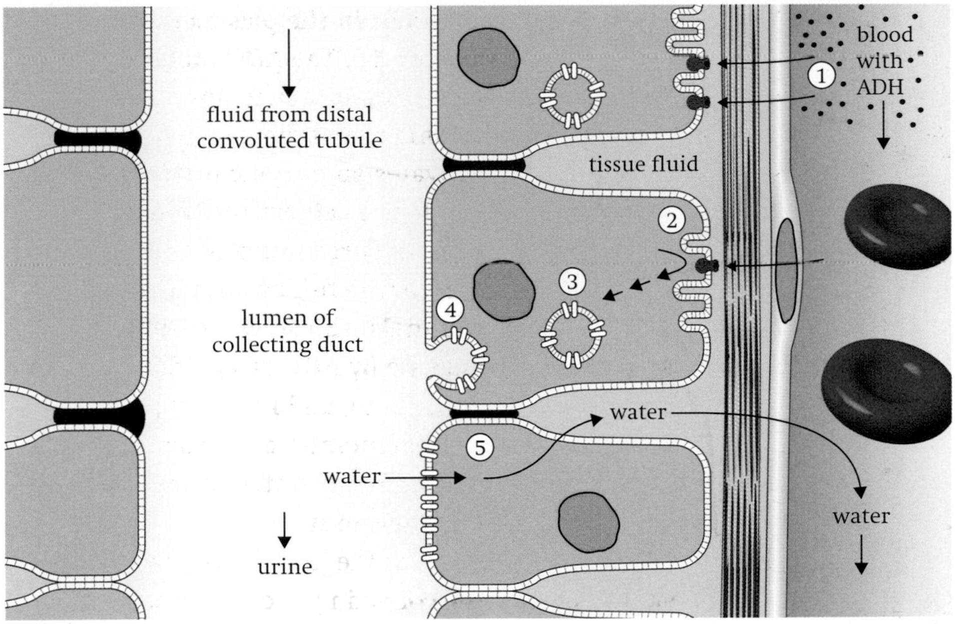

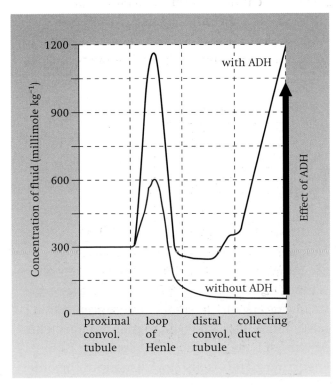

1 ADH binds to receptors in the plasma membrane of the cells lining the collecting duct.
2 This activates a series of enzyme-controlled reactions, ending with the production of an active phosphorylase enzyme.
3 The phosphorylase causes vesicles, surrounded by membrane containing water-permeable channels, to move to the plasma membrane.
4 The vesicles fuse with the plasma membrane.
5 Water can now move freely through the membrane, down its water potential gradient, into the concentrated tissue fluid and blood plasma in the medulla of the kidney.

● **Figure 6.14** How ADH increases water reabsorption in the collecting duct.

● **Figure 6.15** The concentration of fluid in different regions of a nephron, with and without the presence of ADH.

Negative feedback in the control of water content

You have seen how the secretion of ADH, brought about as a result of a low blood water content, causes more water to be absorbed back into the blood from the nephrons in the kidney. Thus the maximum amount of water will be retained in the body.

When the blood water content rises, the osmoreceptors are no longer stimulated, and stop stimulating their neighbouring nerve cells. So ADH secretion slows down. This affects the cells in the walls of the collecting ducts. The water-permeable channels are moved out of the plasma membrane of the collecting duct cells, back into the cytoplasm. Thus, the collecting duct becomes less permeable to water. The liquid flowing down it retains more of its water, flowing into the ureter as a copious, dilute urine.

The collecting duct cells do not respond immediately to the reduction in ADH secretion by the posterior pituitary gland. This is because it takes some time for the ADH already in the blood to be broken down; approximately half of it is destroyed every 15–20 minutes. However, once ADH stops arriving at the collecting duct cells, it takes only 10–15 minutes for the water-permeable channels to be removed from the plasma membrane and taken back into the cytoplasm for storage.

SAQ 6.4
Construct a flow diagram to show how blood water concentration is controlled. Identify clearly the receptors and effectors, and show how negative feedback is involved.

Hormonal communication

Exocrine and endocrine glands

The chemicals, such as ADH, which are used to carry information from one part of a mammal's body to another part are called **hormones**. They are made in **endocrine glands** (*figure 6.16*).

A **gland** is a group of cells which produces and releases one or more sub-stances, a process known as **secretion**. Endocrine glands contain secretory cells which pass their secretions directly into the blood. 'Endocrine' means 'secret-ing to the inside', a reference to the fact that endocrine glands secrete hormones into blood capillaries inside the gland.

Endocrine glands are not the only type of gland. We have many glands in our digestive system, for example, such as the salivary glands which secrete saliva. These glands are **exocrine glands** (*figure 6.16*). 'Exocrine' means 'secreting to the out-side'. The secretory cells of exocrine glands secrete their substances, which are *not* hormones, into a tube or duct, along which the secretion flows. Salivary glands secrete saliva into salivary ducts, which carry the saliva into the mouth.

Hormones

Mammalian hormones have many features in common. They are usually relatively small molecules. Many hormones, such as insulin, are polypeptides or proteins whereas others, such as testosterone, are steroids.

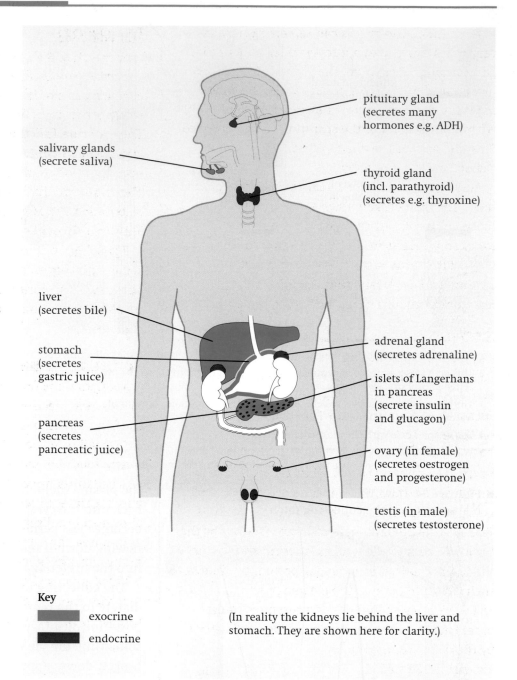

pituitary gland
(secretes many
hormones e.g. ADH)

salivary glands
(secrete saliva)

thyroid gland
(incl. parathyroid)
(secretes e.g. thyroxine)

liver
(secretes bile)

stomach
(secretes
gastric juice)

adrenal gland
(secretes adrenaline)

islets of Langerhans
in pancreas
(secrete insulin
and glucagon)

pancreas
(secretes
pancreatic juice)

ovary (in female)
(secretes oestrogen
and progesterone)

testis (in male)
(secretes testosterone)

Key

exocrine

endocrine

(In reality the kidneys lie behind the liver and stomach. They are shown here for clarity.)

● **Figure 6.16** The positions of some exocrine and endocrine glands in the human body.

After they have been secreted from an endocrine gland, hormones are transported around the body in the blood plasma. The concen-trations of hormones in human blood are very small. For any one hormone, the concentration is rarely more than a few micrograms of hormone per cm^3 of blood. Their rate of secretion from endocrine glands is also low, usually of the order of a few micrograms or milligrams a day. These small quantities of hormone can, however, have very large effects on the body.

Most endocrine glands can secrete hormones very quickly when an appropriate stimulus arrives. For example, adrenaline, the 'fight or flight' hormone secreted in response to a frightening stimulus, is secreted from the adrenal glands within one second of the stimulus being perceived. This means that the effects of hormones can be 'turned on' quite quickly.

Many hormones have a very short life in the body. They are broken down by enzymes in the blood or in cells, or are lost in the urine. Insulin, for example, lasts for only around 10–15 minutes, while adrenaline lasts for between 1 and 3 minutes. This means that the effects of hormones can also be 'turned off' quite quickly.

SAQ 6.5

If you are in a frightening situation, adrenaline will be secreted and cause your heart rate to increase. This can go on for several hours. If adrenaline has such a short life-span in the body, how can its effect continue for so long?

Hormones are transported all through the body in the blood. However, each hormone has a particular group of cells which it affects, called **target cells**. These cells, and only these cells, are affected by the hormone because they contain **receptors** specific to the hormone. The receptors for protein hormones, such as insulin, are on the plasma membrane. These hormones bind with the receptors on the outer surface of the membrane, causing a response by the cell without actually entering it. Steroid hormones, however, are lipid-soluble, and so can pass easily through the plasma membrane into the cytoplasm. The receptors for steroid hormones are inside the cell, in the cytoplasm.

SAQ 6.6

Explain why steroid hormones can pass easily through the plasma membrane, while protein hormones cannot.

The pancreas

Figures 6.17, 6.18 and 6.19 show the structure of the pancreas. The pancreas is a very unusual gland, because parts of it function as an exocrine gland, while other parts function as an endocrine gland. The exocrine function is the secretion of pancreatic juice, which flows along the pancreatic duct into the duodenum, where it helps in digestion. The endocrine function is carried out by groups of cells called the **islets of Langerhans**, which are scattered throughout the pancreas.

The islets contain two types of cells. α **cells** secrete **glucagon**, while β **cells** secrete **insulin**. These two hormones, both small proteins, are involved in the control of blood glucose levels (figure 6.21).

The control of blood glucose

Carbohydrate is transported through the human bloodstream in the form of glucose, in solution in the blood plasma. For storage, glucose can be converted into the polysaccharide **glycogen**, a large, insoluble molecule made up of many glucose units linked together (Biology 1, page 26), which can be stored inside cells, especially liver and muscle cells (figure 6.22).

In a healthy human, each 100 cm³ of blood normally contains between 80 and 120 mg of glucose. If blood glucose level drops below this, then cells may run short of glucose for respiration, and be unable to carry out their normal activities. This is

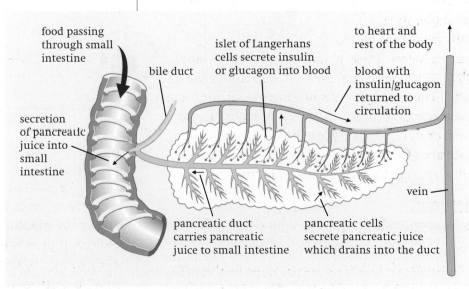

● **Figure 6.17** The pancreas is both an exocrine and endocrine gland.

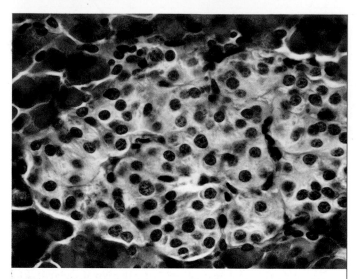

● **Figure 6.18** Light micrograph of pancreas (× 500), showing an islet of Langerhans, containing α and β cells.

especially important for cells that can only respire glucose, such as brain cells. Very high blood glucose levels can also cause major problems, again upsetting the normal behaviour of cells.

After a meal containing carbohydrate, glucose from the digested food is absorbed from the small intestine and passes into the blood. As this blood flows through the pancreas, the α and β cells detect the raised glucose levels. The α cells

respond by stopping the secretion of glucagon, while the β cells respond by secreting insulin into the blood plasma. The insulin is carried to all parts of the body, in the blood (*box 6A* opposite).

Insulin affects many cells, especially those in the liver and muscles. The effects on these cells include:

■ an increased absorption of glucose from the blood into the cells;

■ an increase in the rate of use of glucose in respiration;

■ an increase in the rate at which glucose is converted into the storage polysaccharide glycogen.

All of these processes take glucose out of the blood, so lowering the blood glucose levels. A drop in blood glucose concentration is detected by the α and β cells in the pancreas. The α cells respond by secreting glucagon, while the β cells respond by stopping the secretion of insulin.

The lack of insulin puts a stop to the increased uptake and usage of glucose by liver and muscle cells, although uptake still continues at a more 'normal' rate. The presence of glucagon affects the activities of the liver cells. (Muscle cells are not responsive to glucagon.) These effects include:

■ the breakdown of glycogen to glucose;

■ the use of fatty acids instead of glucose as the main fuel in respiration;

■ the production of glucose from other compounds, such as fats.

As a result, the liver releases glucose into the blood. This blood flows around the body, passing through the pancreas. Here, the α and β cells sense the raised glucose levels, switching off glucagon secretion and perhaps switching on insulin secretion if the glucose levels are higher than normal.

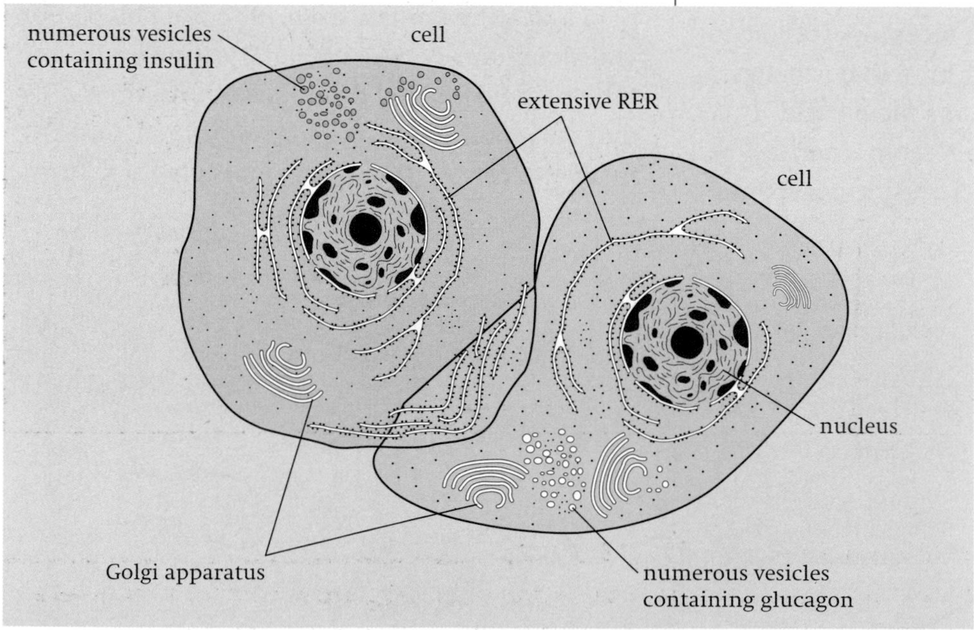

numerous vesicles containing insulin

cell

extensive RER

cell

nucleus

Golgi apparatus

numerous vesicles containing glucagon

● **Figure 6.19** Diagrams, based on electron micrographs, showing the structure of α and β cells from islets of Langerhans of a rat. The structures of these cells vary slightly between species, but here the insulin in the β cells forms dark, crystalline deposits inside the numerous vesicles, while glucagon in the α cells is less visible. In reality, the cells are almost filled with vesicles, though only a few have been shown here.

Box 6A The control of insulin secretion

The β cells in the islets of Langerhans release insulin in response to the presence of high levels of glucose in the blood. How do they sense this, and how is the amount of insulin that is released controlled?

The β cells contain several types of channels in their plasma membranes, each of which allows a particular type of ion to pass through (*Biology 1*, page 55). These include channels that let K^+ ions pass through, and others that let Ca^{2+} pass through.

Normally, the K^+ channels are open, leaving the K^+ ions free to pass through. These positively charged ions diffuse from inside the cell to the outside. This makes the outside of the cell positively charged compared with the inside. We say that there is a **potential difference** across the membrane. The potential difference across the plasma membrane of a resting β cell – that is one that is not secreting insulin – is about −70 mV.

However, when glucose levels around the β cell are high, this starts off a chain of events which alters the situation. The glucose passes into the cell, where it is quickly phosphorylated by the enzyme **glucokinase**. The phosphorylated glucose is then metabolised to produce ATP.

The K^+ channels are sensitive to the amount of ATP in the cell, and they respond to this increase in ATP levels by closing. So now the K^+ ions cannot diffuse out. As a result, the difference in electrical potential on the inside and the outside of the membrane becomes less. It is now only about −30 mV.

Now the Ca^{2+} channels come into the picture. They, unlike the K^+ channels, are normally closed. However, they respond to the change in potential across the membrane by opening. Ca^{2+} ions flood into the cell from the tissue fluid outside it.

The Ca^{2+} ions affect the behaviour of the vesicles containing insulin. These vesicles are moved towards the plasma membrane, where they fuse with the membrane and empty their contents outside the cell.

When you have studied the way in which nerve impulses are generated and transmitted (pages 108–117), you will probably be able to pick out several similarities between that mechanism, and the mechanism by which insulin secretion is controlled.

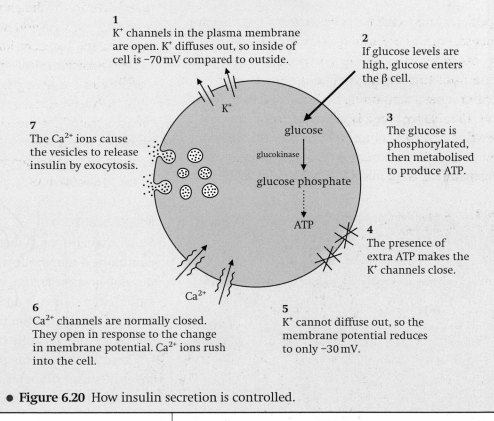

1
K^+ channels in the plasma membrane are open. K^+ diffuses out, so inside of cell is −70 mV compared to outside.

2
If glucose levels are high, glucose enters the β cell.

3
The glucose is phosphorylated, then metabolised to produce ATP.

7
The Ca^{2+} ions cause the vesicles to release insulin by exocytosis.

4
The presence of extra ATP makes the K^+ channels close.

6
Ca^{2+} channels are normally closed. They open in response to the change in membrane potential. Ca^{2+} ions rush into the cell.

5
K^+ cannot diffuse out, so the membrane potential reduces to only −30 mV.

● **Figure 6.20** How insulin secretion is controlled.

Blood sugar levels never remain constant, even in the healthiest person. One reason for this is the inevitable time delay between a change in the blood glucose level and the onset of actions to correct it. Time delays in control systems result in oscillation, where things do not stay absolutely constant, but sometimes rise slightly above and sometimes drop slightly below the 'required' level.

SAQ 6.7

The control of blood glucose concentration uses a negative feedback control mechanism.

a Explain what is meant by negative feedback.

b What are the receptors in this control mechanism?

c What are the effectors?

(You may need to look back to page 88.)

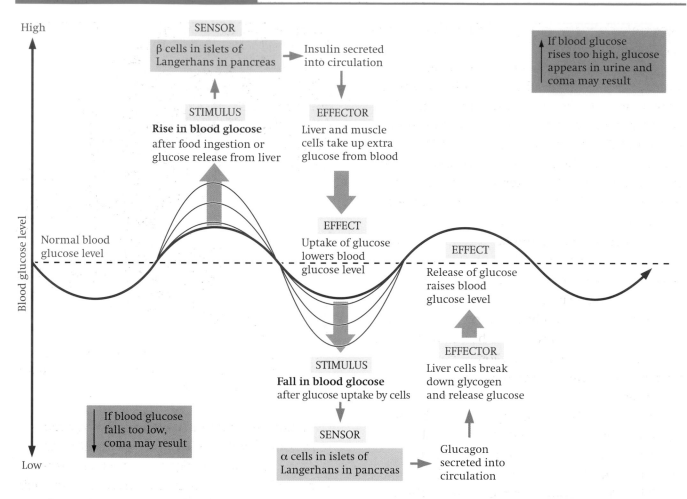

High

SENSOR

β cells in islets of Langerhans in pancreas → Insulin secreted into circulation

If blood glucose rises too high, glucose appears in urine and coma may result

STIMULUS

EFFECTOR

Rise in blood glocose after food ingestion or glucose release from liver

Liver and muscle cells take up extra glucose from blood

Blood glucose level

Normal blood glucose level

EFFECT

Uptake of glucose lowers blood glucose level

EFFECT

Release of glucose raises blood glucose level

If blood glucose falls too low, coma may result

STIMULUS

EFFECTOR

Fall in blood glocose after glucose uptake by cells

Liver cells break down glycogen and release glucose

SENSOR

α cells in islets of Langerhans in pancreas → Glucagon secreted into circulation

Low

● **Figure 6.21** The control mechanism for blood glucose levels.

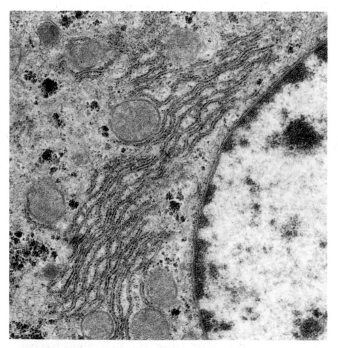

● **Figure 6.22** Electron micrograph of part of a liver cell (× 22 000). The dark spots are glycogen granules in the cytoplasm. Numerous mitochondria can also be seen.

Diabetes mellitus

Sugar diabetes, or diabetes mellitus, is one of the commonest metabolic diseases in humans. In developed countries, approximately 1% of people suffer from diabetes mellitus. The incidence is lower in many developing countries, for reasons which are not yet fully understood.

There are two forms of sugar diabetes. In **juvenile-onset diabetes**, sometimes called **insulin-dependent diabetes**, the pancreas seems to be incapable of secreting sufficient insulin. It is thought that this might be due to a deficiency in the gene which codes for the production of insulin, or because of an attack on the β cells by the person's own immune system. This form of diabetes, as suggested by its name, usually begins very early in life.

The second form of diabetes is called **non-insulin-dependent diabetes**. In this form, the pancreas does secrete insulin, but the liver and muscle cells do not respond properly to it. It frequently begins relatively late in life and is often associated with obesity.

The symptoms of both types of diabetes mellitus are the same. After a carbohydrate meal, blood glucose levels rise and stay high (*figure 6.23*). Normally there is no glucose in urine, but if blood glucose levels become very high, the kidney cannot reabsorb all the glucose so that some passes out in the urine. Extra water and salts accompany this glucose, and the person consequently feels extremely hungry and thirsty.

In a diabetic person, uptake of glucose into cells is slow, even when blood glucose levels are high. Thus cells lack glucose, and metabolise fats and proteins as an alternative energy source. This can lead to a build-up of substances called keto-acids in the blood, which lowers the blood pH. The combination of dehydration, salt loss and low blood pH can cause coma in extreme situations.

Between meals, when blood glucose levels would normally be kept up by mobilisation of glycogen reserves, the blood glucose levels of a person with untreated diabetes may plummet. This is because there is no glycogen to be mobilised. Once again, coma may result, this time because of a lack of glucose for respiration.

SAQ 6.8
Explain why people with diabetes mellitus have virtually no glycogen to be mobilised.

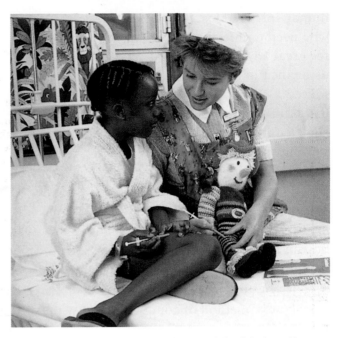

● **Figure 6.24** A nurse teaches a girl with insulin-dependent diabetes to inject insulin. She will have to do this daily, all her life.

In insulin-dependent diabetes, regular injections of insulin, together with a carefully controlled diet, are used to keep blood glucose levels near normal (*figure 6.24*). The person must monitor their own blood glucose level, taking a blood sample several times a day. In non-insulin-dependent diabetes, insulin injections are not normally needed. Control is by diet alone.

SAQ 6.9
a Insulin cannot effectively be taken by mouth. Why is this so?
b Suggest how people with non-insulin–dependent diabetes can control their blood glucose level.

Until the early 1980s, all insulin was obtained from animals such as pigs and cattle. In the 1980s, insulin began to be made using bacteria into which the human insulin gene had been inserted (*Biology 1*, page 76). This insulin is much cheaper than that obtained from animals, and also has the advantage that it is, of course, human insulin, not pig or cow insulin, which differ slightly from

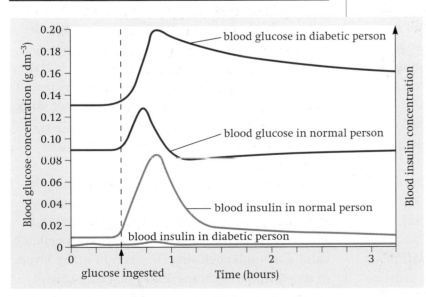

● **Figure 6.23** Blood glucose and insulin levels following intake of glucose in a normal person and a person with insulin-dependent diabetes.

human insulin. Most people who need to inject insulin see great advantages in using insulin from this source, although a few have had problems in making the change from using pig or cattle insulin to using human insulin produced by genetic engineering.

Some of the advantages of using genetically engineered human insulin are:

- more rapid response;
- shorter duration of response;
- less chance of an immune response to the insulin developing;
- effective in people who have developed a tolerance for animal-derived insulin;
- more acceptable to people who feel it is unethical to use pig or cattle insulin.

Nervous communication

Neurones

So far in this chapter we have looked at the way in which hormones are used by mammals to send messages from one part of the body to another. The hormones are carried in the blood, and so spread all through the body. Mammals also have another method of communication within their bodies. This method is faster and more precise and involves the transmission of electrical signals or impulses along precisely constructed pathways. The cells which carry these signals are called nerve cells or **neurones**.

Figure 6.25 shows the structure of a mammalian neurone. This is a **motor neurone** which transmits messages from the brain or spinal cord to a muscle or gland.

The cell body of a motor neurone lies within the spinal cord or brain. The nucleus of a neurone is always in its cell body. Often, dark specks can be seen in the cytoplasm. These are groups of ribosomes involved in protein synthesis.

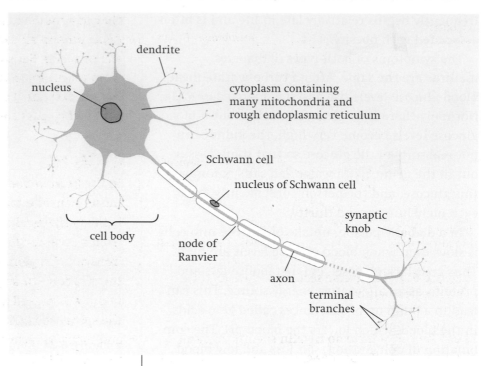

● **Figure 6.25** A motor neurone. The axon may be over a metre long.

Many thin cytoplasmic processes extend from the cell body. In a motor neurone, all but one of these processes are relatively short. They conduct impulses *towards* the cell body, and are called **dendrons** or **dendrites**. One process is much longer, and conducts impulses *away* from the cell body. This is called the **axon**. A motor neurone with its cell body in your spinal cord might have its axon running all the way to one of your toes, so axons may be extremely long. Within the cytoplasm of an axon, all of the usual organelles such as endoplasmic reticulum, Golgi apparatus and mitochondria, are present. Particularly large numbers of mitochondria are found at the tips of the terminal branches of the axon, together with many vesicles containing chemicals called transmitter substances. Their function will be explained later (page 116).

In some neurones, cells called **Schwann cells** wrap themselves around the axon all along its length. *Figure 6.26* shows one such cell, viewed as the axon is cut transversely. The Schwann cell spirals around, enclosing the axon in many layers of its plasma membrane. This enclosing sheath, called the **myelin sheath**, is made largely of lipid, together with some proteins. Not all axons have myelin sheaths. Some invertebrate animals, such

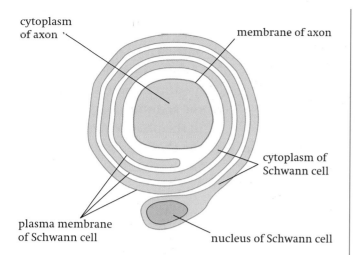

cytoplasm
of axon

membrane of axon

cytoplasm of
Schwann cell

plasma membrane
of Schwann cell

nucleus of Schwann cell

● **Figure 6.26** Transverse section of the axon of a myelinated neurone.

as earthworms, have no myelin sheaths around their neurones. In humans, about one third of our motor and sensory neurones are myelinated. The sheath affects the speed of conduction of the nerve impulse (page 111). The small, uncovered areas of axon between Schwann cells are called **nodes of Ranvier**. They occur about every 1–3 mm in human neurones. The nodes themselves are very small, around 2–3 μm long.

Figure 6.27 shows the different shapes of neurones with different functions. The basic structure of a **sensory neurone** is the same as that of a motor neurone, but it has one long dendron and an axon which is often shorter than the dendron. Sensory neurones bring impulses from receptors (cells which pick up stimuli, such as touch or light) to the brain or spinal cord. There, they pass them on to other neurones.

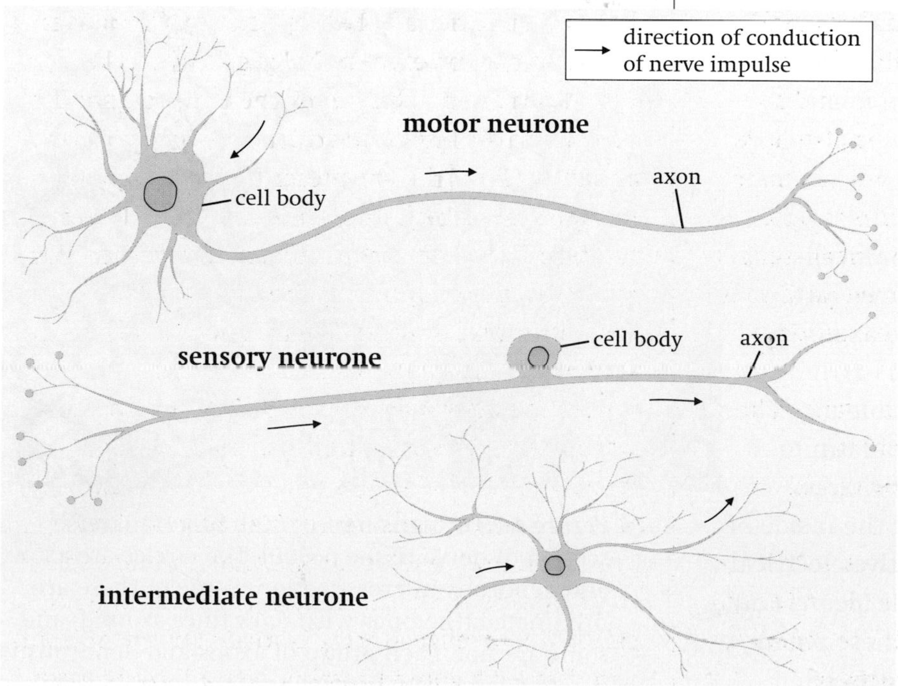

A reflex arc

In the human body, a sensory neurone and a motor neurone may form a reflex arc. A **reflex arc** is the pathway along which impulses are carried from a receptor to an effector, without involving 'conscious' regions of the brain. *Figure 6.28* shows the structure of a spinal reflex arc in which the impulse is passed from neurone to neurone inside the spinal cord. The neurone between the sensory and motor neurones is called an intermediate neurone. Others may have no intermediate neurone, and the impulse passes directly from the sensory neurone to the motor neurone.

Within the spinal cord, the impulse will also be passed on to other neurones which take the impulse up the cord to the brain. This happens at the same time as the message is travelling along the motor neurone to the effector. The effector therefore responds to the stimulus before there is any voluntary response, involving conscious regions of the brain. This type of reaction to a stimulus is called a **reflex action**. It is a fast, automatic response to a stimulus. Reflex actions are a very useful way of responding to danger signals, such as the touch of a very hot object on your skin or the sight of an object flying towards you.

SAQ 6.10

Think of three reflex actions other than the two already mentioned. For each action, state the precise stimulus, name the receptor which first detects this stimulus, name the effector which responds to it, and describe the way in which this effector responds.

direction of conduction
of nerve impulse

motor neurone

cell body

axon

sensory neurone

cell body

axon

intermediate neurone

● **Figure 6.27** Motor, sensory and intermediate neurones.

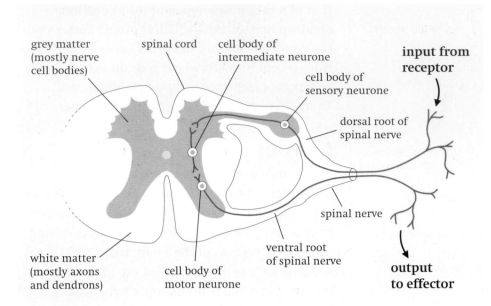

● **Figure 6.28** A reflex arc. The spinal cord is shown in transverse section.

Transmission of nerve impulses

Neurones transmit impulses as electrical signals. These signals travel very rapidly along the plasma membrane from one end of the cell to the other and are *not* a flow of electrons like an electric current. Rather, the signals are very brief changes in the distribution of electrical charge across the plasma membrane, caused by the very rapid movement of sodium and potassium ions into and out of the axon.

Resting potential

Figure 6.29 shows myelinated and nonmyelinated nerve tissue and *figure 6.30* shows just part of a nonmyelinated axon. Some axons in some organisms, such as squids and earthworms, are very wide, and it is possible to insert tiny electrodes into their cytoplasm to measure these changes in electrical charge.

In a resting axon, it is found that the inside of the axon always has a slightly negative electrical potential compared with the outside (*figures 6.30* and *6.31a*). The difference between these potentials, called the **potential difference**, is often around −65 mV. In other words, the electrical

potential of the inside of the axon is 65 mV lower than the outside.

The resting potential is produced and maintained by the **sodium–potassium pump** in the plasma membrane of the axon (*figure 6.31b* and *box 1A* on page 5). Sodium ions, Na^+, are picked up from the cytoplasm inside the axon by a carrier protein in the membrane and carried to the outside. At the same time, potassium ions, K^+, are brought into the cytoplasm from the external fluids. Both of these processes involve moving the ions against their concentration gradients, and so use energy from the hydrolysis of ATP.

The sodium–potassium pump removes three sodium ions from the cell for every two potassium

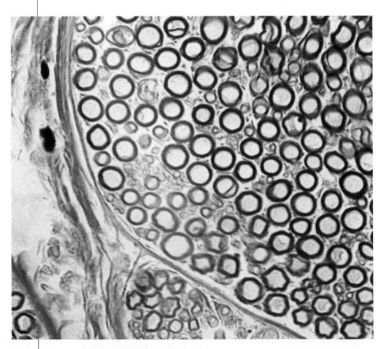

● **Figure 6.29** A light micrograph of a transverse section of nerve tissue (× 500). The circles are axons and dendrons in cross-section. Some of these are myelinated (the ones with dark lines around) and some are not. Each group of axons and dendrons is surrounded by a perineurium (red lines). Several such groups make a complete nerve.

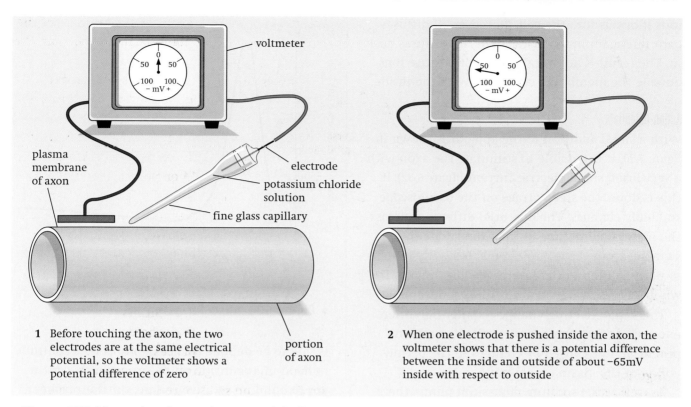

1 Before touching the axon, the two electrodes are at the same electrical potential, so the voltmeter shows a potential difference of zero

portion of axon

2 When one electrode is pushed inside the axon, the voltmeter shows that there is a potential difference between the inside and outside of about −65mV inside with respect to outside

● **Figure 6.30** Measuring the resting potential of an axon.

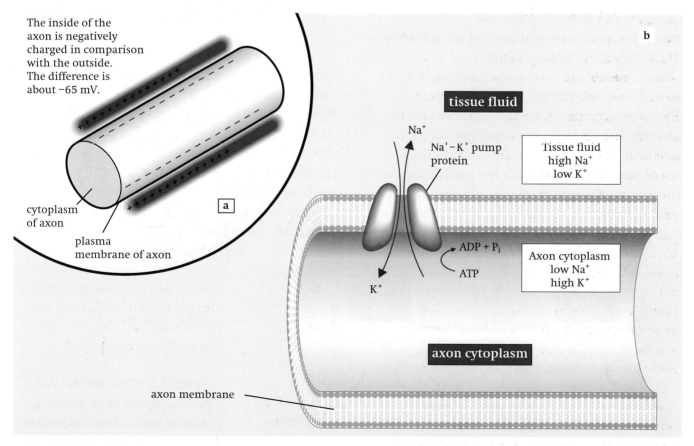

The inside of the axon is negatively charged in comparison with the outside. The difference is about −65 mV.

cytoplasm of axon

plasma membrane of axon

axon membrane

tissue fluid

Na⁺

Na⁺–K⁺ pump protein

Tissue fluid high Na⁺ low K⁺

ADP + P_i

ATP

K⁺

Axon cytoplasm low Na⁺ high K⁺

axon cytoplasm

● **Figure 6.31**
a At rest, an axon has negative electrical potential inside.
b The sodium–potassium pump maintains the resting potential by keeping more sodium ions outside than there are potassium ions inside.

ions it brings into the cell. Moreover, K⁺ diffuses back out again much faster than Na⁺ diffuses back in. The result is an overall excess of positive ions outside the membrane compared with the inside.

Action potentials

With a small addition to the apparatus shown in *figure 6.30*, it is possible to stimulate the axon with a very brief, small electric current (*figure 6.32*). If this is done, the steady trace on the oscilloscope suddenly changes. The potential difference across the plasma membrane of the axon suddenly switches from −65 mV to +40 mV. It swiftly returns to normal after a brief 'overshoot' (*figure 6.33*). The whole process takes about 3 milliseconds (ms).

This rapid, fleeting change in potential difference across the membrane is called an **action potential**. It is caused by changes in the permeability of the plasma membrane to Na⁺ and K⁺.

As well as the sodium–potassium pump, there are other channels in the plasma membrane that allow Na⁺ or K⁺ to pass through. They open and close depending on the electrical potential (or voltage) across the membrane and are therefore said to be **voltage-gated channels**.

First, the electric current used to stimulate the axon causes the opening of the channels in the plasma membrane which allow sodium ions to pass through. As there is a much greater concentration of sodium ions outside the axon than inside, they flood in through the open channels. The now relatively high concentration of positively charged sodium ions inside the axon makes it less negative *inside* than it was before. The membrane

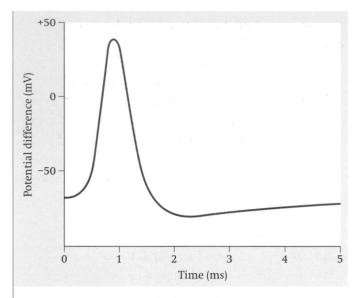

● **Figure 6.33** An action potential.

is said to be **depolarised**. As sodium ions continue to flood in, the inside of the axon swiftly continues to build up positive charge, until it reaches a potential of +40 mV compared with the outside.

At this point, the sodium channels close, so sodium ions stop diffusing into the axon. At the same time, the potassium channels open. Potassium ions therefore diffuse *out* of the axon, down their concentration gradient. The outward movement of potassium ions removes positive charge from inside the axon to the outside, thus beginning to return the potential difference to normal. This is called **repolarisation**. So many potassium ions leave the axon that the potential difference across the membrane briefly becomes even more negative than the normal resting potential. The potassium channels then close, and the sodium–potassium pump begins to act again, restoring the normal distribution of sodium and potassium ions across the membrane, and therefore restoring the resting potential.

Transmission of action potentials

The description of an action potential above concerns events at one particular point in an axon membrane. However, the function of a neurone is to transmit information *along* itself.

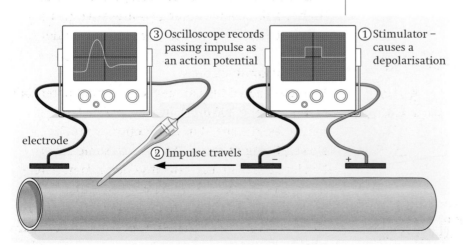

● **Figure 6.32** Recording of an action potential.

How do action potentials transmit information along a neurone?

An action potential at any point in an axon's plasma membrane triggers the production of an action potential in the membrane on either side of it. *Figure 6.34* shows how it does this. The temporary depolarisation of the membrane where the action potential is causes a 'local circuit' to be set up between the depolarised region and the resting regions on either side of it. Sodium ions flow sideways inside the axon, away from the positively charged region towards the negatively charged regions on either side. This depolarises these adjoining regions and so generates an action potential in them.

In practice, if an action potential has been travelling in one direction from a point of stimulation, a 'new' action potential is only generated *ahead* of, and not behind, it. This is because the region behind it will still be recovering from the action potential it has just had and its distribution of sodium and potassium ions will not yet be back to normal. It is therefore incapable of producing a new action potential for a short time. This is known as the **refractory period**.

How action potentials carry information

Action potentials do not change in size as they travel. However long an axon is, the action potential will continue to reach a value of +40 mV inside all the way along. Moreover, the intensity of the stimulus which originally generated the

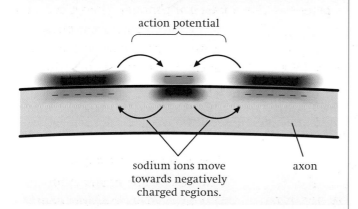

action potential

sodium ions move towards negatively charged regions.

axon

● **Figure 6.34** How action potentials are transmitted along an axon. Local circuits are set up between the region where there is an action potential and the resting regions, causing the resting regions to depolarise.

action potential has absolutely no effect on the size of the action potential. A very strong light shining in your eyes will produce action potentials of precisely the same size as a dim light. Nor does the speed at which the action potentials travel vary according to the size of the stimulus. In any one axon, the speed of axon potential transmission is always the same.

What *is* different about the action potentials resulting from a strong and a weak stimulus is their **frequency**. A strong stimulus produces a rapid succession of action potentials, each one following along the axon just behind its predecessor. A weak stimulus results in fewer action potentials per second (*figure 6.35*).

Moreover, a strong stimulus is likely to stimulate more neurones than a weak stimulus. While a weak stimulus might result in action potentials passing along just one or two neurones, a strong stimulus could produce action potentials in many more.

The brain can therefore interpret the *frequency* of action potentials arriving along the axon of a sensory neurone, and the *number* of neurones carrying action potentials, to get information about the *strength* of the stimulus being detected by that receptor. The *nature* of the stimulus, whether it is light, heat, touch or so on, is deduced from the *position* of the sensory neurone bringing the information. If the neurone is from the retina of the eye, then the brain will interpret the information as meaning 'light'. If for some reason a different stimulus, such as pressure, stimulates a receptor cell in the retina, the brain will still interpret the action potentials from this receptor as meaning 'light'. This is why rubbing your eyes when they are shut can cause you to 'see' patterns of light.

Speed of conduction

In a myelinated human neurone, action potentials travel at up to 100 m s^{-1}. In nonmyelinated neurones, the speed of conduction is much slower, being as low as 0.5 m s^{-1} in some cases. Myelin speeds up the rate at which action potentials travel by insulating the axon membrane. Sodium and potassium ions cannot flow through the myelin sheath, so it is not possible for depolarisation or action potentials to occur in parts of the axon which are surrounded by it. They can only occur at the nodes of Ranvier.

Figure 6.36 shows how an action potential is transmitted along a myelinated axon. The local circuits that are set up stretch from one node to the next. Thus action potentials 'jump' from one node to the next, a distance of 1–3 mm. This is called **saltatory conduction**. It can increase the speed of transmission by up to 50 times that in a nonmyelinated axon of the same diameter.

Diameter also affects the speed of transmission (*figure 6.37*). Thick axons transmit action potentials faster than thin ones. Earthworms, which have no myelinated axons, have a few very thick nonmyelinated ones which run all along their body from head to tail (*figure 6.38*). A bird pecking at an earthworm's head sets up action potentials in these giant axons, which sweep along the length of the body, stimulating muscles to contract. The rapid response which results may enable the earthworm to escape.

What starts off an action potential?

In the description of the generation of an action potential on page 110, the initial stimulus was a small electric current. In normal life, however, action potentials are generated by a wide variety of stimuli, such as light, touch, sound, temperature or chemicals.

A cell which responds to such stimuli by initiating an action potential is called a **receptor cell**. Receptor cells are often found in sense organs. For

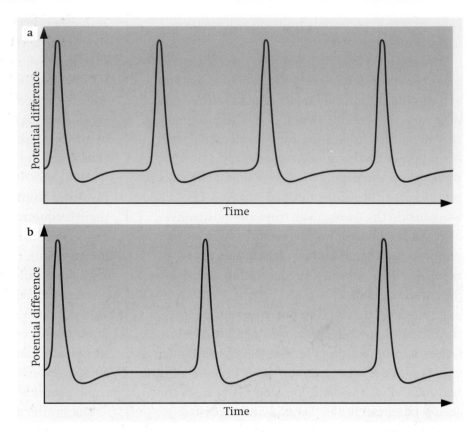

● **Figure 6.35** Action potentials resulting from **a** a strong stimulus and **b** a weak stimulus. Note that the size of each action potential remains the same, only their frequency changes.
a A high frequency of impulses is produced when a receptor is given a strong stimulus. This high frequency carries the message 'strong stimulus'.
b A lower frequency of impulses is produced when a receptor is given a weaker stimulus. This lower frequency carries the message 'weak stimulus'.

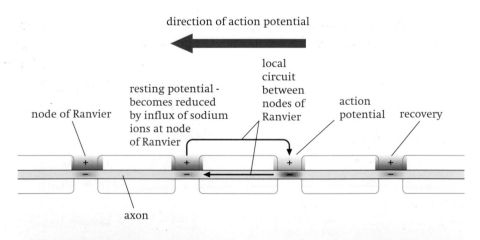

● **Figure 6.36** Transmission of an action potential in a myelinated axon. The myelin sheath acts as an insulator, preventing differences in potential across the parts of the axon membrane surrounded by the sheath. Potential differences can only occur at the nodes of Ranvier. The action potential therefore 'jumps' from one node to the next, travelling much more swiftly than in a nonmyelinated axon.

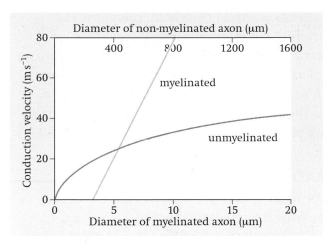

● **Figure 6.37** Speed of transmission in myelinated and nonmyelinated axons of different diameters.

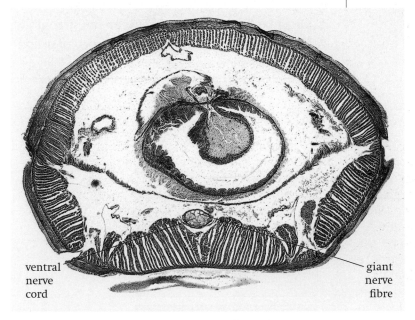

● **Figure 6.38** Transverse section of an earthworm (× 22). The ventral nerve cord contains three giant nerve fibres.

example, light receptor cells are found in the eye and sound receptor cells are found in the ear. Some receptors, such as light receptors, are special cells which generate an action potential and send it on to a sensory neurone, while others, such as some kinds of touch receptors, are simply the ends of the sensory neurones themselves. Receptor cells convert energy in one form – such as light, heat or sound – into energy in an electrical impulse in a neurone (*table 6.2*).

One type of receptor found in the dermis of the skin is a **Pacinian corpuscle** (*figure 6.39*). Pacinian corpuscles contain an ending of a sensory neurone, surrounded by several layers of connective tissue, called a **capsule**. The ending of the sensory neurone inside the capsule has no myelin.

When pressure is applied to a Pacinian corpuscle, the capsule is pressed out of shape, and deforms the nerve ending inside it. This deformation causes sodium and potassium channels to open in the cell membrane, allowing sodium ions to flood in and potassium ions to flow out. This depolarises the membrane. The increased positive charge inside the axon is called a **receptor potential**. The harder the pressure applied to the Pacinian corpuscle, the more channels open and the greater the receptor potential becomes. If the pressure is great enough, then the receptor potential becomes large enough to trigger an action potential (*figure 6.40*).

Receptor	Sense	Form in which energy is received
rod or cone cells in retina	sight	light
taste buds on tongue	taste	chemical potential
olfactory cells in nose	smell	chemical potential
Pacinian corpuscles in skin	pressure	movement and pressure
Meissner's corpuscles in skin	touch	movement and pressure
Ruffini's endings in skin	temperature	heat
proprioceptors (stretch receptors) in muscles	placement of limbs	mechanical displacement – stretching
hair cells in semicircular canals in ear	balance	movement
hair cells in cochlea	hearing	sound

● **Table 6.2** Some examples of energy conversions by receptors. Each type of receptor converts a particular form of energy into electrical energy – that is, a nerve impulse.

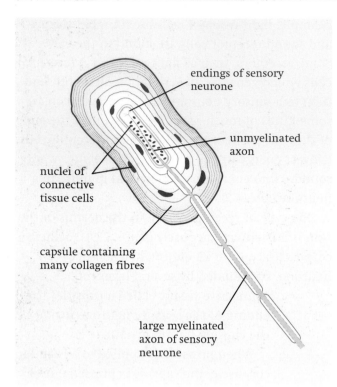

endings of sensory
neurone

unmyelinated
axon

nuclei of
connective
tissue cells

capsule containing
many collagen fibres

large myelinated
axon of sensory
neurone

● **Figure 6.39** A Pacinian corpuscle. These corpuscles
are found in the dermis, and are sensitive to pressure.

Below a certain threshold, therefore, the
pressure stimulus only causes local depolarisation, not an action potential, and therefore no
information is transmitted to the brain. Above
this threshold, action potentials are initiated.
As the pressure increases, the action potentials
are produced more frequently.

SAQ 6.11

Use *figure 6.40* to answer these questions.
a What is a receptor potential?
b Describe the relationship between the pressure
applied to a Pacinian corpuscle and the size of
the receptor potential which is generated.
c What is the threshold receptor potential?
d Describe the relationship between the strength of
the stimulus applied and the frequency of action
potentials generated.

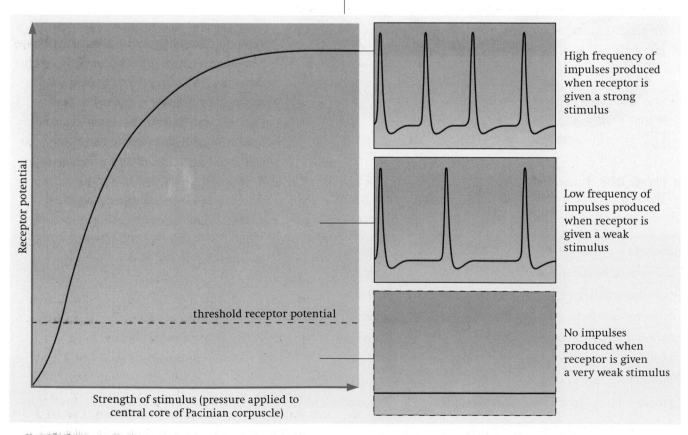

Receptor potential

threshold receptor potential

Strength of stimulus (pressure applied to
central core of Pacinian corpuscle)

High frequency of
impulses produced
when receptor is
given a strong
stimulus

Low frequency of
impulses produced
when receptor is
given a weak
stimulus

No impulses
produced when
receptor is given
a very weak stimulus

● **Figure 6.40** As pressure is applied to the inner capsule of a Pacinian corpuscle, it produces a
depolarisation of the membrane of the sensory nerve ending. This is called the receptor
potential. Greater pressures produce greater receptor potentials. If the receptor potential
reaches a particular size, called the threshold, then an action potential is triggered.

Synapses

Where two neurones meet, they do not quite touch. There is a very small gap, about 20 nm wide, between them. This gap is called the **synaptic cleft**. The parts of the two neurones near to the cleft, plus the cleft itself, make up a **synapse** (*figure 6.41*).

The mechanism of synaptic transmission

Action potentials cannot jump across synapses. Instead, the signal is passed across by a chemical, known as a **transmitter substance**. In outline, an action potential arriving along the plasma membrane of the first, or **presynaptic**, neurone, causes it to release transmitter substance into the cleft. The transmitter substance molecules diffuse across the cleft, which takes less than a millisecond as the distance is so small. This may set up an action potential in the plasma membrane of the second, or **postsynaptic**, neurone.

Let us look at these processes in more detail. The cytoplasm of the presynaptic neurone contains vesicles of transmitter substance (*figure 6.42*). More than 40 different transmitter substances are known; **noradrenaline** and **acetylcholine** are found throughout the nervous system, while

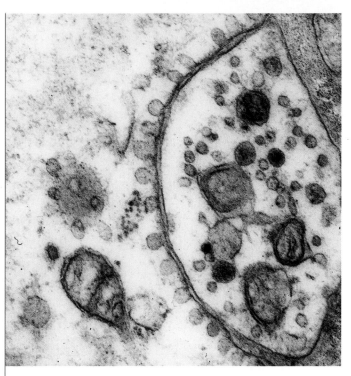

● **Figure 6.42** Electron micrograph of a synapse (× 68 000). The presynaptic neurone is to the right of the picture. Several mitochondria and numerous vesicles, which contain transmitter substance, can be seen.

others such as **dopamine** and **glutamic acid** occur only in the brain. We will concentrate on those synapses which use acetylcholine (ACh) as the transmitter substance. These are known as **cholinergic synapses**.

You will remember that, as an action potential sweeps along the plasma membrane of a neurone, local circuits depolarise the next piece of membrane, opening sodium channels and so propagating the action potential. In the part of the membrane of the presynaptic neurone which is next to the synaptic cleft, the arrival of the action potential also causes **calcium channels** to open. Thus, the action potential causes not only sodium ions but also calcium ions to rush in to the cytoplasm of the presynaptic neurone.

This influx of calcium ions causes vesicles of ACh to move to the presynaptic membrane and fuse with it, emptying their contents into the synaptic cleft (*figure 6.43*). Each action potential causes just a few vesicles to do this, and each vesicle contains up to 10 000 molecules of ACh. The ACh diffuses across the synaptic cleft, usually in less than 0.5 ms.

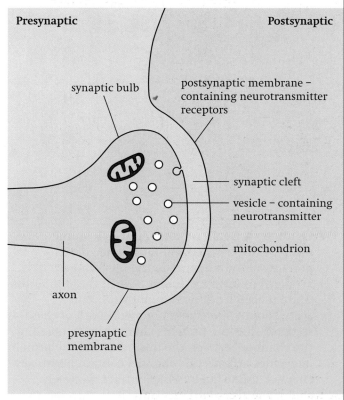

● **Figure 6.41** A synapse.

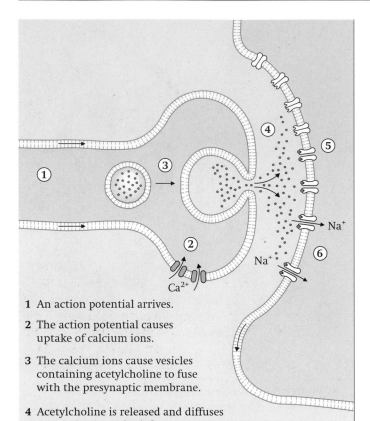

1 An action potential arrives.

2 The action potential causes uptake of calcium ions.

3 The calcium ions cause vesicles containing acetylcholine to fuse with the presynaptic membrane.

4 Acetylcholine is released and diffuses across the synaptic cleft.

5 Acetylcholine molecules bind with receptors in the postsynaptic membrane, causing them to open sodium channels.

6 Sodium ions flood in through the open channels in the postsynaptic membrane. This depolarises the membrane and initiates an action potential.

● **Figure 6.43** Synaptic transmission.

The plasma membrane of the postsynaptic neurone contains **receptor proteins**. Part of the receptor protein molecule has a complementary shape to part of the ACh molecule, so that the ACh molecules can temporarily bind with the receptors. This changes the shape of the protein, opening channels through which sodium ions can pass (*figure 6.44*). Sodium ions rush into the cytoplasm of the postsynaptic neurone, depolarising the membrane and starting off an action potential.

If the ACh remained bound to the postsynaptic receptors, the sodium channels would remain open, and action potentials would fire continuously. To prevent this from happening, and also to avoid wasting the ACh, it is recycled. The synaptic cleft contains an enzyme, **acetylcholinesterase**, which splits each ACh molecule into acetate and choline.

The choline is taken back into the presynaptic neurone, where it is combined with acetyl co-enzyme A to form ACh once more. The ACh is then transported into the presynaptic vesicles, ready for the next action potential. The entire sequence of events, from initial arrival of the action potential to the re-formation of ACh, takes about 5–10 ms.

Much of the research on synapses has been done not at synapses between two neurones, but those between a motor neurone and a muscle.

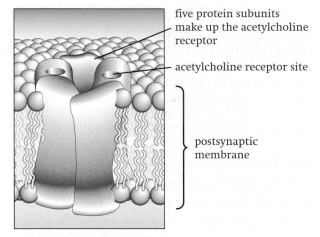

five protein subunits make up the acetylcholine receptor

acetylcholine receptor site

postsynaptic membrane

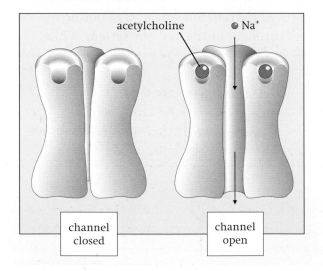

acetylcholine   ● Na⁺

channel closed

channel open

● **Figure 6.44** Detail of how the acetylcholine receptor works. The receptor is made of five protein subunits spanning the membranes arranged to form a cylinder. Two of these subunits contain acetylcholine receptor sites. When acetylcholine molecules bind with both of these receptor sites the proteins change shape, opening the channel between the units. Parts of the protein molecules around this channel contain negatively charged amino acids, which attract positively charged sodium ions and pull them through the channel.

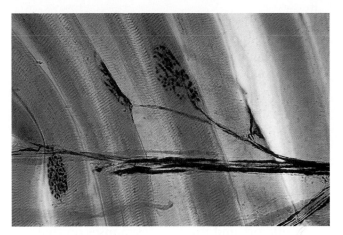

● **Figure 6.45** Light micrograph of neuromuscular junctions (×320). The red tissue in the background is muscle fibres, while the axons show as dark lines. The axons terminate in a number of branches on the surface of the muscle fibre, forming motor end plates. Action potentials are passed from the axon to the muscle, across a synaptic cleft, at these end-plates.

Here, the nerve forms **motor end plates** and the synapse is called a **neuromuscular junction** (*figure 6.45*). Such synapses function in the same way as described above. An action potential is produced in the muscle, which may cause it to contract (*box 1B on page 6*).

SAQ 6.12

Suggest why:

a impulses travel in only one direction at synapses;

b if action potentials arrive repeatedly at a synapse, the synapse eventually becomes unable to transmit the impulse to the next neurone.

The effects of other chemicals at synapses

Many drugs and other chemicals act by affecting the events at synapses.

You will remember that **nicotine** is one of the main chemicals found in cigarette smoke (*Biology 1, page 188*). Part of the nicotine molecule is similar in shape to ACh molecules, and will fit into the ACh receptors on postsynaptic membranes (*figure 6.46*). This produces similar effects to ACh, initiating action potentials in the postsynaptic neurone or muscle fibre. Unlike ACh, however, nicotine is not rapidly broken down by enzymes, and so remains in the receptors for longer than ACh. A large dose of nicotine can be fatal.

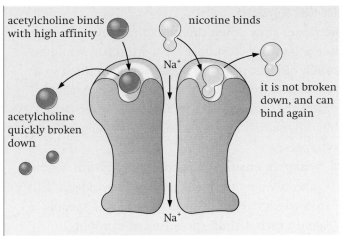

● **Figure 6.46** Nicotine molecules have similarities in shape to acetylcholine molecules, and will fit into some acetylcholine receptor sites, causing sodium channels to open. So nicotine can generate action potentials in postsynaptic neurones. Not all acetylcholine receptors are equally responsive to nicotine; those at neuromuscular junctions have only a low affinity for nicotine.

The **botulinum toxin** is produced by an anaerobic bacterium which occasionally breeds in contaminated canned food. It acts at the presynaptic membrane where it prevents the release of ACh. Eating food that contains this bacterium is frequently fatal. However, the toxin does have important medical uses. In some people, for example, the muscles of the eyelids contract permanently, so that they cannot open their eyes. Injections of tiny amounts of the botulinum toxin into these muscles can cause them to relax, so allowing the lids to be raised.

Organophosphorous insecticides inhibit the action of acetylcholinesterase, thus allowing ACh to cause continuous production of action potentials in the postsynaptic membrane. Many flea sprays and collars for cats and dogs contain organophosphorous insecticides, so great care should be taken when using them, for the health of both the pet and the owner. Contamination from organophosphorous sheep-dip (used to combat infestations by ticks) has been linked to certain illnesses in farm workers. Several **nerve gases** also act in this way. People involved in the production of these chemicals have regular checks of their free acetylcholinesterase levels to monitor their safety.

The roles of synapses

Synapses slow down the rate of transmission of a nerve impulse. Responses to a stimulus would be much quicker if action potentials generated in a receptor travelled along an unbroken neuronal pathway from receptor to effector, rather than having to cross synapses on the way. So why have synapses?

■ **Synapses ensure one-way transmission.** Signals can only pass in one direction at synapses. This allows signals to be directed towards specific goals, rather than spreading at random through the nervous system.

■ **Synapses increase the possible range of actions in response to a stimulus.** Synapses allow a wider range of behaviour than could be generated in a nervous system in which neurones were directly 'wired up' to each other. They do this by allowing the interconnection of many nerve pathways. Think for a moment of your possible behaviour when you see someone you know across the street. You can call out to them and walk to meet them, or you can pretend not to see them and hurry away. What decides which of these two responses, or any number of others, you will make?

Your nervous system will receive information from various sources about the situation. Receptors in your eyes will provide details about who the person is, and whether they have seen you or not. Stored away in your brain will be memories about the person: are they a good friend?.. is there something you want to talk about with them?.. are they boring? Your brain will also have other information to consider: are you in a hurry?.. have you time to spend here? All of these pieces of information will produce action potentials in many neurones in your nervous system. As a result of this, action potentials may or may not be sent to the muscles of your legs to make them turn and carry you across the street.

The way in which the 'turn' and 'not turn' decision is reached in your nervous system depends on what happens at synapses. Each neurone within the brain has many, often several thousand, synapses with other neurones. Action potentials arriving at some of these synapses will **stimulate** an action potential in the neurone, as described on page 114. Action potentials arriving at others will cause the release of transmitter substances which, far from producing an action potential in the neurone, will actually make it *more* difficult to depolarise its plasma membrane, and so **inhibit** the production of an action potential. Whether or not an action potential is produced depends on the summed effect of the number and frequency of action potentials arriving at all the stimulatory and inhibitory synapses on that particular neurone. In very simple terms, if the action potentials carrying 'good friend' information outweigh those carrying 'in a hurry' information, you will probably decide to turn towards the person even if it may make you late for your appointment.

The loss of *speed* in this response is more than compensated for in the possible *variety* of responses which can be made. We *do* have, however, some very rapid and very stereotyped responses. These are called **reflex actions**, and involve quick, automatic responses to stimuli. Two examples are blinking when an object speeds towards your eye, or jumping when you hear an unexpected noise. In a reflex action, there are normally only two or three neurones involved: a sensory neurone and a motor neurone, with perhaps an intermediate neurone in between (*figure 6.28*). These actions are ones where the survival value of a very rapid response is greater than the value of a carefully considered one.

■ **Synapses are involved in memory and learning.** Despite much research, little is yet known about how memory operates. However, there is much evidence that it involves synapses. For example, if your brain frequently receives information about two things at the same time, say a sound of a particular voice and a sight of a particular face, then it is thought that *new* synapses form in your brain that link the neurones involved in the passing of information along the particular pathways from your ears and eyes. In future, when you hear the voice, information flowing from your ears along this pathway automatically flows into the other pathway too, so that your brain 'pictures' the face which goes with the voice.

Plant growth regulators

Plants, like animals, have communication systems that allow coordination between different parts of their bodies. In at least some species, electrical signals rather like action potentials can be detected. For example, in the 'sensitive plant' *Mimosa*, which responds to touch by folding up its leaves, an electrical signal similar to an action potential can be detected, though this travels much more slowly. In the Venus fly-trap (*figure 6.47*), action potentials are set up when an insect touches the sensory hairs in the middle of the trap, and pass into the leaf tissue, causing the trap to close.

However, most communication within plants depends on chemicals. These are known as **plant hormones** or **plant growth regulators**.

Unlike animal hormones, plant growth regulators are not produced in endocrine glands, but in a variety of tissues. They are usually produced in such small quantities that it has proved very difficult to discover exactly where some of them are made. They move in the plant either directly from cell to cell (by diffusion or active transport) or carried in the phloem sap or xylem vessels. Some may not move at all from their site of synthesis.

● **Figure 6.47** The leaves of the Venus fly trap, *Dionaea muscipula*, have a group of stiff, sensitive hairs in their centres. When these are touched, the leaves respond by closing, trapping whatever was crawling over them. Digestive juices are then secreted, and the soluble products absorbed into the leaf cells.

Because they are usually found in only very, very low concentrations it is difficult to determine precisely what some of them do. Moreover, some of them seem to have very different effects when they are present in a relatively low concentration than when they are in a relatively high concentration. They can have different effects in different tissues, in different species, or at different stages of a plant's development. Add to this the fact that two or more plant growth regulators acting together can have very different effects from either of them acting alone, and you can see how difficult it is for plant physiologists to discover exactly what these substances do, where they do it and how.

Here we will look at just one or two roles of three plant growth substances – auxins, gibberellins and abscisic acid.

Auxins and apical dominance

Plants make several chemicals known as **auxins**, of which the principal one is **IAA** (indole 3-acetic acid, *figure 6.48*). Here, we will refer to this simply as 'auxin' in the singular. Auxin is synthesised in the growing tips of roots and shoots, where the cells are dividing. It is transported from here back down the shoot, or up the root, by active transport from cell to cell, and also to a lesser extent in phloem sap.

Auxin seems to be involved in determining whether a plant grows upwards or whether it branches sideways. When a plant has an active growing point at its apex, this tends to stop buds on the side of the stem, called **lateral buds**, from growing. The plant grows upwards rather than branching out sideways. However, if the bud at the tip of the main shoot – the apical bud – is cut off, then the lateral buds start to grow. Clearly, the presence of the **apical bud** is stopping the lateral buds from growing. This is called **apical dominance**.

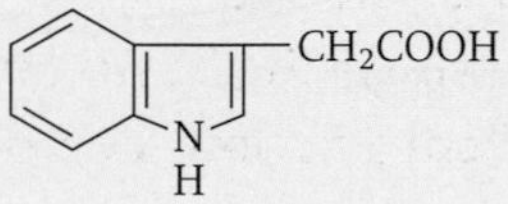

● **Figure 6.48** The molecular structure of indole 3-acetic acid, IAA.

Auxin synthesised in the apical bud is transported down the stem to the lateral buds. One theory to explain apical dominance is that auxin is present in the lateral buds in a concentration that inhibits their growth. Removal of the apical bud causes the concentration of auxin in the lateral buds to drop, so that they can now grow. But the experimental evidence for this is contradictory and uncertain. At the moment, it is not understood how this effect occurs, or exactly what role auxin has in it. It seems likely that other plant growth substances, such as **cytokinins** and **abscisic acid** are also involved (see later).

Gibberellins and stem elongation

Gibberellins are plant growth regulators that are synthesised in most parts of plants. They are present in especially high concentrations in young leaves and in seeds, and are also found in stems, where they have an important role in determining their growth.

The height of some plants is partly controlled by their genes. For example, tallness in peas is affected by a gene with two alleles; if the dominant allele is present, the plants can grow tall, but plants homozygous for the recessive allele always remain short. The dominant allele of this gene regulates the synthesis of an enzyme that catalyses the synthesis of an active form of gibberellin, GA_1. If only the recessive allele is present, then the plant contains only inactive forms of gibberellin. Active gibberellin stimulates cell division and cell elongation in the stem, so causing the plant to grow tall.

Applying active gibberellin to plants which would normally remain short, such as cabbages, can stimulate them to grow tall. As yet, little is known about how gibberellins cause these effects.

Gibberellins and seed germination

In some seeds, gibberellins are involved in the control of germination. *Figure 6.49* shows the structure of a barley seed. When the seed is shed from the parent plant, it is in a state of **dormancy**; that is it contains very little water and is metabolically inactive. This is useful, as it allows the seed to survive in adverse conditions, such as through a cold winter, only germinating when the temperature rises in spring.

The seed contains an **embryo**, which will grow to form the new plant when the seed germinates. The embryo is surrounded by **endosperm tissue** which is a food store, containing the polysaccharide starch. On the outer edge of the endosperm is a protein-rich **aleurone layer**. The whole seed is covered by a tough, waterproof, protective layer.

When the seed absorbs water, this stimulates the production of gibberellin by the embryo, and the gibberellin in turn stimulates the synthesis of **amylase** by the cells in the aleurone layer. The amylase hydrolyses the starch molecules in the endosperm, converting them to soluble maltose molecules. These are converted to glucose and are transported to the embryo, providing a source of carbohydrate that can be respired to provide energy as the embryo begins to grow.

Gibberellin causes these effects by regulating genes that are involved in the synthesis of amylase. In barley seeds, it has

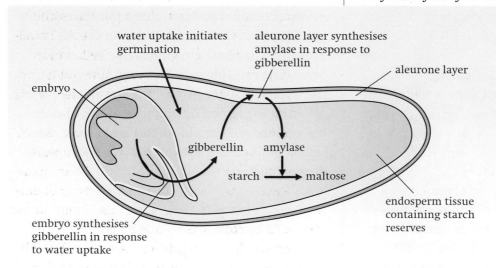

● **Figure 6.49** Longitudinal section through a barley seed, showing how secretion of gibberellins by the embryo results in the mobilisation of starch reserves during germination.

been shown that application of gibberellin causes an increase in the transcription of mRNA coding for amylase.

Abscisic acid and stomatal closure

Abscisic acid, otherwise known as **ABA**, has been found in a very wide variety of plants, including ferns and mosses as well as flowering plants. It can be found in every part of the plant, and is synthesised in almost all cells that possess chloroplasts or amyloplasts (organelles like chloroplasts, but that contain large starch grains and no chlorophyll).

One role of ABA that is well documented is as a so-called **stress hormone**. If a plant is subjected to difficult environmental conditions, such as very high temperatures, or very reduced water supplies, then it responds by secreting ABA. In a plant in drought conditions, the concentration of ABA in the leaves can rise to 40 times that which would normally be present. This high concentration of ABA causes the stomata to close, which reduces loss of water vapour from the leaf.

In chapter 2, we saw how the guard cells control the opening and closure of stomata (*figure 2.9*). Each guard cell has a relatively thick cell wall on the side next to the stoma (the opening between them), and a relatively thin wall on the opposite side. When the guard cells become turgid, they expand into a curved shape, because the inner, thick cell wall resists expansion more than the outer wall. This leaves a space between them – the open stoma. When the guard cells lose water, they become flaccid and collapse together so that the stoma is closed.

The increase in turgor of the guard cells is brought about by the activities of transporter proteins in their plasma membranes. An ATP-powered 'proton pump' in the membrane actively transports hydrogen ions, H^+, out of the guard cells. The lowering of hydrogen ion concentration inside the cells causes potassium channels to open in the plasma membrane, and potassium ions, K^+, move into the cell. They do this because the removal of H^+ ions has left the inside of the cell negatively charged compared with the outside, and as the K^+ ions have a positive charge, they are drawn down an electrical gradient towards the negatively charged region.

The extra K^+ ions inside the guard cells lower the solute potential, and therefore the water potential. Now there is a water potential gradient between the outside and the inside of the cell, so water moves in by osmosis. This increases the turgor of the guard cells, and the stoma opens.

It is not known exactly how ABA achieves the closure of stomata, but the fact that the response is very fast indicates that, unlike the effect of gibberellins in seeds, it is not done by regulating the expression of genes. If ABA is applied to a leaf, the stomata close within just a few minutes. It seems that guard cells have ABA receptors on their plasma membranes, and it is possible that when ABA binds with these it inhibits the proton pump. This would stop the hydrogen ions being pumped out, so potassium ions and water would not enter, and the guard cells would become flaccid and close the stomata.

Leaf abscission

Abscisic acid takes its name from the fact that it was thought to be closely involved in leaf or fruit fall, which is known as **abscission**.

Some trees regularly drop their leaves at certain times in year. In Britain, for example, as in many other temperate countries, deciduous trees such as oak and ash drop their leaves in autumn, as the days grow shorter and cooler.

The leaves fall because the leaf stalk, or petiole, breaks off from the stem (*figure 6.50*). First, useful substances are withdrawn from the leaves and taken back into the stem; this involves the breakdown of some of the pigments in the leaves, changing their green colour to yellow, golds and reds. An **abscission zone** forms where the petiole meets the stem, made up of two layers of cells. Nearest to the leaf is the **separation layer**, which is made of small cells with quite thin cell walls. Nearest to the stem is the **protective layer**, made up of cells whose walls contain **suberin**. (Suberin is a waxy, waterproof substance, also found in the cell walls of cork cells in tree bark.)

Enzymes then break down the cell walls in the separation layer, and the petiole breaks at this point. The protective layer remains, forming a 'scar' on the stem where the leaf used to be. These leaf scars can sometimes be very visible. For example, they form the characteristic horseshoe shapes on twigs of horse chestnut trees.

We still do not know exactly what controls leaf abscission, but it does now seem that abscisic acid has very little to do with it! Abscisic acid does appear to be involved in the senescence (aging) of leaves, but not directly in their falling from the plant. Auxin is a much stronger candidate for this role. Abscission is usually accompanied by a drop in auxin concentration in the leaf, and in many instances abscission can be prevented by applying auxin in the early stages of the process. It is used for this purpose in citrus orchards, where auxin is sprayed onto the trees to prevent the fruit from falling until it can be harvested. Confusingly, however, high concentrations of auxin, applied later, can actually *promote* fruit drop! It is sometimes sprayed in this way onto olive or apple trees to thin the fruit crop, if it looks as though there will be too many small fruits instead of fewer, larger ones.

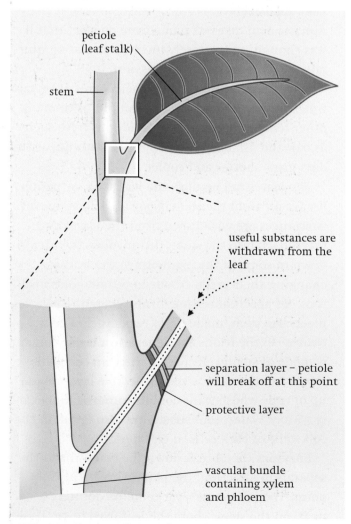

petiole
(leaf stalk)

stem

useful substances are
withdrawn from the
leaf

separation layer – petiole
will break off at this point

protective layer

vascular bundle
containing xylem
and phloem

● **Figure 6.50** Leaf fall.

SUMMARY

◆ Animals and plants have internal communication systems that allow information to pass between different parts of their bodies, and so help them to respond to changes in their external or internal environments.

◆ Mammals keep their internal environment relatively constant, so providing steady and appropriate conditions within which cells can carry out their activities. This is known as homeostasis.

◆ Information transfer and control systems involve receptors and effectors. Regulatory control systems, such as those involved in homeostasis, also involve negative feedback.

◆ Toxic waste products of metabolism, especially carbon dioxide and urea, are removed from the body by the process of excretion. Urea is the main nitrogenous excretory product, formed by the deamination of excess amino acids in the liver. Urea is excreted in solution in water, as urine.

◆ The kidneys regulate the concentration of various substances in the body fluids, by excreting appropriate amounts of them. Each kidney is made up of thousands of nephrons and their associated blood vessels. The kidneys produce urine by ultrafiltration and reabsorption, plus some secretion of unwanted substances. Different regions of a nephron have different functions, and this is reflected in the structure of their walls.

◆ Blood is brought to the glomerulus in the cup of the renal capsule of the nephron in an afferent arteriole. High hydrostatic pressure in the glomerulus forces substances through the capillary walls, the basement membrane and the wall of the renal capsule into the nephron. The basement membrane acts as a filter, allowing only small molecules through. Most reabsorption occurs in the proximal convoluted tubule, by diffusion and active transport, and also in the distal convoluted tubule and collecting duct. The loop of Henle acts as a counter-current multiplier, producing high concentrations of salt in the medulla which can draw out water from the collecting duct and produce a concentrated urine.

◆ The water content of the blood is controlled by changing the amount of water excreted by the urine. This is done by regulating the permeability of the walls of the collecting ducts to water, and hence the amount of water reabsorbed from the collecting ducts into the blood. The permeability is altered by the hormone ADH, which is secreted by the posterior pituitary gland in response to stimulation of osmoreceptors in the hypothalamus.

◆ Hormones are chemicals that are made in endocrine glands and transported in blood plasma to their target cells, where they bind to specific receptors and so affect the behaviour of the cells.

◆ Blood glucose levels are controlled by the action of insulin and glucagon, which are secreted by the islets of Langerhans in the pancreas and affect liver and muscle cells. Negative feedback keeps the blood glucose level from varying too much from the norm.

◆ Neurones are cells adapted for the rapid transmission of electrical signals. Sensory neurones transmit signals from receptors to the central nervous system (brain and spinal cord); motor neurones transmit signals from the central nervous system to effectors; intermediate neurones transmit signals within the central nervous system. In vertebrates, the axons of many neurones are insulated by a myelin sheath which speeds up transmission.

◆ Signals are transmitted as action potentials. A resting neurone has a negative potential inside compared with outside. An action potential is a fleeting reversal of this potential, caused by changes in permeability of the plasma membrane to potassium and sodium ions. Action potentials are always the same size. Information about the strength of a stimulus is given by the frequency of action potentials produced.

◆ Action potentials may be initiated within the brain or at a receptor. Receptors respond to information from the environment. Environmental changes result in permeability changes in the membranes of receptor cells, which in turn produce changes in potential difference across the membrane. If sufficiently great, this will trigger an action potential.

◆ Neurones do not make direct contact with one another, but are separated by a very small gap called a synaptic cleft. Impulses pass across this gap as bursts of transmitter substance, released by the presynaptic neurone when an action potential arrives.

Any one neurone within the central nervous system is likely to have at least several hundred synapses with other neurones, some of which will be stimulatory and some inhibitory. This allows integration within the nervous system, resulting in complex and variable patterns of behaviour, and in learning and memory.

◆ Plants produce several chemicals known as plant growth substances, that are involved in the control of growth and responses to environmental changes. Auxin is synthesised mainly in growing tips of shoots and roots, and appears to be involved in preventing the growth of lateral buds when an intact and active apical bud is present. It is also involved in leaf abscission. Gibberellin is synthesised in young leaves and in seeds. It stimulates growth of stems and germination of seeds. Abscisic acid is synthesised by any cells in a plant that contain chloroplasts or amyloplasts, especially in stress conditions. The presence of large concentrations of abscisic acid in leaves causes stomata to close.

Questions

1 Discuss the ways in which the structures of different parts of a nephron are adapted to their functions.

2 The table shows information about the relative thickness of the medulla of the kidneys, the percentage of the loops of Henle which are long rather than short, and the relative concentration of the urine for three mammals.

Discuss these data.

Mammal	Relative thickness of medulla	Percentage of long loops of Henle	Relative concentration of urine
beaver	1.3	0	650
human	3.0	16	1400
desert mouse	10.7	100	5800

3 Discuss the roles of active transport in the reabsorption of glucose and water in a kidney nephron.

4 Compare the mechanisms for controlling blood glucose levels and water content in body fluids.

5 Most vertebrates use hormones similar to mammalian ADH, to help with water regulation. These hormones do not always work in the same way as described in this chapter. Suggest how each of the following might help the animal to conserve water.

a In reptiles and amphibians the hormones not only increase the permeability of the distal tubules and collecting ducts to water, but also reduce glomerular filtration rate.

b In some amphibians the hormone increases the permeability of the outer surface of the skin to sodium ions.

c In toads the hormone increases the permeability of the walls of the urinary bladder to water.

6 Discuss the ways in which the structure of a motor neurone is related to its function.

7 Compare and contrast the ways in which the nervous system and the endocrine system bring about communication between different parts of the mammalian body.

8 Compare and contrast animal hormones with plant growth substances.

To answer the following questions, you will need to bring together information from other areas of your course, as well as from this chapter.

9 a Describe the structure of a cell membrane.

b Outline the roles of (i) respiration and (ii) carrier proteins in the maintenance of the resting potential in a neurone.

10 a With reference to enzyme function, explain why it is important for mammals to control the temperature and pH of their body fluids.

b Explain how a large increase in blood glucose concentration could affect the water potential of body fluids, and discuss the effects that this could have on body cells.

11 a Describe how genetic engineering has been used to manufacture insulin on a large scale.

b Explain why some diabetics may need to inject insulin, and discuss the advantages to them of using insulin produced by genetic engineering.

12 a Describe how ions such as Na^+ and Ca^{2+} can pass across cell membranes.

b Compare the mechanism by which insulin is released from β cells with that by which transmitter substance is released from a presynaptic neurone.

DNA triplet codes

The table shows all the possible triplets of bases in a DNA molecule and what each codes for. The 3-letter abbreviations for each amino acid are, in most cases, the first three letters of their full name.

First position	Second position				Third position
	A	G	T	C	
A	Phe	Ser	Tyr	Cys	A
	Phe	Ser	Tyr	Cys	G
	Leu	Ser	STOP	STOP	T
	Leu	Ser	STOP	Trp	C
G	Leu	Pro	His	Arg	A
	Leu	Pro	His	Arg	G
	Leu	Pro	Gln	Arg	T
	Leu	Pro	Gln	Arg	C
T	Ile	Thr	Asn	Ser	A
	Ile	Thr	Asn	Ser	G
	Ile	Thr	Lys	Arg	T
	Met	Thr	Lys	Arg	C
C	Val	Ala	Asp	Gly	A
	Val	Ala	Asp	Gly	G
	Val	Ala	Glu	Gly	T
	Val	Ala	Glu	Gly	C

Answers to self-assessment questions

Chapter 1

1.1 $ADP + P_i (H_3PO_4) + 30.5\,kJ \rightarrow ATP + H_2O$

1.2 In polynucleotides, the bases are linked by covalent bonds between phosphate groups and sugars. In NAD, the link is by a covalent bond between two phosphate groups.

1.3 By decarboxylation, citrate, a six-carbon compound, can be converted to five-carbon and four-carbon compounds, finally giving oxaloacetate which can act as an acceptor for an incoming two-carbon unit from acetyl coenzyme A giving citrate again.

1.4 Reduced NAD per glucose:

from glycolysis	2
from the link reaction (1 × 2)	2
from the Krebs cycle (3 × 2)	6
Total	10

Reduced FAD per glucose:

from the Krebs cycle (1 × 2)	2

Remember that two molecules of pyruvate go through the link reaction, and that there are two turns of the Krebs cycle for each molecule of glucose respired.

1.5 Each reduced NAD produces 2.5 ATP in oxidative phosphorylation; each reduced FAD produces 1.5 ATP.

Oxidative phosphorylation gives 28 ATP per molecule of glucose, as follows:

via 2 reduced NAD from glycolysis (2 × 2.5)	5
via 2 reduced NAD from the link reaction (2 × 2.5)	5
via 2 reduced FAD from the Krebs cycle (2 × 1.5)	3
via 6 reduced NAD from the Krebs cycle (6 × 2.5)	15

1.6 Only 2 ATP (1 ATP per turn) are made directly in the Krebs cycle.

Hydrogens are lost at four different stages of each turn of the cycle. Once these have been taken up by hydrogen carriers they can be transferred to the reactions of oxidative phosphorylation to give much more ATP.

1.7 Points should include: the link reaction and Krebs cycle take place in the liquid matrix where enzymes and substrates can freely interact; mitochondria in active tissues are large and have many cristae; the large surface area of cristae for the layout of the sequences/'production lines' of carriers needed for electron transfer; the importance of the membranes and the intermembrane space for building up a hydrogen ion gradient in chemiosmosis; the role of ATP synthase.

1.8 $C_{18}H_{36}O_2 + 26O_2 \rightarrow 18CO_2 + 18H_2O + energy$

$$RQ = \frac{CO_2}{O_2} = \frac{18}{26} = 0.69$$

1.9 Take readings of oxygen consumption at one temperature, say $15\,°C$, including replicate readings to give a mean value. Increase the temperature to, say, $25\,°C$. Leave the organisms at that temperature for about 10 minutes for the rate of respiration to reach an equilibrium. Take readings as before. Repeat at other temperatures.

Chapter 2

2.1 a Both chlorophyll a and b have absorption peaks in the blue (400–450 nm) and red (650 nm) wavelengths. The carotenoids also have two peaks in the blue wavelengths. The action spectrum also peaks in the blue and red wavelengths. It is these absorbed wavelengths that provide energy for photosynthesis.

   b Different pigments have different absorption spectra. The maxima of the action spectrum do not closely match the absorption spectrum of any single pigment. Although the peaks at the two ends of the absorption spectrum are of similar height, the action spectrum has a larger peak at 650 nm. The action spectrum does not perfectly match the absorption spectra since not all absorbed light is used in photosynthesis.

2.2 a The chloroplasts absorb light and split water (photolysis) generating hydrogen ions. This reduces DCPIP from blue to colourless, so that the colorimeter reading falls.

b The chloroplasts in light reduce DCPIP at a steady rate. The chloroplasts in the dark for five minutes do not reduce DCPIP during that time. When placed in the light, reduction occurs at a slightly slower rate. (A possible reason for this is gradual loss of activity by isolated chloroplasts because of damage.)

2.3 The Hill reaction shows that chloroplasts have 'reducing power' necessary to reduce fixed carbon dioxide to carbohydrate. They produce hydrogen ions. This is seen by their reduction of a coloured redox agent (blue DCPIP) to colourless.

2.4 Thylakoid membranes provide a large surface area for many pigments, enzymes and electron carriers and for light absorption.

The arrangement of pigments into photosystems provides efficient light absorption.

Grana with ATP synthase allow ATP synthesis.

The stroma bathes all the membranes and holds the enzymes, reactants and products of the Calvin cycle.

2.5 a Experiments 1 and 2 differ only in temperature and show the limiting effect of temperature. The photosynthetic rate is approximately doubled by each 10 °C temperature rise, both in initial increase in light intensity and at light saturation. The effect is via the light-independent stage since increased temperature increases the rate of these reactions.

b Experiments 1 and 3 differ in carbon dioxide concentration and show limiting effect of that concentration. A tenfold increase of external carbon dioxide concentration produces an approximate doubling of the rate of photosynthesis. The limiting effect is not only external carbon dioxide concentration but the rate at which the leaf can be supplied with carbon dioxide. This depends on the steepness of the diffusion gradient and the permeability of the leaf.

Chapter 3

3.1 a *Eotetranychus* is a primary consumer, while *Typhlodromus* is a secondary consumer.

b Energy is lost as it is transferred between trophic levels. There is therefore less energy to support secondary consumers than primary consumers, so the total biomass of secondary consumers is less than that of primary consumers.

3.2 At the top of the shore, both *Chthamalus* and *Balanus* cannot live higher because here they would be covered by water for only a very short time each day, and they cannot tolerate desiccation or wide temperature fluctuations. *Chthamalus* tolerates these better than *Balanus* and so can live a little higher up the shore.

At the bottom of its range *Chthamalus* has to compete with *Balanus* for space on the rocks, and in this area *Balanus* is the better competitor. So interspecific competition limits the lower range of *Chthamalus*.

At the bottom of its range, where it is covered by water for long periods of time, *Balanus* is more exposed to predation by dogwhelks, and also to competition with algae for space on the rocks. So interspecific competition and predation limit the lower range of *Balanus*.

3.3 Answers will depend on the species chosen.

3.4 a Species cover is the mean percentage cover calculated from the results in all the quadrats. To work this out, add up the percentage cover in each quadrat, and divide by the number of quadrats.

$(25 + 20 + 10 + 25 + 45 + 30 + 15 + 20) \div 12 = 15.8\%$

As the percentage cover in each quadrat was obviously estimated only to the nearest 5%, it is unrealistic to suggest that we can calculate it to one decimal place! It would therefore be sensible to round this figure up to 16%, or even to the nearest 5%, which would give an answer of 15%.

b Species frequency is the percentage of the quadrats in which the species was found. It was found in 8 out of the 12 quadrats, so species frequency is

$(8 \div 12) \times 100 = 66.67\%$

3.5 Where animals graze, their urine and faeces return nitrogen to the soil. When grassland is cut, the nitrogen contained in the grass is removed for hay or silage, and lost to the ecosystem.

Chapter 4

4.1 **a** prophase I (in fact, they pair before this, during interphase but can only be seen for the first time during prophase)

b prophase I

c anaphase I

d anaphase II

e telophase I

4.2 Meiosis could not take place in a triploid, 3n, cell, because there is an odd number of each chromosome so they will not be able to pair up.

In theory, meiosis can take place in a tetraploid, 4n, cell because there is an even number of each kind of chromosome, so they can each find a partner to pair up with. In practice, meiosis is often very difficult in a 4n cell because, if there are four homologous chromosomes present, they all tend to join up with each other. Crossing over between chromatids of different chromosomes results in an inextricable tangle, so meiosis cannot proceed effectively.

4.3 6

4.4 3 homozygous, 3 heterozygous

4.5 **a** Symbols should use the same capital letter, with a different superscript for each allele. For example:

C^R to represent the allele for red coat

C^W to represent the allele for white coat

b $C^R C^R$ red coat

$C^R C^W$ roan coat

$C^W C^W$ white coat

c (i) Red Poll × roan gives $C^R C^R$ (red coat) and $C^R C^W$ (roan coat) in a ratio of 1 : 1.

(ii) Roan × roan gives $C^R C^R$ (red coat), $C^R C^W$ (roan coat) and $C^W C^W$ (white coat) in a ratio of 1 : 2 : 1.

4.6 Symbols should use the same letter of the alphabet, using the capital letter to represent the dominant allele, and the small letter to represent the recessive allele. For example:

B to represent the allele for black eyes

b to represent the allele for red eyes.

The cross would be expected to produce Bb (black-eyed mice) and bb (red-eyed mice) in a ratio of 1 : 1.

4.7 If a cross between an unspotted and spotted plant can sometimes produce offspring which are all unspotted, then unspotted must be the dominant allele. Suitable symbols could be:

A to represent the dominant unspotted allele;

a to represent the recessive spotted allele.

(U and u or S and s are not good choices, as they are difficult to distinguish.)

An unspotted plant could therefore have either the genotype AA or Aa.

A spotted plant could only have the genotype aa.

Therefore, a cross between spotted and unspotted could either be:

Parents　　AA × aa

Offspring　　Aa

or it could be:

Parents　　Aa × aa

Offspring　　Aa and aa in a ratio of 1 : 1.

4.8 She may be right, but not necessarily. It is true that if her bitch were homozygous for the dominant allele for black spots all of her eggs would contain this dominant allele, and therefore all of her offspring would be black no matter what the genotype of the male parent. If the bitch was heterozygous, it might be expected that a mating with a homozygous recessive dog would produce black-spotted and brown-spotted offspring in a ratio of 1 : 1. However, as only three puppies were born, it may just be chance that no brown-spotted puppy was born. The breeder would need to produce more litters from the bitch before she could be sure of her dog's genotype.

4.9 The child with blood group O must have the genotype $I^o I^o$. Therefore, each parent must have one I^o allele. The genotypes are therefore:

Man and the child with blood group B	$I^B I^o$
Woman and the child with blood group A	$I^A I^o$
Child with blood group O	$I^o I^o$

4.10 Suitable symbols for these four alleles could be:

C^A	to represent the agouti allele
C^g	to represent the chinchilla (grey) allele
C^h	to represent the Himalayan allele
C^a	to represent the albino allele

a

$C^A C^A$	agouti
$C^A C^g$	agouti
$C^A C^h$	agouti
$C^A C^a$	agouti
$C^g C^g$	chinchilla
$C^g C^h$	chinchilla
$C^g C^a$	chinchilla
$C^h C^h$	Himalayan
$C^h C^a$	Himalayan
$C^a C^a$	albino

b (i) The genotype of the albino parent must be $C^a C^a$, as the allele C^a is recessive to everything else. Each of the offspring will therefore get a C^a allele from this parent. The offspring are all chinchilla, so their genotypes must all be $C^g C^a$. This means that the chinchilla parent must have given a C^g allele to each offspring, so the chinchilla parent almost certainly has the genotype $C^g C^g$. If it had any other allele in its genotype, this would be expected to show in the phenotype of its offspring.

   When the $C^g C^a$ offspring are crossed, they will produce genotypes of $C^g C^g$, $C^g C^a$ and $C^a C^a$ in a ratio of 1:2:1, that is a ratio of chinchilla to albino in a ratio of 3:1. This is close enough to the actual ratio of 4 chinchilla to 2 albino, as with these very small numbers it is unlikely for ratios to work out exactly.

   (ii) Following similar reasoning to that in (i) above, the agouti rabbit probably has the genotype $C^A C^h$ and the Himalayan parent the genotype $C^h C^h$. This would produce agouti and Himalayan offspring in a ratio of 1:1.

   (iii) As chinchilla rabbits are produced in the first generation, at least one of the agouti parents must carry a chinchilla allele. As a Himalayan rabbit is produced in the second generation, one of the original parents must carry a Himalayan allele. The first cross is therefore:

Parental phenotype	agouti		agouti	
Parental genotype	$C^A C^h$		$C^A C^g$	
Gametes	C^A or C^h		C^A or C^g	
Offspring	$C^A C^A$	$C^A C^h$	$C^A C^g$	$C^h C^g$
	agouti	agouti	agouti	chinchilla

The second cross, between two chinchilla rabbits with the genotype $C^h C^g$, would be expected to produce offspring with the genotypes $C^h C^h$, $C^h C^g$ and $C^g C^g$ in a ratio of 1:2:1, so giving the phenotypic ratio of 3 chinchilla:1 Himalayan.

4.11

Parental phenotype	female		male
Parental genotype	XX		XY
Gametes	all X		X or Y
Offspring	XX	or	XY
	female		male

4.12 a No. The son will receive a Y chromosome from his father, which cannot carry a haemophilia allele.

b Yes. The man could pass on his haemophilia allele to a daughter, who could then pass it on to a son.

4.13 a Suitable symbols could be:

X^N	allele for normal colour vision
X^n	allele for red-green colour blindness
$X^N X^N$	normal female
$X^N X^n$	carrier (normal) female
$X^n X^n$	female with colour blindness
$X^N Y$	normal male
$X^n Y$	male with colour blindness

b

Parental phenotypes	normal	normal
Parental genotypes	X^N Y	X^N X^n
Gametes	X^N Y	X^N X^n

Offspring genotypes and phenotypes

	Genotypes of eggs	
	X^N	X^n
Genotypes of sperm X^N	$X^N X^N$ normal female	$X^N X^n$ carrier female
Y	$X^N Y$ normal male	$X^n Y$ male with colour blindness

This can happen if the woman is heterozygous. The affected child will be male.

c Yes, if the mother has at least one allele for colour blindness, and the father has colour blindness.

4.14 **a** Male cats cannot be tortoiseshell because a tortoiseshell cat has two alleles of this gene. As the gene is on the X chromosome, and male cats have one X chromosome and one Y chromosome, then they can only have one allele of the gene.

b

Parental phenotypes	orange male	tortoiseshell female
Parental genotypes	$X^{C^O}Y$	$X^{C^O}X^{C^B}$
Gametes	X^{C^O} Y	X^{C^O} X^{C^B}

Offspring genotypes and phenotypes

	Genotypes of eggs	
Genotypes of sperm	X^{C^O}	X^{C^B}
X^{C^O}	$X^{C^O}X^{C^O}$ orange female	$X^{C^B}X^{C^O}$ tortoiseshell female
Y	$X^{C^O}Y$ orange male	$X^{C^B}Y$ black male

The kittens would therefore be expected to be in the ratio of 1 orange female : 1 tortoiseshell female : 1 orange male : 1 black male.

4.15 **a** Independent assortment results from the random alignment of the pairs of homologous chromosomes on the equator during metaphase I. It ensures that the chromosomes carrying the A or a alleles behave quite independently from those carrying the D or d alleles. This means that allele A can end up in a gamete with either D or d, and allele a can also end up in a gamete with either D or d. Thus independent assortment is responsible for the fact that each parent can produce four different types of gamete, AD, Ad, aD and ad.

b Random fertilisation means that it is equally likely that any one male gamete will fuse with any female gamete. This results in the 16 genotypes shown in the square. Thus random fertilisation is responsible for the different genotypes of the offspring, and the ratios in which they are found.

4.16 **a** AaBb and Aabb in a ratio of 1:1

b GgHh, Gghh, ggHh and gghh in a ratio of 1:1:1:1

c All TtYy

d EeFf, Eeff, eeFf and eeff in a ratio of 1:1:1:1

4.17 **a** They would all have genotype GgTt, and phenotype grey fur and long tail.

b Grey long, grey short, white long, white short in a ratio of 9:3:3:1.

4.18 Let T represent the allele for tall stem, t the allele for short stem, L^G the allele for green leaves and L^W the allele for white leaves.

Parents	TTL^GL^G	ttL^GL^W
Gametes	TL^G	tL^G or tL^W
Offspring	TtL^GL^G, TtL^GL^W in a ratio of 1:1.	

4.19 **a** If B represents the allele for black eyes and b represents the allele for red eyes, L represents the allele for long fur and l represents the allele for short fur, then the four possible genotypes of an animal with black eyes and long fur are

BBLL, BbLL, BBLl and BbLl.

b Perform a test cross, that is breed the animal with an animal showing both recessive characteristics. If the offspring show one of the recessive characteristics, then the 'unknown' genotype must be heterozygous for that characteristic.

4.20 The expected ratio would be 9 grey long : 3 grey short : 3 white long : 1 white short.

The total number of offspring is 80, so we would expect 9/16 of these to be grey long, and so on.

Expected numbers:

$9 \div 16 \times 80 = 45$ grey long

$3 \div 16 \times 80 = 15$ grey short

$3 \div 16 \times 80 = 15$ white long

$1 \div 16 \times 80 = 5$ white short

Now complete a table like the one on page 60.

Phenotypes of animals	grey, long	grey, short	white, long	white, short
Observed number (O)	54	4	4	18
Expected ratio	9	3	3	1
Expected number (E)	45	15	15	5
O – E	+9	–11	–11	+13
$(O - E)^2$	81	121	121	169
$(O - E)^2/E$	1.8	8.1	8.1	33.8
$\Sigma(O - E)^2/E = 51.8$ $\chi^2 = 51.8$				

This is a huge value for χ^2.

Now look at *table 4.1* on page 60. We have four classes of data, so there are 3 degrees of freedom. Looking along this line, we can see that our value for χ^2 is much greater than any of the numbers there, and certainly well above the value of 7.82, which is the one indicating a probability of 0.05 that the difference between the observed and expected results is due to chance. Our value is way off the right hand end of the table, so we can be certain that there is a **significant difference** between our observed and expected results. Something must be going on that we had not predicted.

(Note: if you study *Applications of Genetics* later in your course, you will find out what may be causing these rather unexpected results!)

4.21 The Human Genome Project aims to identify all of the genes on the human chromosomes. If the base sequence of the alleles that cause the inherited disease are discovered, then a sample of DNA from each prospective parent can be taken and tested to see if either or both of them have this allele. They then have the fullest possible information about the likelihood of any of their children having the disease. It may even be possible to treat or prevent the disease. However, living with this extra information may be more stressful than not knowing and it might disadvantage them when dealing with life or health insurance companies.

4.22 Synthesising enzymes which have no use would be a waste of materials (amino acids) and energy.

Chapter 5

5.1 Characteristics are passed from parents to offspring in their genes. Variation caused by the environment does not change the DNA of an organism.

5.2 a There seems to be no selection pressure against unusual colours, as there are no predators.
   b Possibilities include ability to cope with a limited food or water supply, ability to cope with the limited breeding space, and susceptibility to disease such as myxomatosis if this is present on the island.

5.3 a The more frequently antibiotics are used, the more frequently resistant bacteria will be selected for. If antibiotic use is infrequent, then other selection pressures will be more important in bacterial populations, decreasing the likelihood of resistant bacteria surviving.
   b Changing the antibiotic changes the selection pressure. Different strains of bacteria will be selected for when a different antibiotic is used, decreasing the likelihood of a resistant strain for each antibiotic becoming widespread.
   c It is far less likely that any individual bacterium will be resistant to two antibiotics than to any single antibiotic, so decreasing the chance of any bacteria surviving in an environment where two antibiotics are used together.

Chapter 6

6.1 a From the glomerulus.
   b Proteins.
   c It will increase the solute concentration of the blood plasma therefore lowering its water potential and increasing the water potential gradient between the filtrate and the blood.

6.2 A large percentage (60%) of the water in the fluid is reabsorbed in the proximal convoluted tubule; thus the amount of water in which the urea is dissolved decreases. This increases the concentration of urea in the fluid.

6.3 **a** Flow rate is highest at the beginning of the proximal convoluted tubule, where fluid is entering via filtration into the renal capsule. As the fluid flows along the proximal convoluted tubule, a large percentage of it is reabsorbed, thus decreasing its volume. There is thus less fluid to flow, so less passes a given point in unit time: in other words, its flow rate decreases.

This reabsorption continues all along the nephron, which is why the flow rate continues to drop. The rate of flow decreases rapidly in the collecting duct, as a high proportion of water may be reabsorbed here.

b (i) Glucose concentration drops rapidly to zero as the fluid passes through the proximal convoluted tubule, because all of it is reabsorbed into the blood at this stage.

(ii) Urea concentration increases because water is reabsorbed from the tubule.

(iii) The concentration of sodium ions remains constant in the proximal convoluted tubule, as, although some sodium is reabsorbed here, this is balanced by the reabsorption of water. In the loop of Henle, the counter-current multiplier builds up sodium ion concentration in the lower parts of the loop; the concentration drops as you pass up the ascending limb towards the distal convoluted tubule, as sodium ions are lost from the tubule. In the distal convoluted tubule, sodium ions are actively pumped out of the tubule, so you might expect their concentration to drop. However, this is counterbalanced by the continued removal of water from the tubule, which results in an increasing concentration.

(iv) As for sodium ions, until the distal convoluted tubule, where potassium ions are actively transported into the tubule, so increasing their concentration more than that of sodium.

6.4 There are many possible ways in which this flow diagram could be constructed. It should show the following: input (change in blood water concentration) to sensor (osmoreceptor cells); resulting in secretion of ADH from posterior pituitary if water concentration low; producing output (change in rate of water reabsorption) by effector (walls of collecting duct); and negative feedback to sensor.

6.5 The adrenal glands may continue to secrete adrenaline over a long period, for as long as the stimulus to do so continues.

6.6 The plasma membrane is a bilayer of phospholipids. Steroids can dissolve in these lipids, and so pass through.

6.7 **a** In negative feedback, a change initiates a response that brings things back to normal. So, in the case of blood glucose concentration, a rise in the concentration brings mechanisms into play that reduce it.

b The α and β cells in the islets of Langerhans in the pancreas.

c The effectors are the α and β cells themselves (because they respond by secreting or not secreting glucagon and insulin), and also the cells in the liver and muscles.

6.8 The lack of insulin, or the lack of response to insulin, means that cells either do not take up extra glucose when it is in excess, or they do not convert it to glycogen stores.

6.9 **a** Insulin is a protein. Its molecules would be hydrolysed to amino acids in the digestive system.

b People with non-insulin-dependent diabetes are encouraged to test their blood or urine regularly for glucose. They can adjust their diet accordingly. They should eat small amounts of carbohydrate fairly regularly, rather than large quantities at any one time. High-sugar foods, such as confectionary, should be avoided, as these may result in a rapid and dangerous rise in blood glucose levels.

6.10 A wide variety of answers is possible, some of which are suggested below:

Stimulus	Receptor	Effector	Response
sudden loud sound	hair cells in cochlea of ear	various muscles especially in legs	rapid contraction producing movement
smell of food cooking	chemoreceptors in nose	salivary glands	secretion of saliva
sharp tap on knee	stretch receptors	thigh muscle	contraction, causing lower leg to be raised

6.11 **a** A receptor potential is an electrical potential generated in a receptor such as a Pacinian corpuscle. It is produced by the opening of sodium channels which results in a depolarisation of the nerve ending, that is a less negative potential inside the axon than when it is at rest.

b Increasing pressure produces an increasing receptor potential. At low levels of pressure, a small increase in pressure results in a relatively large increase in receptor potential. At higher levels of pressure, the increase in receptor potential is less. (The functional significance of this pattern, which is found in most receptors, could be discussed; it results in a relatively high level of sensitivity to low-level stimuli as long as they are above the critical threshold).

c The threshold receptor potential is the smallest receptor potential at which an action potential is generated.

d The greater the strength of the stimulus applied, the greater the frequency of action potentials generated.

6.12 **a** At the synapse, vesicles of transmitter substance are only present in the presynaptic neurone, not in the postsynaptic neurone.

b Repeated action potentials may cause the release of transmitter substance into the cleft at a greater rate than it can be replaced in the presynaptic neurone.

Glossary

α **cell**	a cell in the islets of Langerhans in the pancreas that senses when blood glucose levels are low and secretes glucagon in response.
abiotic factor	the physical characteristics of a habitat, such as temperature, light intensity and soil pH.
abscisic acid (ABA)	a plant growth regulator that causes closure of stomata in dry conditions, and inhibits seed germination.
abscission	the dropping of leaves or fruits from a plant.
absorption spectrum	a graph of the absorbance of different wavelengths of light by a compound such as a photosynthetic pigment.
accessory pigment	a pigment that is not essential to photosynthesis but which absorbs light of different wavelengths and passes the energy to chlorophyll *a*.
acetylcholine	a transmitter substance found, for example, in the presynaptic neurone at neuromuscular junctions.
acetylcholinesterase	an enzyme that rapidly breaks down acetylcholine at synapses.
action potential	a fleeting reversal of the resting potential across the plasma membrane of a neurone, which rapidly travels along its length.
action spectrum	a graph of the rate of photosynthesis at different wavelengths of light.
activation energy	the energy that must be provided to make a reaction take place.
ADP	adenosine diphosphate.
adrenaline	a hormone secreted by the adrenal glands in times of stress or excitement.
afferent	leading towards, e.g. the afferent blood vessel leads towards a glomerulus.
alcoholic fermentation	anaerobic respiration in which glucose is converted to ethanol.
aleurone layer	a layer of tissue around the endosperm in a cereal seed that synthesises amylase during germination.
allele	a particular variety of a gene.
allopatric speciation	speciation that takes place as a result of two populations living in different places and having no contact with each other.
allopolyploid	possessing more than two sets of chromosomes, where the chromosomes come from two different species.
anabolic reaction	synthesis of complex substances from simpler ones.
antibiotic	a substance produced by a living organism that kills or inhibits the growth of bacteria.
antidiuretic hormone (ADH)	a hormone secreted from the pituitary gland that increases water reabsorption in the kidneys and therefore reduces water loss in urine.
apical dominance	the tendency for the apical bud of a plant to grow, while the lateral buds do not; removal of the apical bud stimulates growth of the lateral buds.
artificial selection	the selection by humans of organisms with desired traits.
ATP	adenosine triphosphate – the universal energy currency of cells.
ATP synthase	the enzyme catalysing the phosphorylation of ADP to ATP.

autopolyploid	possessing more than two sets of chromosomes, where all the sets are from the same species.
autosomes	all the chromosomes except the X and Y (sex) chromosomes.
autotroph	an organism that can trap an inorganic carbon source (carbon dioxide) using energy from light or from chemicals.
auxin	a plant growth substance synthesised in the growing regions of shoots and roots.
axon	a long cytoplasmic process of a neurone, that conducts action potentials away from the cell body.
β cell	a cell in the islets of Langerhans in the pancreas that senses when blood glucose levels are high and secretes insulin in response.
β galactosidase	an enzyme which catalyses the hydrolysis of lactose to glucose and galactose.
binomial	the two-word Latin name (genus plus species) of a species.
biochemical oxygen demand (BOD)	the rate at which oxygen is used up in a sample of water; a high BOD indicates a rapid rate of aerobic respiration by bacteria.
biotic factor	a factor which affects a population or a process, that is caused by other living organisms; examples include competition, predation and parasitism.
Bowman's capsule	*see* renal capsule.
calorimeter	the apparatus in which the energy value of a compound can be measured by burning it in oxygen.
Calvin cycle	a closed pathway of reactions in photosynthesis in which carbon dioxide is fixed into carbohydrate.
cancer	a disease that results from the breakdown of the usual control mechanisms of mitosis.
carotenoid	a yellow, orange or red plant pigment used as an accessory pigment in photosynthesis.
carrying capacity	the maximum size of a population that can be supported sustainably (that is over a long time period) in a particular habitat.
chemiosmosis	the synthesis of ATP using energy stored as a difference in hydrogen ion concentration across a membrane in a chloroplast or mitochondrion.
chi-squared (χ^2) test	a statistical test that can be used to determine if any difference between observed results and expected results is significant, or due to chance.
chitin	a carbohydrate-like substance that is found in fungal cell walls and insect exoskeletons.
chlorophyll	a green pigment responsible for light capture in photosynthesis in algae and higher plants.
chloroplast	the photosynthetic organelle in eukaryotes.
cholinergic synapse	a synapse at which the transmitter substance is acetylcholine.
chromosome mutation	a random and unpredictable change in the structure or number of chromosomes in a cell.
clear-felling	cutting down all the trees in an area of woodland.
climax community	the final community in a succession.
codominance	alleles are said to be codominant when both alleles have an effect on the phenotype of a heterozygous organism.
collecting duct	the last section of a nephron, from which water can be absorbed back into the blood stream before the urine flows into the ureter.
community	all the living organisms in a particular habitat.
competition	when a particular resource is in short supply, organisms requiring that resource are said to compete with each other.
coppicing	cutting down trees or shrubs very close to the ground, leaving only a short trunk or stems called a coppice stool; the plant will regrow from this stool and can be coppiced again in several years' time.

counter-current multiplier	an arrangement in which fluid in adjacent tubes flows in opposite directions, allowing relatively large differences in concentration to be built up.
creatinine	a nitrogenous excretory substance produced from the breakdown of creatine.
crista (*pl.* cristae)	a fold of the inner membrane of the mitochondrial envelope on which are found stalked particles of ATP synthase.
crop rotation	growing different crops in a field in successive years.
crossing over	an event that occurs during meiosis I, when chromatids of two homologous chromosomes break and rejoin so that a part of one chromatid swaps places with the same part of the other.
cytokinins	plant growth regulators that stimulate cell division.
deamination	the breakdown of excess amino acids in the liver, by the removal of the amine group; ammonia and eventually urea are formed from the amine group.
dendrite	a short cytoplasmic process of a neurone, that conducts action potentials towards the cell body.
dendron	a long cytoplasmic process of a neurone, that conducts action potentials towards the cell body.
depolarisation	the reversal of the resting potential across the plasma membrane of a neurone or muscle cell, so that the inside becomes positively charged compared with the outside.
diabetes	an illness in which the pancreas does not make sufficient insulin, or where cells do not respond appropriately to insulin.
dihybrid cross	a genetic cross in which two different genes are considered.
diploid	possessing two complete sets of chromosomes.
directional selection	a type of selection in which the most common varieties of an organism are selected against, resulting in a change in the features of the population.
diuresis	the production of large volumes of dilute urine.
dominance	an allele is said to be dominant when its effect on the phenotype of a heterozygote is identical to its effect in a homozygote.
dormancy	a state of 'suspended animation', in which metabolism is slowed right down, enabling survival in adverse conditions.
ecosystem	all of the living organisms of all species, and all of the non-living components, that are found together in a defined area and that interact with each other.
effector	an organ or tissue that responds to a stimulus, for example a muscle.
efferent	leading away from.
electron transport chain	chain of adjacently arranged carrier molecules in the inner mitochondrial membrane along which electrons pass by redox reactions.
endocrine gland	a gland that secretes its products, which are always hormones, directly into the blood.
endosperm	a tissue made of triploid cells that stores food in some seeds, such as cereal grains.
endothelium	a tissue that lines the inside of a structure, such as the inner surface of a blood vessel or a nephron.
epithelium	a tissue that covers the outside of a structure.
eukaryotic cell	a cell, such as plant or animal cell, that has a nucleus and many membrane-bound organelles.
eutrophication	a process in which enrichment of water with nutrients leads to an increase in algae and bacteria, and a reduction in oxygen content.
excretion	the removal of toxic or excess products of metabolism from the body.

exocrine gland	a gland that secretes substances into a duct, for example the salivary glands.
factor VIII	one of several substances that must be present in blood in order for clotting to occur.
fixation, of nitrogen	the conversion of gaseous nitrogen, N_2, into a more reactive form such as nitrate or ammonia.
gene mutation	a change in the base sequence in part of a DNA molecule.
genotype	the alleles possessed by an organism.
gibberellin	a plant growth regulator that increases growth in genetically dwarf plants, and that stimulates germination.
glomerular filtration rate	the rate at which fluid passes from the glomerular capillaries into the renal capsules in the kidneys.
glomerulus	a knot of capillaries in the 'cup' of a renal capsule.
glucagon	a small peptide hormone secreted by the α cells in the islets of Langerhans in the pancreas that brings about an increase in the blood glucose level.
glycogen	a polysaccharide, made of many glucose molecules linked together, that stores glucose in liver and muscle cells.
glycolysis	the splitting (lysis) of glucose.
granum (*pl.* **grana**)	a stack of thylakoids in a chloroplast.
guard cell	a sausage-shaped epidermal cell found in pairs bounding a stoma and controlling its opening or closure.
haemophilia	a genetic disease in which there is an insufficient amount of a clotting factor, such as factor VIII, in the blood.
haploid	possessing one complete set of chromosomes.
heterotroph	an organism needing a supply of organic molecules as its carbon source.
heterozygous	having two different alleles of a gene.
homeostasis	maintaining a constant environment for the cells within the body.
homologous chromosomes	two chromosomes that carry the same genes in the same positions (loci).
homologous features	features of an organism that appear to have been derived from the same ancestral structure, for example the limbs of vertebrates.
homozygous	having two identical alleles of a gene.
hormone	a substance secreted by an endocrine gland, that is carried in blood plasma to another part of the body where it has an effect.
IAA	a type of auxin.
independent assortment	the way in which different alleles of genes on different chromosomes may end up in any combination in gametes, resulting from the random alignment of bivalents on the equator during meiosis I.
industrial melanism	an increase in the frequency of dark individuals in a population, for example the peppered moth, as a result of selection pressures favouring these forms in areas polluted by industrial emissions.
inorganic fertiliser	a fertiliser containing inorganic ions, such as nitrate, ammonium, potassium and phosphate ions.
insulin	a small peptide hormone secreted by the β cells in the islets of Langerhans in the pancreas that reduces blood glucose levels.
intensive farming	farming using high inputs, such as fertilisers and pesticides, and high stocking densities, in order to achieve high yields.

intermediate neurone	a neurone whose cell body and many dendrites are all within the brain or spinal cord; it receives action potentials from a sensory neurone and transmits action potentials to a motor neurone
interspecific competition	competition between members of different species.
intraspecific competition	competition between members of the same species.
islets of Langerhans	groups of cells in the pancreas which secrete insulin and glucagon.
Krebs cycle	a closed pathway of reactions in aerobic respiration in a mitochondrion in which hydrogens pass to hydrogen carriers for subsequent ATP synthesis and some ATP is synthesised directly.
lactose permease	an enzyme secreted by some bacteria, such as *E. coli*, which enables the cell to absorb lactose.
lag phase	the early stages of population growth, in which little or no growth is evident, as the organisms adjust to a new environment.
lamina	the blade of a leaf.
limiting factor	the one factor, of many affecting a process, that is nearest its lowest value and hence is rate-limiting.
link reaction	decarboxylation and dehydrogenation of pyruvate and formation of acetyl coenzyme A, linking glycolysis with the Krebs cycle.
log phase	the stage of population growth that follows the lag phase, during which the population repeatedly doubles per unit time.
loop of Henle	the part of the nephron between the proximal and distal convoluted tubules; in humans, about 14% of the loops of Henle are long and reach down into the medulla of the kidney.
meiosis	the type of cell division that results in a halving of chromosome number and a reshuffling of alleles; in humans, it occurs in the formation of gametes.
mesophyll	the internal tissue of a leaf blade with chloroplasts for photosynthesis and consisting of an upper layer of palisade cells (the main photosynthetic tissue) and a lower layer of spongy mesophyll with large air spaces for gas exchange.
mitochondrion	the organelle in eukaryotes in which aerobic respiration takes place.
monohybrid cross	a cross in which the inheritance of one gene is considered.
motor end plate	the ending of an axon of a motor neurone, where it forms a synapse with a muscle.
motor neurone	a neurone whose cell body is in the brain or spinal cord, and that transmits action potentials to an effector such as a muscle or gland.
multiple alleles	the existence of three or more alleles of a gene, as, for example, in the determination of A,B,O blood groups.
mutagen	a substance that can cause mutation.
mutation	an unpredictable change in the structure of DNA, or in the structure and number of chromosomes.
mycelium	the main body of a fungus, made up of a network of threads called hyphae.
myelin	a substance that surrounds many axons and dendrons, made up of many layers of the plasma membranes of Schwann cells.
natural selection	the way in which individuals with particular characteristics have a greater chance of survival than individuals without those characteristics, which are therefore more likely to breed and pass on the genes for these characteristics to their offspring.
negative feedback	a process in which a change in some parameter, such as blood glucose level, brings about processes which move its level back towards normal again.

nephron	a kidney tubule.
nerve	a bundle of numerous axons and dendrons of many different neurones, surrounded by a sheath called the perineurium.
neuromuscular junction	a synapse between the axon of a motor neurone and a muscle.
neurone	a nerve cell; a cell which is specialised for the conduction of action potentials.
niche	the particular role filled by a species in an ecosystem.
nicotine	a chemical found in tobacco smoke that can bind with acetylcholine receptors on the postsynaptic membrane of cholinergic synapses.
nitrogenous excretory product	an unwanted product of metabolism that contains nitrogen, for example ammonia, urea or uric acid.
node of Ranvier	a short gap in the myelin sheath surrounding an axon.
noradrenaline	a neurotransmitter substance.
operator	part of an operon to which a repressor protein can bind, so preventing the expression of the structural gene in that operon.
operon	a length of DNA containing genes coding for one or more proteins, plus other regions which control whether or not these genes will be expressed.
organic fertiliser	a fertiliser containing organic substances such as urea, for example farmyard manure or mushroom compost.
organic molecule	a compound containing carbon and hydrogen.
osmoreceptor	a receptor cell that is sensitive to the water potential of the blood.
osmoregulation	the control of the water content of the fluids in the body.
oxidative phosphorylation	synthesis of ATP from ADP and P_i using energy released by the electron transport chain in aerobic respiration.
oxygen debt	the volume of oxygen that is required at the end of exercise to metabolise lactate that accumulates as a result of anaerobic respiration in muscles.
palisade cell	*see* mesophyll.
pancreas	an organ lying close to the stomach that functions both as an exocrine gland (secreting pancreatic juice) and an endocrine gland (secreting insulin and glucagon).
percentage frequency	the percentage of samples in which a particular species was found.
petiole	a leaf stalk.
phenotype	the characteristics of an organism, often resulting from an interaction between its genotype and its environment.
phenylketonuria (PKU)	a genetic disease resulting from a mutation in a gene that codes for an enzyme involved in the metabolism of phenylalanine.
phosphorylation	the transfer of a phosphate group to an organic compound.
photolysis	the splitting of water using light energy: $H_2O \rightarrow 2H^+ + 2e^- + \frac{1}{2}O_2$
photophosphorylation	the synthesis of ATP from ADP and P_i using light energy in photosynthesis.
photosynthesis	the fixation of carbon from carbon dioxide into organic molecules using light energy.
photosystem	a cluster of light-harvesting accessory pigments surrounding a primary pigment or reaction centre.
phylogeny	the evolutionary history of a species.
pioneer plant	a plant which can colonise newly-cleared or disturbed ground.
plant growth regulator	the chemicals produced in plants that affect their growth and development; they include auxins, gibberellins, cytokinins and abscisic acid.

podocyte	one of the cells which make up the endothelium of a renal capsule.
point quadrat	a quadrat whose sides are so small that it covers only a single point; especially useful when sampling percentage cover in relatively thickly-growing vegetation.
polyploidy	possessing more than two complete sets of chromosomes.
population	all the individuals of a species living in an area at the same time and that can interbreed with one another.
positive feedback	a process in which a change in some parameter brings about processes that move its level even further in the direction of the initial change.
postsynaptic neurone	the neurone on the opposite side of a synapse to the neurone in which the action potential arrives.
predator	an animal that feeds by killing other organisms.
presynaptic neurone	a neurone at a synapse from which neurotransmitter is secreted when an action potential arrives.
prey	an animal that is eaten by predators.
primary pigment	*see* reaction centre.
primary succession	the succession that occurs on an area where no living things were originally present.
promoter	the part of an operon to which RNA polymerase must bind before transcription of the structural genes can begin.
quadrat	a square area within which sampling of a community can take place.
reabsorption	taking back into the blood some of the substances in a kidney nephron.
reaction centre	a molecule of chlorophyll *a* that receives energy from the light absorbed by surrounding accessory pigments in a photosystem.
receptor potential	a change in the normal resting potential across the membrane of a receptor cell, caused by a stimulus.
receptor	a cell which is sensitive to a change in the environment that may generate an action potential as a result of a stimulus.
recessive	an allele is said to be recessive if it is only expressed when no dominant allele is present.
redox reaction	an oxidation–reduction reaction involving the transfer of electrons from a donor to an acceptor.
reflex action	a fast, automatic response to a stimulus; reflex actions may be innate (inborn) or learned (conditioned);
reflex arc	the pathway taken by an action potential leading to a reflex action; the action potential is generated in a receptor, passes along a sensory neurone into the brain or spinal cord and then along a motor neurone to an effector.
refractory period	a period of time during which a neurone is recovering from an action potential, and during which another action potential cannot be generated.
regulator gene	part of a DNA molecule that codes for a protein that controls the expression of another gene.
renal capsule	the cup-shaped part at the beginning of a nephron; sometimes known as Bowman's capsule.
repolarisation	getting the resting potential of a neurone back to normal after an action potential has passed.
repressor	a protein that can bind to part of a DNA molecule, preventing expression of a nearby gene.

reproductive isolation	the inability of two groups of organisms to breed with one another, for example because of geographical separation, or because of behavioural differences.
respiration	enzymatic release of energy from organic compounds in living cells.
respiratory quotient (RQ)	the ratio of the volume of carbon dioxide given out in respiration to that of oxygen used.
respirometer	the apparatus for measuring the rate of oxygen consumption in respiration or for finding the RQ.
resting potential	the difference in electrical potential that is maintained across a neurone when it is not transmitting an action potential; it is normally about $-60\,mV$ inside and is maintained by the sodium–potassium pump.
saltatory conduction	conduction of an action potential along a myelinated axon or dendron, in which the action potential jumps from one node of Ranvier to the next.
sampling	collecting information from just a part of the whole, for example collecting ecological data from just part of a field; care must be taken to ensure that the sample is reasonably large and representative of the whole.
Schwann cell	a cell which is in close association with a neurone, whose plasma membrane wraps round and round the axon or dendron of the neurone to form a myelin sheath.
secondary succession	the succession taking place in an area where some vegetation was already present.
secretion	the release of a useful substance from a cell or gland.
selection pressure	an environmental factor that confers greater chances of survival and reproduction on some individuals than on others in a population.
selective breeding	choosing only organisms with desirable features, from which to breed.
selective cutting	felling only certain carefully chosen trees in a woodland.
sensory neurone	a neurone that transmits action potentials from a receptor to the central nervous system.
sex chromosomes	the pair of chromosomes that determine the gender of an individual; in humans, they are the X and Y chromosomes.
sex linked gene	a gene that is carried on an X chromosome but not on a Y chromosome.
sexual reproduction	reproduction involving meiosis, gametes, fertilisation and the production of zygotes.
sickle cell anaemia	a genetic disease caused by a faulty gene coding for haemoglobin, in which haemoglobin tends to precipitate when oxygen concentrations are low.
sickle trait	a person who is heterozygous for the sickle cell allele is said to have sickle trait; there are normally no symptoms, except occasionally in very severe conditions of oxygen shortage.
silent mutation	a mutation in which the change in the DNA has no discernible effect on an organism.
sodium–potassium pump	a membrane protein (or proteins), that moves sodium ions out of a cell and potassium ions into it, using ATP.
speciation	the production of new species.
species frequency	another term for percentage frequency, that is the percentage of samples within which a species is found.
stabilising selection	a type of natural selection in which the status quo is maintained because the organisms are already well adapted to their environment.
stationary phase	the stage in the lifetime of a population in which no growth or decrease takes place; the rate of production of new individuals exactly matches the rate of death.
stimulus	a change in the environment that is detected by a receptor, and which may cause a response.
stoma	a pore in the epidermis of a leaf bounded by two guard cells.

stroma	the matrix of a chloroplast in which the light-independent reactions of photosynthesis occur.
suberin	a waxy, waterproof substance found in some plant cell walls, for example cells in bark.
succession	a directional change in a community, in which changes in the environment cause changes in the community, which in turn cause further changes in the environment.
sympatric speciation	the emergence of a new species from another species where the two are living in the same place; it can happen, for example, as a result of polyploidy.
synapse	a point at which two neurones meet but do not touch; the synapse is made up of the end of the presynaptic neurone, the synaptic cleft and the end of the postsynaptic neurone.
synaptic cleft	a very small gap between two neurones at a synapse.
target cell	a cell that is affected by a hormone; target cells have receptors with which the hormone is able to bind.
test cross	a genetic cross in which an organism showing a characteristic caused by a dominant allele is crossed with an organism that is homozygous recessive; the phenotypes of the offspring can be a guide to whether the first organism is homozygous or heterozygous.
tetraploid	possessing four complete sets of chromosomes.
thylakoid	a flattened membrane-bound, fluid-filled sac, which is the site of the light-dependent reactions of photosynthesis in a chloroplast.
transect	a line along which sampling of a habitat is carried out.
transmitter substance	a chemical that is released from a presynaptic neurone when an action potential arrives that then diffuses across the synaptic cleft and may initiate an action potential in the postsynaptic neurone.
triploid	possessing three complete sets of chromosomes.
trophic level	the position in a food chain at which an organism feeds; for example, herbivores are primary consumers, carnivores may be secondary or tertiary consumers.
ultrafiltration	filtration on a molecular scale, for example the filtration that occurs as fluid from the blood passes through the basement membrane of a renal capsule.
urea	a nitrogenous excretory product produced in the liver from the deamination of amino acids.
ureter	a tube that carries urine from a kidney to the bladder.
urethra	a tube that carries urine from the bladder to the outside.
uric acid	the main nitrogenous excretory product of birds; some uric acid is also excreted by humans.
voltage-gated channel	a protein channel through a cell membrane that opens or closes in response to changes in electrical potential across the membrane.
water potential	the tendency of a solution to lose or gain water; water moves from high water potential to low water potential.
work	all energy transfers other than those involving thermal energy.
zygote	a cell formed by the fusion of two gametes; if the gametes are haploid, then the zygote is diploid.

Index

Terms shown in **bold** also appear in the glossary (see pages 135–143). Pages in *italics* refer to figures.